Learn to Implement Games with Code

John M. Quick

CRC Press
Taylor & Francis Group
Boca Raton   London   New York

CRC Press is an imprint of the
Taylor & Francis Group, an **informa** business

AN A K PETERS BOOK

CRC Press
Taylor & Francis Group
6000 Broken Sound Parkway NW, Suite 300
Boca Raton, FL 33487-2742

© 2017 by Taylor & Francis Group, LLC
CRC Press is an imprint of Taylor & Francis Group, an Informa business

No claim to original U.S. Government works

Printed at CPI on sustainably sourced paper
Version Date: 20160414

International Standard Book Number-13: 978-1-4987-5338-8 (Paperback)

Library of Congress Cataloging-in-Publication Data

Names: Quick, John M., author.
Title: Learn to implement games with code / John M. Quick.
Description: Boca Raton : Taylor & Francis Group, LLC, CRC Press is an imprint of Taylor & Francis Group, [2017] | Includes bibliographical references and index.
Identifiers: LCCN 2016007414 | ISBN 9781498753388
Subjects: LCSH: Computer games--Programming.
Classification: LCC QA76.76.C672 Q53 2017 | DDC 794.8/1536--dc23
LC record available at https://lccn.loc.gov/2016007414

**Visit the Taylor & Francis Web site at
http://www.taylorandfrancis.com**

**and the CRC Press Web site at
http://www.crcpress.com**

*This book is dedicated to the future
game developers of the world.*

Contents

8. A Proper Introduction   219

9. A Proper Transition   229

Preface

Game development is one of the most rewarding crafts of modern times. Not only is making games a wonderful lifelong hobby, but employment opportunities exist at many levels. Some solo independent developers (indies) make computer and mobile games that reach thousands of players. Meanwhile, game development studios can range in size from a few close friends to worldwide corporations with thousands of employees. Furthermore, governments worldwide are encouraging their citizens to learn to code. Indeed, computer programming is likely to become one of the world's key disciplines for people of all kinds in the near future.

If you want to learn to code, then making games is an excellent place to start. Yet, creating games is a challenging endeavor. You can expect to put many hours into your craft before finally releasing your first game. However, your efforts are sure to be personally fulfilling, especially when your game spreads joy to players. Fortunately, this book will guide you through the development process as you put together a release-ready game. It is written in a friendly and conversational tone, which is suitable for a wide audience of aspiring game developers, such as yourself. You will gain practical, hands-on experience with implementing game components using code. You will gradually build a complete game that you can be proud of. After reading *Learn to Implement Games with Code*, you will be prepared to start making games of your very own design.

Is This Book for You?

You are already familiar with the basics of coding. This includes topics such as variables, loops, arrays, conditional statements, and functions. Perhaps you have looked into C#, Unity, and game development. Every little bit helps, but this is not strictly necessary. Nevertheless, you are dedicated and ready to create unique solutions to the challenges that lie ahead. Most of all, you are interested in experiencing a practical, hands-on approach to learning. If this describes you, then *Learn to Implement Games with Code* will help you become a better game developer.

On the other hand, you may be brand new to coding. In that case, you should first read *Learn to Code with Games*, which is also written by John M. Quick. It follows the same practical, hands-on learning approach, but is designed for first-time coders. After you finish, feel free to return to this book for more advanced game development topics. The reference for *Learn to Code with Games* follows:

Quick, J. M. 2015. *Learn to Code with Games*. Boca Raton, FL: CRC Press. ISBN: 9781498704687.

Challenges

This book is structured using the concept of challenges. In each chapter, one or more challenges are presented to you. Each challenge helps you learn to implement a game component by presenting a problem that needs to be solved. Thereafter, you are inspired to develop your own logical solution and code to solve the problem. Hints are provided along the way to help guide you through the process. You will grow as a game developer as you progress through the challenges of this book. Ultimately, you will put together an entire game. Better yet, the well-crafted, reusable implementations that you create in this book will serve you well in future game development projects.

Goals

Every chapter has a set of goals. These represent the game implementation techniques that you will be able to apply once the chapter is completed. Look for them in the "Goals" section near the beginning of each chapter.

Required Files

A "Required Files" section is placed near the beginning of each chapter. This specifies which of the provided files you need to access during the chapter. A "Software" folder is included for every chapter (https://www.crcpress.com/Learn-to-Implement-Games-with-Code/Quick/p/book/9781498753388). Inside, you will find a "Challenge" folder, which is your starting point for each chapter. This is the project that you will work with to implement your solution. Meanwhile, the "Solution" folder contains a complete example project that demonstrates one way to solve the challenge. This is handy for comparing your solution to the example solution.

Unity Game Engine

The challenges in this book make use of the Unity game engine. Although you will pick up some useful Unity tips throughout the course of this book, the primary focus is on coding game implementations. Therefore, you can think of Unity as the catalyst that rapidly gets you into making games. Accordingly, you need to download and install Unity from http://unity3d.com to complete the challenges in this book. It is available in a free personal version for both Mac and PC.

Although we will use Unity, note that the coding implementations that you create are independent of any platform. You are learning about processes and techniques that facilitate the creation of all kinds of games. You can transfer your implementations to other projects and platforms in the future. Hence, the experience that you gain through coding game implementations is the greatest value from this book. Once you know how to implement games, you will be able to apply your experience to new projects, regardless of platform.

Code Editor

Unity includes the MonoDevelop code editor by default. However, you may use any code editor that you prefer. This choice is a personal preference that doesn't impact your ability to succeed at completing the challenges in this book. For PC, you might consider Visual Studio or NotePad++; for Mac, Xamarin Studio, Sublime Text, and TextWrangler are some viable options.

Acknowledgment

Thanks to Carrie Heeter, PhD, Professor of Media and Information at Michigan State University, whose advice transformed the course of this book for the better.

Author

John M. Quick, PhD, is an expert in the strategic enhancement of motivation, learning, and performance. He collaborates with industry and university clients to strategically solve their greatest challenges.

John earned a PhD in educational technology at Arizona State University, Tempe, Arizona, where he researched enjoyment and individual differences in games. He created the Gameplay Enjoyment Model (GEM) and Gaming Goal Orientations (GGO) models to guide the design of effective game-based solutions.

John has released more than 15 digital games. His games focus on innovative topics, such as learner engagement, employee performance improvement, and cutting-edge interfaces.

John has over 5 years of classroom experience at the higher education level. He has instructed courses on computer literacy, game design, and programming at Michigan State University, Arizona State University, and DigiPen Institute of Technology Singapore.

John is the author of *Learn to Code with Games* (ISBN: 9781498704687) and *Statistical Analysis with R* (ISBN: 9781849512084).

1 The World Beyond the Screen

Not too long ago, Luna (Figure 1.1) began her quest upon the surface world. Luna grew up among the Dark Elves of Clandis. Her people live entirely underground and shun anyone who would leave the city. However, Luna has a curious and brave soul. One day, she secretly left the underground city and ventured to the surface. Until now, Luna's adventures have been filled with the excitement of new people and places.

Yet, Luna has a bit of a problem. She has outgrown her original quest. She knows that there is more to see and do in the world. She runs up, down, left, and right, as far as she can. However, no matter how hard she tries, she cannot move past the boundaries of the screen. Perhaps you can use your knowledge of the surface world to help Luna continue on her quest.

▌▌ Goals

By the end of this chapter, you will be able to apply these game implementation techniques:

- Implement a camera that follows the player

- Lock camera movement to the boundaries of the game world

- Design smooth camera movement for a pleasant player experience

Figure 1.1 Luna is embarking on an epic quest that you will create through code!

- Create your own C# scripts, variables, and functions

- Determine logical solutions to computer problems prior to implementing them

- Leverage Unity features to improve your development process

▌▌ Required Files

In this chapter, you will use the following files from the *Software > Chapter_01* folder (https://www.crcpress.com/Learn-to-Implement-Games-with-Code/Quick/p/book/9781498753388).

- The contents of the Challenge folder to create, code, and test your solution

- The contents of the Solution folder to compare your solution to the example solution

▌▌ Unity Game Engine

The challenges in this book make use of the Unity game engine. You can download the Unity installer from http://unity3d.com. To install Unity, open the installer on your computer and follow the instructions. Soon after, you will be making games with Unity.

▌▌ Test the Example Solution

A Solution folder is included with each chapter. This folder contains a working example of how the challenges in the chapter can be solved. All of the scripts and

Figure 1.2 Press the play button near the top of the Unity interface to test the current version of your game.

project files are included. At the start of the chapter, it is recommended that you test the solution to see how it works. You can do this by opening the project in Unity and clicking on the play button (Figure 1.2) near the top of the interface. Afterwards, the game will run inside the Game window.

For example, open the *Software > Solution > Assets > Scenes > Map.unity* file in Unity. Press the play button to launch the game. Use the WASD or arrow keys to move Luna around the screen. As you can see, the camera pleasantly follows Luna around and allows her to explore the entire world map. This represents what you will create in this chapter.

▐ Build Your Solution

A Challenge folder is included with each chapter. This folder contains all the scripts and project files that you begin the chapter with. Throughout the chapter, you will build upon these files to implement your own solutions to the challenges. By the end of the chapter, you will create your own working version of the game.

For instance, open the *Software > Challenge > Assets > Scenes > Map.unity* file in Unity. Press the play button to launch the game. Use the WASD or arrow keys to move Luna around the screen. Notice that Luna is stopped at the edges of the screen. Your challenge in this chapter is to implement a camera that allows Luna to explore the entire game world.

▐ Put Logic before Syntax

You can think of every computer code implementation as having two parts: the logic and the syntax. The logic forms an overall plan for what you will implement. It defines what you will create and how you will create it. Logic represents a generic solution that can be translated into any computer language. Meanwhile, the syntax represents a specific implementation of computer code in a language of choice. Syntax brings one instance of our implementation to life. Both logic and syntax are necessary to succeed in any implementation. However, the order in which you implement logic and syntax can either support or hinder your progress.

For every challenge in this book, as well as your future coding career, you should take the opportunity to focus on logic prior to syntax. Since logic represents a solution to a problem regardless of any specific language, it makes for an excellent implementation guide. Defining your logic first will help you immensely when it comes to writing the syntax for a specific implementation. By contrast, if you dive directly into the syntax without planning your logic, you may find yourself confused and frustrated in a sea of code. Using logic to guide your syntax will help you to stay focused and work efficiently toward a solution.

There are no strict guidelines on how to formulate your logic. However, you need to find a way to coherently plan a solution to a problem. Further, you should ensure that your plan helps you implement code efficiently and effectively.

Two helpful techniques that you can use to formulate your logic are *pseudocode* and *process mapping*. Brief descriptions and examples of these techniques are provided here. For a more extended discussion of pseudocode and process mapping for coding, see *Learn to Code with Games* (Quick 2015).

Pseudocode

Pseudocode is a logic technique in which human language is used to describe a solution that will be implemented in a computer language. Consider the implementation of "move the character up and down using the arrow keys." One person's pseudocode may closely resemble human language, like this:

```
IF the player holds the up arrow, THEN increase the character's y
   axis value.
IF the player holds the down arrow, THEN decrease the character's y
   axis value.
```

Meanwhile, another person's pseudocode more closely resembles computer language, like this:

```
IF Input.UpArrow:
    Character.y++
ELSE IF Input.DownArrow:
    Character.y--
```

Notice the use of keywords like *if*, *then*, and *else*. These are the key pieces of logic that describe how the code will function. For either version of the pseudocode, the implemented code might look something like this:

```
if (Input.GetKey(KeyCode.UpArrow) {

    character.y++;
}
else if (Input.GetKey(KeyCode.DownArrow) {

    character.y--;
}
```

Regardless of whether your pseudocode is closer to human language or to computer language, what matters most is that it helps you clearly define the logic for your implementation. Indeed, well-written pseudocode is easily translated into the computer code. This makes pseudocode especially well-suited to implementations with detailed steps and complex calculations.

Process Mapping

Process mapping is a logic technique in which symbols are used to represent the function of a system. Consider the implementation of "show the win screen once the player has won the game." An example process map for this implementation is shown in Figure 1.3.

Notice the use of common symbols. Rectangles represent processes or states. Diamonds are decision points with multiple potential outcomes. Arrows show how information flows from one place to another.

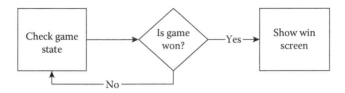

Figure 1.3 A process map illustrates the logic behind determining the game state. You can use process mapping to guide the design of your code.

Once again, the exact format is not important. What matters is that you can apply process mapping to clearly organize the logic behind your implementation. Process maps are especially useful for demonstrating the overall flow of information throughout a system. Thus, you may use process maps when emphasizing how information is passed through or states are managed in your code.

▮ Challenge Context

Before discussing your challenge, let's introduce what you are provided with already. Return to the challenge project in Unity. Look in the Project window to find the Assets folder. There are several folders inside Assets, including Prefabs, Scenes, Scripts, and Sprites (Figure 1.4).

Prefabs

The basic building block in Unity is the `GameObject`. Every `GameObject` has a Transform component that defines its position, rotation, and scale. Furthermore, a `GameObject` can have any number of optional components added to it. These components represent different types of functionality that the object can have. For example, a `SpriteRenderer` is used to display an image, while a `BoxCollider2D` is used to detect collisions. Feel free to make your own `GameObject` by selecting GameObject > Create Empty (Figure 1.5) from the Unity menu. You will see a new `GameObject` appear in the Hierarchy window (Figure 1.6). Click on this object and look at the Inspector window. There, you will see the `Transform` component. If you click on the Add Component button, you can attach a wide variety of additional components to the `GameObject` (Figure 1.7). Feel free to experiment with this `GameObject`, and delete it once you are finished. This represents the basic process of building a game in Unity. A complete game is made by assembling a variety of objects and components with different functions and responsibilities.

Figure 1.4 Find the Assets folder and its subfolders inside the Unity Project window.

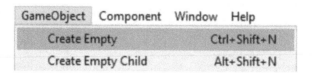

Figure 1.5 Create your own GameObject by selecting GameObject > Create Empty from the Unity menu.

Figure 1.6 After creating a new GameObject, it will appear in the Hierarchy window.

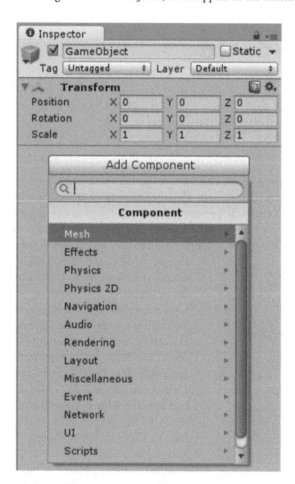

Figure 1.7 View information about your GameObject and its components in the Inspector window. Use the Add Component button to attach additional components to your GameObject.

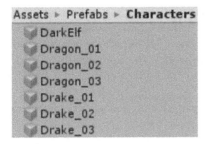

Figure 1.8 The *Assets > Prefabs* folder contains a collection of characters and objects that you can use to create your game.

Figure 1.9 All of the objects that compose your scene can be viewed in the Hierarchy window.

In Unity, a prefab is like a preconfigured `GameObject` with all of its various components and settings. Prefabs are an excellent choice for anything that will be reused or duplicated throughout a game. For instance, collectable objects and characters are often reused. Storing these objects as prefabs makes them easy to clone later. In addition, any time a prefab is edited from inside the Assets folder, all copies of that prefab throughout the game are automatically updated. To create a prefab, first make a `GameObject` in the Hierarchy window. Afterwards, click and drag it into the Assets folder to turn it into a prefab. Inside the *Assets > Prefabs* folder is a collection of the various characters and objects that you can use to create your game (Figure 1.8). You will modify and apply these prefabs throughout the challenges in this book.

Scenes

In the *Assets > Scenes* folder, you will find the Map scene. In the Hierarchy window (Figure 1.9), you can see the various objects and components of the Map scene. For example, the Canvas object displays how many collectables Luna has found during the game. The Background > BgMap object is responsible for randomly generating the tiled grass background for the scene. The Foreground > Player object represents Luna and is controlled by the player of our game. Explore the various objects and components in this scene to see how it is assembled.

The Map is our only scene thus far. It is the starting area for our game. Scenes represent different areas of our game, such as levels or menus. Eventually, you will create several different scenes, including dungeons to explore, places for characters to interact, and menus.

Scripts

Inside the *Assets > Scripts* folder, you will find several code files. You will become very familiar with scripts, since coding game implementations is the primary emphasis of this book. An individual script represents one piece of functionality, such as moving a character or generating a tile map. You will create many scripts as you create your game and solve the challenges in this book. Along the way, you will be learning to code your own game implementations. Double-click on a script to open it in your code editor. Review the existing scripts to understand how each of them works. The functionality of each script is briefly described:

- AIMove: controls the movement patterns of non-player characters (NPCs)

- CollectableInventory: represents Luna's inventory of collectable objects

- LevelGenerator: generates an entire scene, complete with its various objects

- MapSpawn: clones a prefab and randomly positions it on a tile map

- RandomMap: creates a random tile map from a collection of prefabs

- StateManager: manages the overall game state and the switching of scenes

- UserCollision: detects when Luna collides with various in-game objects and triggers subsequent events

- UserMove: allows the player to move Luna around the screen using the keyboard

Sprites

Just two images, or sprites, are used to compose all of the visuals in our game. The BgCanvas sprite will be used as the background for various user interface elements in the game. It uses nine-slice scaling to conveniently stretch to fit any rectangular shape or size. The SpriteSheet image contains all of the characters and objects in the game (Figure 1.10). All of our game's characters and objects are composed of individual 64 × 64 pixel tiles. Thus, they can be conveniently arranged into a single page, called a sprite sheet. The Unity Sprite Editor can then be used to separate the sprite sheet into individual images (Unity Technologies 2015j). Art asset management is beyond the scope of this book, so the necessary items will be provided to you. Let's get to coding.

▮▮ Challenge: Move the Camera with Luna

Open the challenge project in Unity by double-clicking on *Software > Challenge > Assets > Scenes > Map.unity*. Press the play button to launch the game. Use the arrow keys to move Luna around the screen. Notice that she can collect the small hearts, but cannot move past the edges of the screen. Right now, the game is only in the earliest stages of development. Throughout this book, you will build upon this project to create a release-ready version of the game.

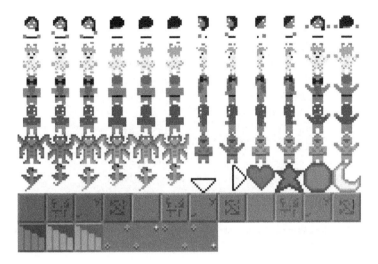

Figure 1.10 The sprite sheet contains all of the characters and objects used in the game.

Recall that Luna's adventurous spirit is driving her to explore the world beyond the edges of the screen. Your challenge is to code a script that moves the camera as Luna moves, thus allowing her to further explore the world. Read the challenge requirements that follow. Before proceeding to code your solution, remember to sort out your logic first. Then, try to implement the solution yourself. As needed, use the hints to help guide you toward a successful implementation. The requirements for this challenge are:

1. Create a script named CamFollow.

2. Attach your script to the camera in the Map scene.

3. Ensure that the camera moves as Luna moves.

Hint: Create a New Script

To begin this challenge, you need to create a new script. Inside the Project window, navigate to the *Assets > Scripts* folder (Figure 1.11). Select Assets > Create > C# Script from the Unity menu (Figure 1.12). A script called NewBehaviourScript will be added to your *Assets > Scripts* folder. You can rename the script by clicking on its name and typing in a new name. Try changing the name of the script to CamFollow. Double-click on your script to open it in your code editor. You now have a brand new, empty script that is ready to be coded. You will be creating your own scripts throughout the challenges in this book, so you will become quite familiar with this process.

Hint: Attach the Script to an Object

Although you have created a script, it will not impact your game until it has been added to an object. Recall that Unity is a system of objects with different

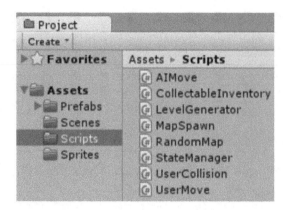

Figure 1.11 Before creating a new script, navigate to your *Assets > Scripts* folder inside the Project window.

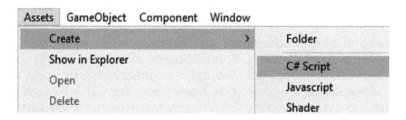

Figure 1.12 Create a new script by selecting Assets > Create > C# Script from the Unity menu.

components attached to them. Scripts are one kind of component that can add functionality to an object. In the case of this challenge, we want our CamFollow script to control the movement of our camera. In the Hierarchy window of the Map scene, you will find a `GameObject` named Main Camera. This is the camera that makes our scene visible to the player. It is also the camera that we want to control with our CamFollow script.

Click on the Main Camera `GameObject` and look at the Inspector window. Toward the bottom, press the Add Component button and select Scripts > Cam Follow from the menu (Figure 1.13). The CamFollow script appears attached to the Main Camera in the Inspector window (Figure 1.14). Thus, from this point forward, the code in the CamFollow script will add functionality to the Main Camera `GameObject`. Once again, this process of adding components to objects will become very familiar to you. Essentially, any time you create a new script, you want to add it to the objects that require its functionality.

Hint: Pin the Camera to Luna

With your script created and attached to the camera, it's finally time to begin coding. As an initial step toward your camera implementation, see if you can get the camera to follow Luna as she moves around the screen. Consider that

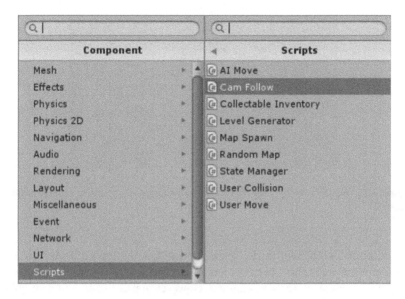

Figure 1.13 Add the CamFollow script to the Main Camera by clicking on the Add Component button and selecting Scripts > Cam Follow from the menu.

Figure 1.14 After adding the CamFollow script, it will appear attached to the Main Camera in the Inspector window.

our entire game world is on a two-dimensional (2D) grid. Therefore, the position of Luna and the camera can be represented by x and y coordinates. How can you use code to make the camera position match Luna's position? How will you ensure that the camera position always matches Luna's positon, even as she moves throughout the game world?

Think about what happens to Luna's position as she moves. Recall that all Unity objects have a `Transform` component, which stores x and y position values. To get an idea of how Luna's position changes as she moves, try running the game. Click on the Player `GameObject` in the Hierarchy window. Focus on the

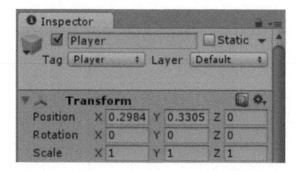

Figure 1.15 Watch how the `Transform` values change as you move Luna around the screen.

`Transform` component in the Inspector window (Figure 1.15). As you move Luna around, watch how her position values change. At the same time, notice that the camera position never changes. However, you can code your CamFollow script to ensure that the camera moves along with Luna.

Hint: Access Unity Objects and Components

Since you may be unfamiliar with Unity, let's cover a few ways to access objects and components in your code. One common task is to access the `GameObject` to which a script is attached. This can be done by typing `GameObject` into your code:

```
//access the GameObject to which this script is attached
gameObject
```

From here, you can use dot notation to access the `Transform` component and its variables, such as the position of the object:

```
//access the Transform component
gameObject.transform
```

```
//access the position variable
gameObject.transform.position
```

Sometimes, you need to access objects that are not directly attached to a script. For instance, you may want to retrieve the Player `GameObject` from inside your CamFollow script. One way to do this is to use the `GameObject.FindWithTag()` function (Unity Technologies 2015e). Note that the Player `GameObject` in our Map scene has been marked with the "Player" tag (Figure 1.16). Thus, we can use `GameObject.FindWithTag()` to retrieve the Player `GameObject` from any script:

```
//retrieve the Player GameObject from the scene
//provide GameObject.FindWithTag() with a string that matches
  the tag
GameObject.FindWithTag("Player")
```

Figure 1.16 The Player GameObject in our scene has been marked with the "Player" tag, allowing it to be easily retrieved by the GameObject.FindWithTag() function.

```
//store the retrieved object in a local variable
GameObject player = GameObject.FindWithTag("Player");
```

Furthermore, you can use the GetComponent() function (Unity Technologies 2015f) to retrieve any component attached to a GameObject:

```
//access any component attached to a GameObject using
  GetComponent()
//for example, retrieve the SpriteRenderer from the Player
  GameObject
player.GetComponent<SpriteRenderer>()
```

Naturally, these snippets only demonstrate the basics of how to access information from objects. You still need to store information in variables, write functions, and modify objects to make your CamFollow script work.

Hint: Apply Unity Control Functions

Unity comes with several handy control functions that are specifically designed to support game development. You will use these functions in nearly all of your scripts. One such function is Start(). The Start() function is called just one time, when a script is enabled for the first time (Unity Technologies 2015h). Thus, Start() is an excellent place to initialize variables and execute code that is required for the rest of our script to run. The Start() function is structured like any normal C# function:

```
void Start() {
    /*
    Initialize variables and execute any
    necessary setup code in this function.
    */
}
```

Another common Unity control function is Update(). The Update() function repeats every single frame throughout the lifetime of our script (Unity Technologies 2015i). Indeed, almost all games are designed to repeat certain actions over and over again. In a single frame, only the slightest change may take place, such as Luna taking one step. By putting many frames together, we create an action sequence, such as Luna running across the screen. Generally, this process of continuously controlling gameplay is known as the *game loop*. Unity's Update() function provides a convenient way to add functionality to our game loop. It is also structured like a standard C# function:

```
void Update() {
    /*
    Place any code that you want to
    execute every single frame in
    this function.
    */
}
```

At this point, perhaps you have an idea of what needs to be done to succeed in this challenge. Try implementing your own solution before proceeding. Afterwards, compare your implementation to the provided example solution.

Example Solution: Move the Camera with Luna

Before we discuss the example solution, please note that it represents just one potential implementation. Throughout the book, your implementations may or may not closely resemble the example solutions. There is no one correct way to implement a game. Thus, your solutions may be just as good or better than the example solutions. The example solutions are provided to help you learn. You should always push yourself to define your own unique solution to each challenge prior to examining the example solution. After you have created a working solution, review the example solution. Look for opportunities to examine the challenge from a different perspective, experiment with an alternative coding method, and improve your own implementation. The ongoing process of defining a logical solution to a challenge, implementing it through code, and reflecting upon it in comparison to the example will help you become better at making games. Take every opportunity to follow this learning process throughout the challenges presented in this book.

Your initial challenge was to get the camera and Luna moving together using your CamFollow script. While you could directly retrieve the Player GameObject in your script, you can also generically store camera's target object in a variable:

```
//target object to follow
public GameObject targetObj;
```

This public variable is treated differently by Unity. Unity allows many data types to be manipulated in the visual interface when they are set to public. Add this variable to your current CamFollow script and save it. Then, click on the Main Camera object in your scene and look at the Inspector window. You will see that the targetObj variable shows up in the Unity interface (Figure 1.17). From here, you can visually assign any GameObject to the targetObj variable. For instance, you can drag the Player GameObject into the targetObj box (Figure 1.18). This sets the targetObj variable equal to your Player GameObject.

Making our targetObj variable public leverages one of the convenient features of Unity. By allowing any GameObject to be assigned to our targetObj variable, our CamFollow script can be easily reused without having to change its code each time. Imagine that you make a different game in the future where you want the camera to follow something other than the player.

Figure 1.17 After creating a `public` variable named `targetObj` in our CamFollow script, it appears in the Inspector window.

Figure 1.18 Drag the Player `GameObject` into the CamFollow script's `targetObj` box to set the `targetObj` variable equal to the Player `GameObject`.

You can use the same CamFollow script, but simply change the `targetObj` to something else. Always look for opportunities like this to make your code reusable.

Proceed to update the position of the camera in the `Start()` function. Here, we immediately set the camera's position to equal Luna's position:

```
void Start() {

    //retrieve target pos
    Vector3 targetPos = targetObj.transform.position;

    //set camera to start from target pos
    targetPos.z = gameObject.transform.position.z;
    gameObject.transform.position = targetPos;
}
```

The position of the target (Luna) is stored in a `Vector3` variable (Unity Technologies 2015m). Subsequently, the camera position is set equal to the target position. This immediately positions the camera over Luna at the start of our game.

Note that this code preserves the camera's original z coordinate. When working in 2D, the z coordinate controls the depth and layering of objects. Our camera is in front of everything in our game world, because it must display everything on the screen. Meanwhile, Luna is positioned at a greater depth, along with the various objects inside our game world. We do not want to disturb this balance. Therefore, we only set the camera's x and y coordinates to match Luna's, while preserving the camera's original z coordinate.

Moving on, we ensure that the camera always matches Luna's position inside the Update() function:

```
private void Update () {

    //retrieve target position
    Vector3 targetPos = targetObj.transform.position;

    //retrieve camera position
    Vector3 camPos = gameObject.transform.position;

    //update camera position based on target position
    camPos.x = targetPos.x;
    camPos.y = targetPos.y;

    //update position
    gameObject.transform.position = camPos;

}
```

In every frame, this Update() function retrieves Luna's position. It then updates the camera's x and y coordinates to match Luna's. Thus, the camera position always matches Luna's, even as she moves throughout the game world.

Congratulations on completing your initial challenge! Run your game in Unity and see that you can move Luna throughout the game world, which is much larger than the size of a single screen. The camera follows her along the way.

However, you likely noticed something less than ideal about our current implementation. As Luna reaches the edges of the game world, the camera displays the void space that lies beyond it. Certainly, we want to fix this.

■ Challenge: Stop the Camera at the Boundaries

Your camera is pinned to Luna's position as she moves around the screen. However, the camera is always centered directly on Luna's position. Once Luna moves toward the edges of the screen, the void space surrounding the game world becomes visible to the camera. We would never want a player of our game to see this happen. Instead, we should prevent the camera from displaying the space outside the boundaries of our game world. Yet, at the same time, we still want the camera to follow Luna as she moves around inside the game world. How can we do this?

Often, it is helpful to draw a picture to visualize the logic of your implementation. Think about the different elements involved in this challenge: Luna's

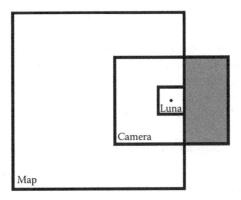

Figure 1.19 The camera is centered over Luna. Thus, as Luna reaches the edge of the world map, the camera's field of view extends beyond the world map. The shaded area represents the amount by which the camera extends beyond the world map.

position, the camera's field of view, and the world map. Presently, the camera's field of view is pinned to Luna's position. Thus, when Luna moves to the edge of the world map, the camera's field of view partially moves outside the boundaries. This situation is visualized in Figure 1.19. Our implementation would be much improved if we prevented the camera view from moving outside the boundaries of the map. The requirements for this challenge are:

1. Determine the boundaries of the world map.

2. Check the camera's field of view against the boundaries.

3. Prevent the camera's field of view from moving outside the boundaries.

Hint: Find the Map Boundaries

Test your game in Unity and look at the Hierarchy window. Expand the Background > BgMap GameObject. You will see a long list of objects with names similar to *Grass_01(Clone)*. Each of these objects is a cloned prefab tile from the *Assets > Prefabs* folder. The RandomMap script attached to our BgMap GameObject clones a large number of tile prefabs to form the world map for our game. Thus, if we want to know the boundaries of our world map, we must determine the cumulative bounds of its individual tiles.

Unity has a Bounds class (Unity Technologies 2015a) that suits our purpose. Conveniently, the Bounds class represents an axis-aligned bounding box (AABB), which is a rectangle that is perfectly parallel to the x and y axes. Similarly, our world map is one large square that is parallel to the axes of our 2D coordinate system. Hence, we can use the Bounds class to represent the overall size of our map.

While Bounds can be used to represent the overall map size, we still need a method to incorporate the size of each individual tile. After all, the size of our world map is the total size of the individual tiles that compose it. Look at the Grass_01 tile in the *Assets > Prefabs > Objects* folder of the Unity Project window. Notice that it has only `Transform` and `SpriteRenderer` components. The `Transform` component determines the tile's position, whereas the `SpriteRenderer` displays the tile's image. Fortunately, the `SpriteRenderer` class (Unity Technologies 2015k) has Bounds associated with it. Thus, you can determine the overall Bounds of the world map by iterating through all of the individual tiles and adding up their Bounds.

Hint: Apply the Boundary Limits

Once you calculate the size of the world map, you need to determine its precise boundaries and apply them to your position calculations. By default, objects in Unity have a center origin point. This means that the (0, 0) coordinate for the object is placed precisely at the center of the object. For instance, Luna's origin appears in the middle of her image, rather than at the top-left corner, bottom-right corner, or anywhere else. Different software uses different origin points, so it is important to consider that Unity defaults to a center origin point. The origin point of an object is critical to consider when calculating its boundaries.

In our case, we need to determine the top, bottom, left, and right boundaries of our world map. Again, visualizing the situation will help you determine a logical solution. Draw a square that represents the bounds of your world map, and put a point in the center to represent its origin (Figure 1.20). Think in terms of a 2D coordinate system. If you start from the origin point at (0, 0), what is the distance to the right edge of the map? What about the top, bottom, and left edges?

Go through the same process again, but instead visualize your camera's field of view. The origin of the camera is also located at its center. What is the distance from the origin point to the top, bottom, left, and right edges of the camera?

Imagine that Luna is running from left to right across the map and the camera is following her. Currently, once Luna reaches the edge of the map, the camera follows right along with her. However, instead of setting the camera's

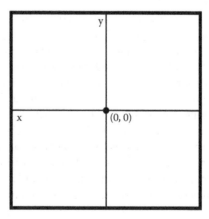

Figure 1.20 Use a visualization to help determine your logic. Draw a square to represent the world map and axes to form a 2D coordinate system. The center of the map is at the point (0, 0). Can you calculate the top, bottom, left, and right edge coordinates?

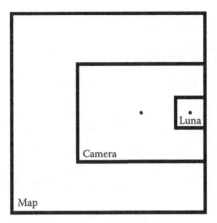

Figure 1.21 As Luna reaches the edge of the world map, the camera stops. With proper boundary checks, the camera is never allowed to move beyond the edges of the world map.

position exactly equal to Luna's position, you should make some adjustments. Think about Luna standing at the right edge of your world map. Right now, your camera hangs over the edge (Figure 1.19). However, you want the camera's right edge to stop at the map's right edge, as depicted in Figure 1.21. Remember to consider that the camera's position in the game world is determined by its center origin point. How can you adjust your position calculations to ensure that the camera never exceeds the boundaries of the world map?

Example Solution: Stop the Camera at the Boundaries

With a few updates to your CamFollow script, you can ensure that the camera never exceeds the boundaries of the world map. Start by determining the boundaries of the world map. Recall that the BgMap object in our scene is the container for the tiles that compose our world map. We want to reference this object in our CamFollow script. Thus, it can be stored in a `public` variable at the top of our script. In addition, we also need to store the `Bounds` of our map:

```
//boundary object
public GameObject boundsObj;

//boundaries
private Bounds _bounds;
```

Much like the `targetObj` variable that we created earlier, the `boundsObj` variable can be set in the Unity Inspector window. Just drag the BgMap GameObject from the Hierarchy window into the `boundsObj` box in our CamFollow script (Figure 1.22). Subsequently, our private _bounds variable needs to be initialized in the `Start()` function:

```
//excerpt from Start() function
//retrieve bounds
_bounds = FindBounds(boundsObj);
```

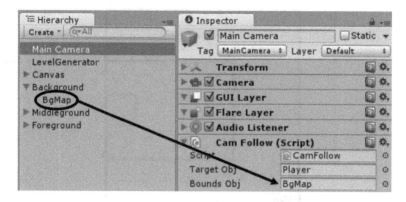

Figure 1.22 Drag the BgMap `GameObject` into the CamFollow script's `boundsObj` box to set the `boundsObj` variable equal to the BgMap `GameObject`.

Here, we set our `_bounds` variable equal to the result of the `FindBounds()` function. This is a custom function designed to add up the size of all of our map tiles. While it is not necessary to write a custom function for this purpose, it helps to keep our code clean. Let's examine the `FindBounds()` function:

```
private Bounds FindBounds(GameObject theParent) {

    //store bounds
    Bounds bounds = new Bounds(Vector3.zero, Vector3.zero);

    //retrieve renderers for all children
    Renderer[] allChildren = theParent.GetComponentsInChildren<Rend
        erer>();

    //search all children
    foreach (Renderer aChild in allChildren) {

        //add child bounds to total
        bounds.Encapsulate(aChild.bounds);

    }

    //return
    return bounds;

}
```

The `FindBounds()` function receives a parent `GameObject` as an argument. It begins with an empty bounds rectangle of size 0. The `Renderer` components of all of the parent's children are retrieved using the `GetComponentsInChildren()` function (Unity Technologies 2015d) and stored in an array. Afterwards, a `foreach` loop iterates through all of the children's `Renderer` components. The `Encapsulate()` function (Unity Technologies 2015b) adds each child's size to the overall `bounds` variable. Subsequently, the `bounds` variable is returned.

Hence, the `_bounds` variable in our `Start()` function represents the entire size of our world map. Recall that the BgMap `GameObject` is stored in our boundsObj variable, which gets passed into the FindBounds() function. The FindBounds() function searches through the individual tiles contained in the BgMap GameObject, adds up their size, and returns the final value to the _bounds variable.

At this point, we're prepared to modify our position calculations. Instead of placing all of this code inside the Update() function, a custom function named UpdatePos() was created. The Update() function now only makes a call to UpdatePos().

```
void Update() {

    //update position
    UpdatePos();

}
```

The existing as well as modified calculations, all take place in our UpdatePos() function.

```
private void UpdatePos() {

    //retrieve target position
    Vector3 targetPos = targetObj.transform.position;

    //retrieve camera position
    Vector3 camPos = gameObject.transform.position;

    //update camera position based on target position
    camPos.x = targetPos.x;
    camPos.y = targetPos.y;

    //if pos would cause camera to exceed bounds, lock to bounds
    //bounds size
    float halfBoundsW = _bounds.size.x / 2;
    float halfBoundsH = _bounds.size.y / 2;

    //camera size
    float halfCamW = Camera.main.orthographicSize * Screen.width /
      Screen.height;
    float halfCamH = Camera.main.orthographicSize;

    //x axis
    if (camPos.x < -halfBoundsW + halfCamW) {

        //lock to left bound, offset for half camera width
        camPos.x = -halfBoundsW + halfCamW;

}
    else if (camPos.x > halfBoundsW - halfCamW) {

        //lock to right bound
        camPos.x = halfBoundsW - halfCamW;
    }

    //y axis
    if (camPos.y < -halfBoundsH + halfCamH) {
```

```
        //lock to bottom bound
        camPos.y = -halfBoundsH + halfCamH;
    }

    else if (camPos.y > halfBoundsH - halfCamH) {

        //lock to top bound
        camPos.y = halfBoundsH - halfCamH;
    }

    //update position
    gameObject.transform.position = camPos;

}
```

Let's break down each piece of the UpdatePos() function. Just as before, we begin by retrieving the target and camera positions, then set them equal to one another.

```
//excerpt from UpdatePos() function
//retrieve target position
Vector3 targetPos = targetObj.transform.position;

//retrieve camera position
Vector3 camPos = gameObject.transform.position;

//update camera position based on target position
camPos.x = targetPos.x;
camPos.y = targetPos.y;
```

Next, we calculate the boundaries of our world map and camera relative to their center origin points:

```
//excerpt from UpdatePos() function
//bounds size
float halfBoundsW = _bounds.size.x / 2;
float halfBoundsH = _bounds.size.y / 2;

//camera size
float halfCamW = Camera.main.orthographicSize * Screen.width /
Screen.height;
float halfCamH = Camera.main.orthographicSize;
```

The map size is stored in the _bounds variable, so we take half of its width and height to represent the distance from the center origin of the map to its edges. For our 2D orthographic camera (Unity Technologies 2015c), the calculation is slightly different. The orthographic size of the camera happens to be half of its height. To find half of the width, multiply the orthographic size by the aspect ratio. We use these values to check whether the updated camera position would exceed the map's boundaries. If so, we prevent it from happening by stopping the camera at the boundaries.

```
//excerpt from UpdatePos() function
//x axis
if (camPos.x < -halfBoundsW + halfCamW) {
```

```
    //lock to left bound
    camPos.x = -halfBoundsW + halfCamW;
}
else if (camPos.x > halfBoundsW - halfCamW) {

    //lock to right bound
    camPos.x = halfBoundsW - halfCamW;
}

//y axis
if (camPos.y < -halfBoundsH + halfCamH) {

    //lock to bottom bound
    camPos.y = -halfBoundsH + halfCamH;
}
else if (camPos.y > halfBoundsH - halfCamH) {

    //lock to top bound
    camPos.y = halfBoundsH - halfCamH;
}
```

Consider these calculations carefully. For example, the first else if statement asks whether the camera's x position is greater than half of the map width minus half the camera width. Think about these calculations in the context of Figure 1.21. From the map's origin, half the width is equal to the right boundary. Meanwhile, the camera's position is determined by its origin point, which is half of its width. If we want the camera's right edge to perfectly align to the map's right boundary, we must take the x value of the map's right boundary and subtract half of the camera's width. This subtraction compensates for the center origin point of the camera. An adjustment such as this is made for each boundary. Make sure to review this code and work out the calculations yourself before proceeding.

Generally speaking, the distance from the center origin point of an object to its left or right edge is half of its width, while the distance to its top or bottom edge is half of its height. However, an object is positioned according to its center origin point. For instance, if you position an object at (0, 0) in your game world, you are setting its center equal to (0, 0). Thus, if you want to make sure the edge of an object is positioned in a particular way, you must adjust for the object's width or height relative to its origin point. When working in Unity with objects that have a center origin point, you will frequently make calculations such as these.

Once we have ensured that the camera will never exceed the map's boundaries, we safely update its position

```
//excerpt from UpdatePos() function
//update position
gameObject.transform.position = camPos;
```

Another challenge is complete. Run your game now to see that, as Luna approaches the boundaries of the world map, the camera stops following her. Yet, while she is moving safely in the center of the map, the camera continues to follow her as normal. Thus, the camera locks only at the point where it would expose the void space beyond our world map. Otherwise, it follows Luna normally.

Although our camera is functioning quite well, there are a few finishing touches we can put on it to make it especially pleasant for players. Let's proceed to the final challenge for this chapter.

▌ Challenge: Give the Camera Smooth Movement

Two relatively minor adjustments can be made to our camera to give it a more professional appeal. First, the camera's movement can be smoothed. Currently, the camera always moves at a constant speed. While this works perfectly fine, we can create a more pleasant effect for the player by smoothing the camera movement. Thus, instead of moving at a constant speed, the camera will gradually accelerate and decelerate as it follows Luna. The second feature that would improve our camera experience is to set a distance threshold for following Luna. In other words, we allow some space for Luna to move around without the camera following her. At present, the camera follows Luna the instant she begins to move. Once we establish a distance threshold, or dead zone, the camera will not follow Luna until after she moves a certain amount. Build upon your CamFollow script to implement these camera features. The requirements for this challenge are:

1. Set a minimum distance at which the camera begins to follow Luna.

2. Smooth the camera's movement so it gradually accelerates and decelerates as it follows Luna.

Hint: Determine the Camera Properties

Think about what you need to know in order to implement the required features. On the one hand, you know that the camera needs to follow Luna at a certain speed. Most likely, you will want to manipulate this speed to control the design of your camera's movement. On the other hand, you also need to specify a distance at which the camera will ignore Luna's movement. Likewise, you will want to adjust this variable. Therefore, it makes sense that you store these pieces of information as variables in your CamFollow script. You might add variables such as these to the top of your script:

```
//excerpt from CamFollow script
//follow speed
public float followSpeed;

//minimum distance at which camera begins to follow
public float minFollowDist;
```

Here, both variables are designated as public. Recall that public variables are visible in the Unity interface. These variables are initialized in the Unity Inspector window, rather than inside your script. This makes it especially easy for you to experiment with different values as you work to optimize your game's design. Thus, you can rapidly test and tune your variable values by setting them in the Inspector and running your game. Repeat this process until you get them just right.

Hint: Apply Smoothing to the Camera Movement

Currently, your camera moves at a constant speed. Find the area in your CamFollow script's `UpdatePos()` function where the camera's position is set. It should look something like this:

```
//excerpt from UpdatePos() function
//update camera position based on target position
camPos.x = targetPos.x;
camPos.y = targetPos.y;
```

Initially, you set the camera's position (`camPos`) exactly equal to Luna's position (`targetPos`). Subsequently, your `UpdatePos()` function makes boundary checks to ensure that the camera's view doesn't move outside of the world map. These boundary checks can remain the same. However, you no longer want to exactly set the camera position equal to Luna's position. Instead, you should use your `followSpeed` variable, as well as any necessary calculations, to gradually move the camera toward Luna's position. Once complete, you should be able to test your game and see that the camera accelerates and decelerates as it approaches Luna. You can fully implement this feature by manipulating how you calculate the new camera position, without needing to change other aspects of your script.

For an extra hint, consider how you can calculate the camera's new position relative to its current position and Luna's position. You always start from the camera's current position. You know that the camera should ultimately end at Luna's position. Thus, you can calculate the total distance that the camera needs to move to get from its current position to Luna's position. However, you only want to move part of the way there each frame. Meanwhile, the `followSpeed` variable determines exactly how fast the camera approaches Luna's position.

Hint: Account for the Distance Threshold

The final adjustment to your camera involves setting a distance threshold. If Luna moves less than this amount, the camera will not move. In contrast, once Luna's movement exceeds the distance threshold, the camera will follow her. Clearly, you will need to calculate the distance between the camera and Luna to implement this feature. That way, you can tell whether or not the camera needs to follow Luna. The exact distance at which the camera should start following Luna is controlled by your `minFollowDist` variable.

Notably, all of your camera's movement calculations are already implemented and do not need to be changed. In fact, you can think of this feature as telling the camera to move or not to move under certain circumstances. Thus, your task involves controlling if and when the camera's position is updated, rather than calculating the position itself. How might you control these factors in your code?

Again, you can make some minor adjustments to your `UpdatePos()` function in order to implement this feature. Once finished, you will be able to move Luna a certain distance without seeing any reaction from the camera. Yet, once she moves too far, the camera will follow her smoothly.

Example Solution: Give the Camera Smooth Movement

Your challenge was to add two features to the camera: smooth movement and a distance threshold. To smooth the camera's movement, you might use a calculation such as this inside your `UpdatePos()` function:

```
//calculate the camera's new position with smoothing applied
Vector3 newCamPos = camPos + (targetPos - camPos) * followSpeed *
Time.deltaTime;
```

In this code snippet, a `Vector3` variable named `newCamPos` stores the new camera position. It is calculated as the current camera position (`camPos`) plus the distance between Luna and the camera (`targetPos - camPos`) times the `followSpeed` times `Time.deltaTime`. On a side note, `Time.deltaTime` represents the time elapsed in the last frame (Unity Technologies 2015l). In Unity, we multiply by `Time.deltaTime` whenever we want to establish frame-rate independence, which is always a good idea when developing games. Hence, multiplying the distance between the camera and Luna by the `followSpeed` controls how fast the camera approaches Luna. Try increasing or decreasing the value of the `followSpeed` variable and testing your game to witness this effect. Through testing, you should be able to determine a value that makes the camera's movement pleasant to the eye. By the way, if you want to see smooth acceleration and deceleration, ensure that your `(targetPos - camPos) * followSpeed * Time.deltaTime` calculation yields a value between 0 and 1. If 1 or greater, the camera will warp directly to Luna or travel too far. If 0 or less, the camera either won't budge or will comically move in the wrong direction!

As for the minimum distance threshold, you need to determine how far the camera is from Luna. Since we're working with a 2D coordinate system, both the camera and Luna have x–y positions. Thus, you calculate the distance between two points as $\sqrt{(x_2 - x_1)^2 + (y_2 - y_1)^2}$, where the camera's position is (x_1, y_1) and Luna's position is (x_2, y_2). In code, the calculation would look like this:

```
//excerpt from UpdatePos() function
//calculate the distance between the camera and the target
float dist = Mathf.Sqrt(
    Mathf.Pow((targetPos.x - camPos.x), 2) +
    Mathf.Pow((targetPos.y - camPos.y), 2)
    );
```

Unity's `Mathf` library contains many common mathematical functions (Unity Technologies 2015g). In this case, the `Sqrt()` function is used to take a square root, while the `Pow()` function is used to raise values to a given power. Many useful functions are included in `Mathf`, and you will likely encounter them in your future coding.

With the distance between Luna and the camera calculated, you can assess whether the distance is large enough to warrant moving the camera. This is where a simple `if` statement and your `minFollowDist` variable come into play:

```
//excerpt from UpdatePos() function
//if distance to target is greater than minimum
```

```
if (targetDist > minFollowDist) {
    /*
    Place your existing camera position calculation
    and boundary check code inside this statement.
    */
}
```

With this check in place, the camera's position only updates if the distance to Luna is greater than the threshold you set. If it is, the camera's position is updated using your existing calculations. If it isn't, the camera's position is not updated at all. Thus, you have implemented a threshold distance at which the camera follows Luna. Try experimenting with different values for your `minFollowDist` variable to see what impact it has on the camera's movement.

Yet, one finishing touch can be placed on our minimum distance threshold. When Luna stops moving, the camera stops just inside the distance threshold. Indeed, this is what we told it to do with our code. However, it would be much nicer if the camera continued to center itself over Luna after she stops moving. To implement this, we need to store Luna's previous position in our CamFollow script, like so:

```
//excerpt from CamFollow script
//previous position of the target
private Vector3 _targetPrevPos;
```

Next, we initialize this variable to Luna's current position inside the `Start()` function. The updated code is shown in bold:

```
//excerpt from Start() function
//store target pos
Vector3 targetPos = targetObj.transform.position;
_targetPrevPos = targetPos;
```

Then, we make sure to update Luna's previous position at the end of every frame. To do so, add this code at the very end of the `UpdatePos()` function:

```
//excerpt from UpdatePos() function
//update previous target position
_targetPrevPos = targetPos;
```

Lastly, we can utilize Luna's current and previous position to determine whether the camera should center over her. Modify the `if` statement in your `UpdatePos()` function, like so:

```
//excerpt from UpdatePos() function
//if distance to target is greater than minimum
//or target is idle
if (targetDist > minFollowDist || targetPos == _targetPrevPos) {
    /*
    Your existing camera position calculation
    and boundary check code is inside this statement.
    */
}
```

By adding the check to compare Luna's current and previous position, we allow the camera to keep moving in the event that she has stopped. We know that she has stopped when her previous position is equal to her current position. Thus, the camera smoothly centers itself over her whenever she is not moving. Nevertheless, we continue to allow the camera to move while Luna is outside the distance threshold, but still prohibit the camera from moving while she is inside the distance threshold. At last, we have a fully functional, professional-looking camera.

Finally, the entire CamFollow script is provided. Compare your own solution to this example and make any desired adjustments to your implementation:

```
public class CamFollow : MonoBehaviour {
    //follow speed
    public float followSpeed;

    //minimum distance at which camera begins to follow
    public float minFollowDist;

    //target object to follow
    public GameObject targetObj;

    //previous position of target
    private Vector3 _targetPrevPos;

    //boundary object
    public GameObject boundsObj;

    //boundaries
    private Bounds _bounds;

    //init
    void Start() {

        //store target pos
        Vector3 targetPos = targetObj.transform.position;
        _targetPrevPos = targetPos;

        //set camera to start from target pos
        targetPos.z = gameObject.transform.position.z;
        gameObject.transform.position = targetPos;

        //retrieve bounds
        _bounds = FindBounds(boundsObj);
    }

    //update
    void Update() {

        //update position
        UpdatePos();
    }

    //update position based on target movement
    private void UpdatePos() {

        //retrieve camera position
        Vector3 camPos = gameObject.transform.position;
```

```
//retrieve target position
Vector3 targetPos = targetObj.transform.position;

//check distance to target
float targetDist = Mathf.Sqrt(

    Mathf.Pow((targetPos.x - camPos.x), 2) +
    Mathf.Pow((targetPos.y - camPos.y), 2)
    );

//if distance to target is greater than minimum
//or target is idle
if (targetDist > minFollowDist || targetPos == _
  targetPrevPos) {

    //calculate new position
    Vector3 newCamPos = camPos + (targetPos - camPos) *
      followSpeed * Time.deltaTime;
    newCamPos.z = camPos.z;

    //if new pos would cause camera to exceed bounds, lock
      to bounds
    //bounds size
    float halfBoundsW = _bounds.size.x / 2;
    float halfBoundsH = _bounds.size.y / 2;

    //camera size
    float halfCamW = Camera.main.orthographicSize * Screen.
      width / Screen.height;
    float halfCamH = Camera.main.orthographicSize;

    //x axis
    if (newCamPos.x < -halfBoundsW + halfCamW) {

        //lock to left bound
        newCamPos.x = -halfBoundsW + halfCamW;
    }
    else if (newCamPos.x > halfBoundsW - halfCamW) {

        //lock to right bound
        newCamPos.x = halfBoundsW - halfCamW;
    }

    //y axis
    if (newCamPos.y < -halfBoundsH + halfCamH) {

        //lock to bottom bound
        newCamPos.y = -halfBoundsH + halfCamH;
    }
    else if (newCamPos.y > halfBoundsH - halfCamH) {

        //lock to top bound
        newCamPos.y = halfBoundsH - halfCamH;
    }

    //update position
    gameObject.transform.position = newCamPos;
}
```

```
        //update previous target position
        _targetPrevPos = targetPos;
    }

    //find bounds for object based on children
    private Bounds FindBounds(GameObject theParent) {

        //store bounds
        Bounds bounds = new Bounds(Vector3.zero, Vector3.zero);

        //retrieve renderers for all children
        Renderer[] allChildren = theParent.GetComponentsInChildren<
          Renderer>();

        //search all children
        foreach (Renderer aChild in allChildren) {

            //add child bounds to total
            bounds.Encapsulate(aChild.bounds);
        }

        //return
        return bounds;
    }

} //end class
```

Summary

Congratulations on completing your first set of challenges! You have implemented a camera that pleasantly follows Luna around the screen and allows her to explore the entire game world. With this chapter complete, you should be able to apply all of these game implementation techniques:

- Implement a camera that follows the player

- Lock camera movement to the boundaries of the game world

- Design smooth camera movement for a pleasant player experience

- Create your own C# scripts, variables, and functions

- Determine logical solutions to computer problems prior to implementing them

- Leverage Unity features to improve your development process

Luna is excited by the opportunity to explore the entire game world, thanks to your camera implementation. Take a moment to test your game and explore the world. Look closely, and you may find that the Red Knight is awaiting Luna's arrival somewhere on the map. He has important information to share about Luna's quest. Your coding journey continues in the next chapter.

References

Quick, J. M. 2015. *Learn to Code with Games.* Boca Raton, FL: CRC Press. ISBN: 9781498704687.

Unity Technologies. 2015a. Bounds. http://docs.unity3d.com/ScriptReference/Bounds. html (accessed December 8, 2015).

Unity Technologies. 2015b. Bounds.Encapsulate. http://docs.unity3d.com/ScriptReference/ Bounds.Encapsulate.html (accessed December 8, 2015).

Unity Technologies. 2015c. Camera.orthographic. http://docs.unity3d.com/ScriptReference/ Camera-orthographic.html (accessed December 8, 2015).

Unity Technologies. 2015d. Component.GetComponentsInChildren. http://docs. unity3d.com/ScriptReference/Component.GetComponentsInChildren.html (accessed December 8, 2015).

Unity Technologies. 2015e. GameObject.FindWithTag. http://docs.unity3d.com/ ScriptReference/GameObject.FindWithTag.html (accessed December 8, 2015).

Unity Technologies. 2015f. GameObject.GetComponent. http://docs.unity3d.com/ ScriptReference/GameObject.GetComponent.html (accessed December 8, 2015).

Unity Technologies. 2015g. Mathf. http://docs.unity3d.com/ScriptReference/Mathf. html (accessed December 8, 2015).

Unity Technologies. 2015h. MonoBehaviour.Start. http://docs.unity3d.com/ ScriptReference/MonoBehaviour.Start.html (accessed December 8, 2015).

Unity Technologies. 2015i. MonoBehaviour.Update. http://docs.unity3d.com/ ScriptReference/MonoBehaviour.Update.html (accessed December 8, 2015).

Unity Technologies. 2015j. Sprite Editor. http://docs.unity3d.com/Manual/SpriteEditor.html (accessed December 8, 2015).

Unity Technologies. 2015k. SpriteRenderer. http://docs.unity3d.com/ScriptReference/ SpriteRenderer.html (accessed December 8, 2015).

Unity Technologies. 2015l. Time.deltaTime. http://docs.unity3d.com/ScriptReference/ Time-deltaTime.html (accessed December 8, 2015).

Unity Technologies. 2015m. Vector3. http://docs.unity3d.com/ScriptReference/Vector3. html (accessed December 8, 2015).

2 A Dialogue with the Red Knight

Upon exploring the full range of the world map, Luna made her first encounter. Strangely, the Red Knight is of few words. In fact, he appears to have no words for Luna. Although there is surely information to share, the Red Knight seems unable to say anything. This is where your coding skills come into play. You can script a dialogue box that allows the Red Knight to speak with Luna. Henceforth, your dialogue box will display critical information to the player of your game.

▮ Goals

By the end of this chapter, you will be able to apply these game implementation techniques:

- Implement a dialogue box to notify the player about important information

- Update a dialogue box based on changing game conditions

- Create a dialogue box that can be dismissed automatically or through user input

- Use a scrolling effect to update the dialogue box as new information arrives

- Manage function execution using coroutines

▮ Required Files

In this chapter, you will use the following files from the *Software > Chapter_02* folder (https://www.crcpress.com/Learn-to-Implement-Games-with-Code/Quick/p/book/9781498753388).

- The contents of the Challenge folder to create, code, and test your solution

- The contents of the Solution folder to compare your solution to the example solution

▮ Challenge Context

The provided challenge project mostly picks up from where you left off in the previous chapter. All of your assets, including the CamFollow script, are present. However, a few additions have been made. To review the project provided as your starting point in this chapter, open the *Challenge > Assets > Scenes > Map.unity* scene in Unity.

Dialogue Box Panel

Expand the Canvas object in the Hierarchy window. An object named PnlDialogue has been added to the scene and contains a TxtDialogue child object (Figure 2.1). This represents the dialogue box that we will use to present information to the player. Examine the Inspector window for PnlDialogue (Figure 2.2). Several components have been arranged. Notably, the `RectTransform` component determines the positioning and sizing of our dialogue box. The `Image` component stores our BgCanvas sprite, which forms the background for our dialogue box. Meanwhile, the `Vertical Layout Group` and `Canvas Group` components fine-tune the presentation of our dialogue box.

Similarly, the TxtDialogue object has been set up with its components. Most importantly, the `Text` component determines the text that will appear in our dialogue box, as well as its formatting (Figure 2.3).

Together, the PnlDialogue and TxtDialogue objects compose the visual aspects of our dialogue box. Your challenge will be to code a script to manage the underlying functionality of the dialogue box.

Unity User Interface System

Notice the Canvas object in the Hierarchy window (Figure 2.4). Our game will thoroughly make use of the Canvas to display user interface (UI)

Figure 2.1 Expand the Canvas object to find the newly added PnlDialogue and TxtDialogue objects. These objects represent our dialogue box.

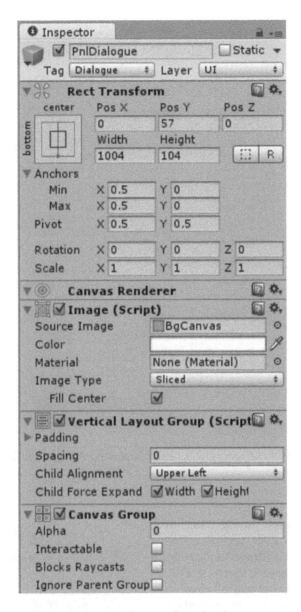

Figure 2.2 The PnlDialogue object has been configured with `RectTransform`, `Image`, `Vertical Layout Group`, and `Canvas Group` components.

items to the player. For example, a tally of the collectable objects Luna has found is displayed in the top-right corner of the screen, thanks to the PnlInventory object. As mentioned, the visuals of our dialogue box are determined by the PnlDialogue object. More such UI elements will be added to our Canvas as we develop our game.

Our Canvas object and its children make use of Unity's UI system (Unity Technologies 2015n). Starting from version 4.6, the Unity UI system provides

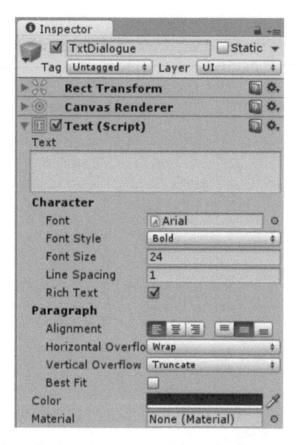

Figure 2.3 The TxtDialogue object's Text component will be used to store the text for our dialogue box.

numerous ways to conveniently design game visuals, such as menus and overlays. The details of the Unity UI system are beyond the scope of this book. Thus, prearranged UI elements will be provided for you throughout the challenges. The focus of this book is on coding game implementations. Hence, your responsibility is to write code that manipulates UI elements in the context of developing your game.

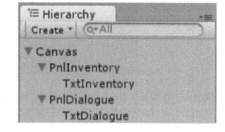

Figure 2.4 The Canvas object contains the user interface elements for our game.

Nevertheless, if you continue to use Unity in the future, it would be worthwhile to learn more about the UI system. For the time being, feel free to manipulate the settings of the provided UI components. Test your game afterward to see how your changes impact the UI.

■ Challenge: Notify the Player Using a Dismissible Dialogue Box

Run your project in Unity. As before, you can move Luna around the screen. Yet, when you encounter the Red Knight, nothing happens. Ultimately, when Luna collides with the Red Knight, you want to display a message to the player.

Think about the features that your dialogue box needs to have. For instance, your dialogue box needs text to display. It might be useful to be able to show and hide your dialogue box on demand. This would allow the player to see messages only at relevant times. Moreover, one way to handle removing the dialogue box is to accept user input. For example, the player could press a key to dismiss the dialogue box after reading it. Fully consider the design of your dialogue box before attempting to code it. For each of the challenge requirements, think about the logic that you will use to implement your dialogue box successfully. The requirements for this challenge are:

1. Create a Dialogue script to manage the information presented to the player.

2. Permit the dialogue text to be updated.

3. Allow the visibility of the dialogue box to be changed.

4. Dismiss the dialogue box based on user input.

5. Detect Luna's collision with the Red Knight to trigger the dialogue box.

Hint: Update the Dialogue Text

Assuming you have created your Dialogue script and attached it to the PnlDialogue object in your scene, you are prepared to begin implementing your dialogue box. If you need a reminder on how to create and attach scripts, review the sections titled *Hint: Create a New Script* and *Hint: Attach the Script to an Object* in Chapter 1.

Without text, there is little reason to have a dialogue box. We could create an entirely new dialogue box every time a new message needs to be shown to the player. However, it would be more efficient for us to reuse one dialogue box throughout the game. Every time we want to display something new, we simply update the text in the dialogue box.

You already have a Dialogue script attached to your PnlDialogue object. The PnlDialogue object has a child object named TxtDialogue, which has a Text component. Recall that these objects leverage Unity's UI system. In order to access components from the UI system, you need to include this using statement (Microsoft Corporation 2015b) at the top of your Dialogue script:

```
//required to access Unity UI system
//place at top of script
using UnityEngine.UI;
```

This statement grants you access to the content included in Unity's UI system. If you didn't include this statement and tried to access UI components in your code, an error would occur.

Once you have access to Unity's UI system in your Dialogue script, you can retrieve the Text component attached to your TxtDialogue object. For example, you could use the GetComponentInChildren() function (Unity Technologies 2015c) to retrieve the Text component and store it in a variable.

```
//use GetComponentInChildren() to retrieve the Text component
//store the Text component in a variable
Text txt = gameObject.GetComponentInChildren<Text>();
```

At this point, your Dialogue script has a method for retrieving the Text component from the PnlDialogue > TxtDialogue object. Why not write a function in your Dialogue script that allows you to update the dialogue box's text whenever you need to?

Hint: Change the Visibility of the Dialogue Box

At times, you want to display your dialogue box to players. At other times, you want to hide the dialogue box from view so it doesn't distract the player from other aspects of your game. Therefore, it makes sense to build the capacity to show and hide the dialogue box into your Dialogue script. One option for showing and hiding the dialogue box involves leveraging the Canvas Group component (Unity Technologies 2015a) attached to your PnlDialogue object (Figure 2.5). Notice that an alpha variable is included in the Canvas Group component. The alpha variable controls the transparency of the entire PnlDialogue object. If the alpha is 0, the dialogue box is fully transparent (invisible). If the alpha is 1, the dialogue box is fully opaque (visible). In-between alpha values will yield a partially transparent dialogue box. Thus, you can retrieve the Canvas Group component in your Dialogue script and set the alpha component, like so:

```
//retrieve the Canvas Group component
CanvasGroup canvasGroup = gameObject.GetComponent<CanvasGroup>();

//set the alpha to 0 (invisible)
canvasGroup.alpha = 0;

//set the alpha to 1 (opaque)
canvasGroup.alpha = 1;
```

You may want to code functions to control the alpha transparency of your dialogue box. Experiment with different alpha values to find the ideal transparency for your dialogue box.

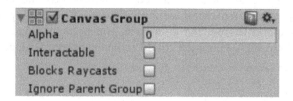

Figure 2.5 The Canvas Group component's alpha value controls the transparency of the entire object. A value of "0" renders the object invisible, while a value of "1" renders the object opaque.

2. A Dialogue with the Red Knight

Hint: Dismiss the Dialogue Box Based on User Input

Imagine your dialogue box appearing on the screen and delivering critical information to the player. Eventually, the player will finish accessing the information presented in the dialogue box. At that moment, you want to dismiss the dialogue box, so it does not become a distraction. A user-friendly option is to allow the player to dismiss the dialogue box through user input, such as a key press or button click. You can already show and hide your dialogue box. Dismissing the dialogue box is equivalent to hiding it when the proper circumstances arise. Thus, you need to add code to your Dialogue script that determines when the dialogue box should be dismissed.

Unity Input Functions

In Unity, you can check for user input with the Input.GetKeyDown(), Input.GetKeyUp(), and Input.GetKey() functions (Unity Technologies 2015g, 2015h, 2015i). All of these functions receive a KeyCode (Unity Technologies 2015j), which is an identifier that indicates which type of input was received. In return, the functions provide a Boolean value that indicates whether the input occurred during the current frame. The only difference between the functions is how they are triggered. Input.GetKeyDown() is triggered immediately when a key is pressed, Input.GetKeyUp() is triggered when a key is released, and Input.GetKey() is triggered when a key is held. For instance, this code sample demonstrates how to check whether the spacebar is released:

```
//if the spacebar is released
if (Input.GetKeyUp(KeyCode.Space)) {

    /*
    Place code to execute when
    user input is received in
    this section.
    */
}
```

Note that Unity's input functions operate on a frame-by-frame basis. That is, they will return a Boolean value for each individual frame they are called. Thus, if you want to continually check for user input throughout the game, you should make sure to call your functions inside Update().

Coroutines

An alternative way to handle user input for your dialogue box would be to implement a coroutine. A coroutine is a function that can execute over multiple frames (Unity Technologies 2015e). After being called, most functions execute in their entirety over the course of a single frame. However, coroutines are capable of pausing their execution in one frame and continuing it in a future frame. While a coroutine is paused, the other code in your game loop continues to execute. Thus, coroutines are extremely useful for managing time-sensitive events. For example, we need to allow the user to dismiss the dialogue box, but we don't know when that will happen. A coroutine allows our game to execute as normal, while simultaneously waiting for user input to occur. Whenever user input occurs, the coroutine can take the necessary actions.

Let's consider the fundamental coroutine implementation in C# and Unity. We begin with a function that returns the IEnumerator type. This function can be executed over a series of frames and paused at any time by including a yield statement (Unity Technologies 2015e). When managing our game code, we will typically use yield along with return and a value. Commonly, yield return 0 is used to delay the execution of a coroutine. While the return value has no special meaning in this case, yield return 0 causes a coroutine to cease its execution and allow the rest of the game loop to continue. Alternatively, we can also return specific values, functions, or even other coroutines. Hence, sophisticated control systems can be implemented using coroutines. For the time being, let's consider a simple coroutine implementation:

```
//example coroutine implementation
//return IEnumerator when creating a coroutine
IEnumerator ExampleCoroutine() {

        //whether the coroutine is running
        bool isRunning = true;

        //while coroutine is running
        while (isRunning) {

                /*
                Place the frame-by-frame
                execution code here. For
                example, update the game
                state in some way and
                check whether the end
                conditions are met.
                */

                if (CONDITIONS == TRUE) {

                        /*
                        Ultimately, once certain
                        conditions are met, we
                        allow the coroutine to end.
                        */

                        //end coroutine
                        isRunning = false;
                }

                /*
                Otherwise, while the end
                conditions are not met,
                we pause the coroutine
                until the next frame.
                */

                //pause coroutine
                yield return 0;
        }
}
```

This sample coroutine starts by initializing a Boolean variable called isRun-ning. This variable flags whether the coroutine is or is not in progress. Next, a while statement iterates over the isRunning variable. Since isRunning was set to true, the while statement runs indefinitely. Inside, we place any code that we want to execute while the coroutine is running. Then, we must include conditions that will either end or pause the coroutine. To end the corou-tine, we set our isRunning variable to false. This ensures that our function completes its final loop during the present frame. Most likely, we want to set our isRunning variable to false inside a conditional statement. This ensures that our coroutine only ends if specific conditions are met. Lastly, to pause the coroutine, we place yield return 0 at the very end of the while statement. If our coroutine gets to this point in a given frame, it will pause its execution and continue during the following frame.

One other necessity is starting our coroutine in the first place. To begin a coroutine, use Unity's StartCoroutine() function (Unity Technologies 2015l). Any time you want a coroutine to begin, you must use the StartCoroutine() function. If you forget to use StartCoroutine() and try to call your corou-tine like a normal function, it will not run. Our example coroutine would be called using this code:

```
//start the example coroutine
StartCoroutine(ExampleCoroutine());
```

Using your knowledge of coroutines and user input, you should be able to write a function that allows the user to dismiss the dialogue box. By the way, coroutines are useful for many other things besides user input. Later on, our game will extensively leverage coroutines to manage games states and turn-based interactions.

Hint: Detect the Collision

At last, we return to Luna's encounter with the Red Knight. Test your game in Unity and move Luna over the Red Knight's position. Still, nothing appears to happen. Yet, if you open the Console window, you will find a message (Figure 2.6).

Unity Console Window

The Unity Console window displays errors, warnings, and other messages associated with your game (Unity Technologies 2015d). You can send your own custom messages to the Console window using the Debug.Log() command

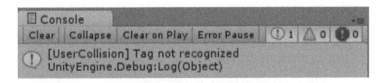

Figure 2.6 When Luna collides with the Red Knight, a message is printed to the Console window.

(Unity Technologies 2015f). Printing messages to the Console window is especially useful for debugging purposes, because it can help you identify bugs and keep track of the various bits of code that execute during gameplay.

Unity Trigger Collisions

Navigate to the *Assets > Scripts* folder and open the UserCollision file in your code editor. Scroll to the bottom of the file to find this line of code:

```
Debug.Log("[UserCollision] Tag not recognized");
```

Indeed, this is the line of code that sent the very same message to the Console window earlier (Figure 2.6). Examine the rest of the UserCollision file. It consists of only one function: OnTriggerEnter2D() (Unity Technologies 2015k). This is a built-in Unity function that detects a trigger collision between two objects at the very moment they intersect. A trigger collision ignores Unity's physics engine features, such as gravity and friction. There are other varieties of collisions available in Unity too, but we only need to use trigger collisions in the context of our game. In addition, trigger functions are available to detect the moment that a collision ends (OnTriggerExit2D()) and sustained collisions over multiple frames (OnTriggerStay2D()).

To detect a trigger collision in Unity, one object must have a Rigidbody2D (Unity Technologies 2015m) component and a collider (Unity Technologies 2015b), such as a BoxCollider2D. Our Player object has both (Figure 2.7). Any other object that we wish to detect collisions with must at least have a collider with the Is Trigger box checked. For example, our Red Knight has a BoxCollider2D component (Figure 2.8).

The UserCollision script is attached to our Player GameObject. Thus, the OnTriggerEnter2D() function is continuously checking for collisions between Luna and other objects in our game world. Whenever Luna collides with another object that has a collider, the OnTriggerEnter2D() function is executed. Inside the function, a switch statement checks the tag of the object that Luna collided with. Depending on the tag, our function executes the appropriate actions in our game world. For instance, this excerpt handles collisions with collectables:

```
//UserCollision script
//excerpt from OnTriggerEnter2D() function
//collectable collisions
case "Collectable":

        //inventory has space remaining
        if (inventory.numObjects < inventory.maxObjects) {

                //add collectable to inventory
                inventory.AddItem();

                //destroy
                Destroy(theCollider.gameObject);
        }

        break;
```

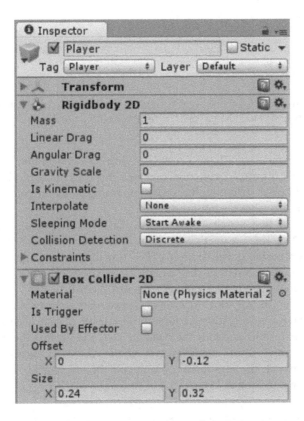

Figure 2.7 The Player object has `Rigidbody2D` and `BoxCollider2D` components, which allow it to collide with other objects.

Figure 2.8 The Red Knight object has a `BoxCollider2D` component with the `Is Trigger` box checked, which allows it to be detected in trigger collisions.

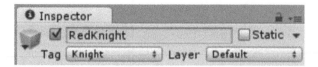

Figure 2.9 The Red Knight object has been given the "Knight" tag, which makes it easy to incorporate into your existing `OnTriggerEnter2D()` function.

Hence, whenever Luna collides with a collectable object, our `OnTriggerEnter2D()` function executes this code. Specifically, this code ensures that Luna's inventory has space remaining, adds the collectable to her inventory, and removes it from the scene.

Inspect the Red Knight object to see that it has been given the "Knight" tag (Figure 2.9). This means that you can incorporate the Red Knight collision into your existing `OnTriggerEnter2D()` function. Simply add a case to your `switch` statement to handle the "Knight" tag. Afterward, your "Knight" case will be executed when Luna encounters the Red Knight.

From here, you only need to write the appropriate code for your Red Knight collision. You should already have functions available in your Dialogue script to update the text, show and hide the dialogue box, and dismiss the dialogue box based on user input. Think about how you can use your `OnTriggerEnter2D()` function to execute the appropriate code in your Dialogue script when Luna collides with the Red Knight.

Example Solution: Notify the Player Using a Dismissible Dialogue Box

You were challenged to code a dialogue box with updateable text, visibility settings, and dismissal through user input. In addition, your dialogue box should be put into action when Luna collides with the Red Knight on the world map. Let's review the example solution.

Most aspects of this challenge can be handled in the Dialogue script, which you created and attached to your PnlDialogue object. To start, you need to update the dialogue box text. This can be handled in a function:

```
public void CreateDialogueWithText(string[] theText) {

        //retrieve text
        Text txt = gameObject.GetComponentInChildren<Text>();

        //set initial text
        txt.text = theText[0];

        //for each text item provided
        for (int i = 1; i < theText.Length; i++) {

                //add line break
                txt.text += "\n";
```

```
        //add text
        txt.text += theText[i];
    }
}
```

This `CreateDialogueWithText()` function accepts an array of strings as an argument. The `Text` component attached to the PnlDialogue > TxtDialogue object is stored in a variable using the `GetComponentInChildren()` function. The dialogue box's text is initially set to the first string in the array. Subsequently, a `for` loop iterates through the remaining strings and adds each one as a new line of text. Of course, this is just one of many potential ways to update the dialogue text. For example, we could update the text with a single formatted string. However, the nice thing about this approach is that it allows us to specify separate lines of text. Thus, we can easily create messages that are formatted in multiple lines within our dialogue box.

Another important feature is the ability to show and hide our dialogue box as needed. This can be accomplished using two functions:

```
public void Show() {

    //set alpha to visible
    gameObject.GetComponent<CanvasGroup>().alpha = 0.8f;
}

public void Hide() {

    //set alpha to invisible
    gameObject.GetComponent<CanvasGroup>().alpha = 0.0f;
}
```

Our `Show()` and `Hide()` functions retrieve the `Canvas Group` component attached to our PnlDialogue object and manipulate its `alpha` value. In this example, the `Show()` function sets the `alpha` to 0.8 instead of 1. This way, the player can still see the portion of the game world that gets covered up by the dialogue box. If the `alpha` were set to 1, the dialogue box would completely cover the game world. Yet, if the `alpha` is too low, the text becomes unreadable, so there is a balance at play. Meanwhile, our `Hide()` function sets the `alpha` to 0, which ensures that it is completely hidden when not in use. Feel free to experiment with your own alpha values.

To complete this iteration of the Dialogue script, we let the user dismiss our dialogue box by implementing a coroutine:

```
public IEnumerator HideOnInput() {

    //whether dialogue is dismissed
    bool isDismissed = false;

    //while not dismissed
    while (isDismissed == false) {

        //check input
        if (Input.GetKeyUp(KeyCode.Space)) {
```

```
                //hide
                Hide();

                //toggle flag
                isDismissed = true;
            }

            //keep waiting
            yield return 0;
        }
    }
```

The HideOnInput() coroutine uses the isDismissed Boolean flag to determine whether the dialogue box has been dismissed. While the dialogue box is present, the coroutine checks each frame for the spacebar to be pressed using Input.GetKey(KeyCode.Space). If the key is pressed, the dialogue box is hidden by calling the Hide() function. The isDismissed flag is also set to true, effectively ending the coroutine. However, if the key is not pressed, the coroutine pauses until the next frame via yield return 0.

Rather than constantly checking for user input in Update(), an advantage of using a coroutine is that we can control when it begins. Importantly, we must remember to call StartCoroutine() precisely when we want to let the player dismiss the dialogue box. For instance, we can start our coroutine just after presenting a new dialogue box to the player. Thereafter, the player can dismiss it when desired.

With that said, our final step for this challenge is to present the dialogue box to the player. To do so, we expand our UserCollision script's OnTriggerEnter2D() function:

```
//UserCollision script
//excerpt from OnTriggerEnter2D() function
//place this code inside the switch statement
//knight collision
case "Knight":

        //retrieve dialogue
        Dialogue dialogue = GameObject.FindWithTag("Dialogue").
          GetComponent<Dialogue>();

        //update dialogue text
        dialogue.CreateDialogueWithText(new string[] {
                "I am the Red Knight.",
                "Nice to meet you!",
                "Good luck on your quest."
        });

        //show
        dialogue.Show();

        //hide on input
        StartCoroutine(dialogue.HideOnInput());

        break;
```

To detect the collision between Luna and the Red Knight, we add the "Knight" tag to our `OnTriggerEnter2D()` function's switch statement. First, the Dialogue script is retrieved from the PnlDialogue object and stored in a variable named `dialogue`. Next, the `CreateDialogueWithText()` function is used to compose the Red Knight's message to Luna. Since this only updates the dialogue box's text, we then call `Show()` to make it visible to the player. Finally, `StartCoroutine()` is used in conjunction with `HideOnInput()` to allow the player to dismiss the dialogue box.

Run your game now and direct Luna to the Red Knight on the world map. Once they collide, you will see your dialogue box appear on the screen. The Red Knight can finally communicate with Luna! After you read the message, press the spacebar to dismiss the dialogue box.

While it is most exciting to have implemented a functional dialogue box, there is much we can do to refine it. In the upcoming challenges, we will focus on improving our dialogue box implementation.

▌ Challenge: Notify the Player Using a Timed Dialogue Box

Timing is another way to handle the dismissal of our dialogue box. Instead of requiring the player to press a key, we can specify a time at which our dialogue box automatically disappears. This feature can be put into your existing Dialogue script, thus providing an additional option for dismissing your dialogue box. The requirements for this challenge are:

1. Introduce a timed delay before dismissing your dialogue box.

2. Write a coroutine to manage your timed delay.

Hint: Introduce a Timed Delay

You can implement a coroutine to handle the timing for your dialogue box. Think of the duration of your dialogue box as a delay introduced before hiding it. Writing a coroutine such as this allows you to specify any number of seconds to delay:

```
private IEnumerator Delay(float theDelay) {

        //process delay
        float duration = 0;
        while (duration < theDelay) {

                //increment duration
                duration += Time.deltaTime;

                //continue
                yield return 0;
        }
}
```

This coroutine keeps track of how much time has elapsed since it began. For each frame, `Time.deltaTime` (the duration of the most recent frame) is added to the cumulative duration, and the coroutine pauses. Once the cumulative duration exceeds the specified limit, the coroutine ends. To execute the delay in the context of your dialogue box, you can place it inside another coroutine, such as this:

```
public IEnumerator HideAfterDelay(float theDelay) {

    //handle delay
    yield return StartCoroutine(Delay(theDelay));

    //hide
    Hide();
}
```

The `HideAfterDelay()` function is our first example of a coroutine inside another coroutine. This is perfectly valid code and quite useful. The `HideAfterDelay()` function yields to the entire `Delay()` coroutine before calling `Hide()`. Thus, the dialogue box is hidden after the delay time has passed. Indeed, we can create sophisticated behaviors by chaining together multiple coroutines. Keep this in mind as we progress through the development process.

Hint: Use the `WaitForSeconds()` Function

Although you have already written your own delay coroutine, it is worth noting that Unity has a useful built-in function called `WaitForSeconds()` (Unity Technologies 2015o). This function receives a number of seconds as an argument. You can return `WaitForSeconds()` inside a coroutine to produce the delay. Hence, `WaitForSeconds()` is essentially identical to the custom delay function that you just saw. The following sample code demonstrates `WaitForSeconds()` implemented inside our `HideAfterDelay()` coroutine:

```
public IEnumerator HideAfterDelay(float theDelay) {

    //handle delay
    yield return new WaitForSeconds(theDelay);

    //hide
    Hide();
}
```

Example Solution: Notify the Player Using a Timed Dialogue Box

With your `HideAfterDelay()` coroutine and either a custom delay function or `WaitForSeconds()`, you have completed the challenge of creating a timed dialogue box. If needed, review the preceding hints to see the code behind these functions. To implement the timed dialogue box, return to the "Knight" case in your UserCollision script:

```
//UserCollision script
//excerpt from OnTriggerEnter2D() function
```

```
case "Knight":

        //retrieve dialogue
        Dialogue dialogue = GameObject.FindWithTag("Dialogue").
         GetComponent<Dialogue>();

        //update dialogue text
        dialogue.CreateDialogueWithText(new string[] {
                "I am the Red Knight.",
                "Nice to meet you!",
                "Good luck on your quest."
        });

        //show
        dialogue.Show();

        //hide after delay
        StartCoroutine(dialogue.HideAfterDelay(3.0f));

        break;
```

As you can see, the only change entails calling our `HideAfterDelay()`
coroutine when Luna collides with the Red Knight. Run your game and move
Luna to the Red Knight. Your dialogue box should appear, and then automatically disappear after a few seconds. You are now capable of dismissing your dialogue box through user input or after a certain amount of time passes. These are
both useful options to have for displaying information in your game.

▮ Challenge: Update the Dialogue Box with a Scrolling Text Effect

Currently, your dialogue box is used to present a single notification at a single
time. While this is reasonable behavior, suppose that you want to get even more
utility out of your dialogue box. Think about using your dialogue box in situations such as these:

- Present multiple lines of text over a period of time

- Update the dialogue text as new information arrives

- Preserve existing lines of text while introducing new ones

For example, imagine having a turn-based interaction sequence between the
characters in your game. You could display information about this unfolding
sequence of events in your dialogue box. After each character takes a turn, you
present a line of text describing what happened. Once the dialogue box runs out
of space, the oldest line of text is removed to make room for the newest line. This
process is demonstrated:

```
//example interaction sequence
//dialogue box with 3 lines of text
//start of Luna's turn
```

```
[Line 1]: Luna's turn…
[Line 2]:
[Line 3]:

//after Luna's turn
[Line 1]: Luna's turn…
[Line 2]: Luna gave the Red Knight a hug!
[Line 3]:

//start of Red Knight's turn
[Line 1]: Luna's turn…
[Line 2]: Luna gave the Red Knight a hug!
[Line 3]: Red Knight's turn…

//after Red Knight's turn
[Line 1]: Luna gave the Red Knight a hug!
[Line 2]: Red Knight's turn…
[Line 3]: Red Knight screamed!
```

As you can see, the dialogue box gradually fills its empty lines. Once all lines are filled, the oldest line is removed and the newest line is added to the bottom. Your challenge is to implement these capabilities in your dialogue box. This will yield a versatile dialogue box that is sure to come in handy as you continue to develop your game. The requirements for this challenge are:

1. Store multiple lines of text in your dialogue box.

2. Allow the text in the dialogue box to be updated.

3. Apply a scrolling effect to your text, such that the oldest lines are gradually removed as new lines are added.

Hint: Store Each Line of Text

Thus far, our Dialogue script has managed the single Text component attached to our PnlDialogue > TxtDialogue object. Interestingly, even though we wish to manipulate the several lines in our dialogue box, we do not have to make any changes to our scene. We can continue to work with a single Text component. However, our Dialogue script must make a logical distinction between the different lines in order to manage them properly. You can do this by storing the individual lines of text displayed in your dialogue box. For example, an array or similar collection of strings would do the trick:

```
//Dialogue script
//store individual lines of text in an array
public string[] lines;
```

If you use a public array such as this one, be sure to set the number of lines stored in your dialogue box from the Unity Inspector window. Click on PnlDialogue and find its Dialogue script in the Unity Inspector. Expand the Lines array and set the Size value equal to the number of lines you want to appear in your dialogue box (Figure 2.10).

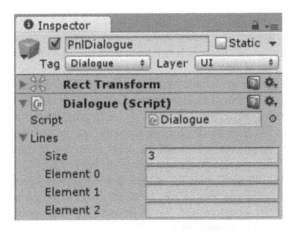

Figure 2.10 Remember to set the number of lines your dialogue box will hold inside the Unity Inspector. For example, a value of "3" is used here.

On a side note, the dialogue box provided to you in the Map scene is large enough to hold three lines of text at the current settings. Feel free to manipulate the font or the dimensions of the dialogue box to accommodate more or fewer lines of text. Once your Dialogue script is finished, you should be able to use any number of lines for your dialogue box. The only limitations are practical in nature, such as screen space and a suitable font size for healthy reading.

After establishing an array to store the lines of text, you can consider how to create the scrolling effect for your dialogue box. The array allows you to individually manipulate each line of text in the dialogue box. Think about how you will keep track of these lines and adjust them as the dialogue box is updated with new information.

Hint: Update the Lines of Text

You have stored individual lines of text. Think about what needs to happen when your dialogue box is updated with a new line of text. What do you need to know about your dialogue box to place this line of text correctly? It may be helpful to consider the possibilities through pseudocode:

```
IF all empty lines:
      ADD line to array at index 0
ELSE IF >= 1 empty lines:
      ADD line to array at first open index
ELSE IF 0 empty lines:
      REMOVE line at index 0
      SHIFT remaining lines up by 1 index
      ADD line to array at last index
```

From these conditions, you can deduce how to update the lines of text in your Dialogue script. Think of your array as holding the topmost line at index 0, the following line at index 1, and so on. If any empty line is available, the newest line is always added to the array at the first available index position. For example, if the array is empty, the line would be placed at index 0. If another line already exists, it would instead be added at index 1.

Eventually, your dialogue box is going to fill up. At that point, you need to apply a different set of logic. When you have no lines available, you need to remove the oldest line from the array. Since our top line is at index 0 and our lines are being added from top to bottom, the oldest line will always be found at index 0.

After clearing the top line at index 0, we shift all of the remaining lines upward by one. Mathematically, this means reducing the index position of each remaining line by one, such that one becomes zero, two becomes one, and so forth. Furthermore, we add the newest line at the last index position in the array. Indeed, this shifting and replacing of lines is what creates our scrolling effect. With each update of our dialogue box, we delete the top line, move the remaining lines up, and insert a bottom line. Taken in sequence, this appears as a smooth flow of text across our dialogue box.

Now that you have identified the logic, you need to implement the scrolling lines in your Dialogue script. You will likely want to code one or more functions to produce the desired behavior. Recall that one part of your challenge involves managing the underlying array of lines, while another involves visually updating the on-screen text. Once your Dialogue script is complete, return to the "Knight" case in your UserCollision script and put your scrolling dialogue box into action!

Example Solution: Update the Dialogue Box with a Scrolling Text Effect

Let's examine one way that you can implement a dialogue box with multiple lines of scrolling text. Recall that your Dialogue script needs to store individual lines of text in an array:

```
//excerpt from Dialogue script
public string[] lines;
```

Further, it would be helpful to write custom functions for updating your dialogue box text. One function can be used to update your on-screen Text component:

```
private void UpdateText() {

        //retrieve text
        Text txt = gameObject.GetComponentInChildren<Text>();

        //clear text
        txt.text = "";

        //iterate through lines
        for (int i = 0; i < lines.Length; i++) {

                //add text
                txt.text += lines[i];

                //add line break
                txt.text += "\n";
        }
}
```

This UpdateText() function is quite similar to the CreateDialogueWithText() function we previously wrote. However, instead of receiving an array of strings as an argument, UpdateText() uses the text already stored in our lines array to update the dialogue box. Specifically, this function retrieves the Text component using GetComponentInChildren() and sets it equal to an empty string. It then loops through the lines array and adds each item as a new line of text. Thus, whenever we call UpdateText(), we refresh the dialogue box with the text stored in our lines array.

While UpdateText() focuses on the visual aspect of our dialogue box, we must also manage the code underlying our lines array. Think back to the conditions for our scrolling text effect from the *Hint: Update the Lines of Text* section. To accompany UpdateText(), we can use a second function that handles the scrolling conditions:

```
public void UpdateDialogueWithText(string theText) {

        //whether text has been placed on line
        bool isTextPlaced = false;

        //start by trying to fill the first blank line
        //iterate through lines
        for (int i = 0; i < lines.Length; i++) {

                //check for blank
                if (String.IsNullOrEmpty(lines[i])) {

                        //set text
                        lines[i] = theText;

                        //toggle flag
                        isTextPlaced = true;

                        //break
                        break;
                }
        }

        //if no blank lines are available
        if (isTextPlaced == false) {

                //reduce index of existing lines by 1
                for (int j = 0; j < lines.Length - 1; j++) {

                        //set current line equal to following line
                        lines[j] = lines[j + 1];
                }

                //update last line with provided text
                lines[lines.Length - 1] = theText;
        }

        //update text
        UpdateText();

}
```

Since `UpdateDialogueWithText()` has quite a few parts, let's break it down one piece at a time. Here, `UpdateDialogueWithText()` receives a new line of text as an argument. A Boolean flag named `isTextPlaced` keeps track of whether or not the line has found a home in our dialogue box.

```
//excerpt from UpdateDialogueWithText() function
public void UpdateDialogueWithText(string theText) {

        //whether text has been placed on line
        bool isTextPlaced = false;
```

Initially, we attempt to find an empty space to put our new line of text. A `for` loop searches through each item in our `lines` array and checks whether it is available via `String.IsNullOrEmpty()` (Microsoft Corporation 2015a). Should an available line be found, that line is set equal to the new line of text, the `isTextPlaced` flag is set to `true`, and the loop is immediately exited with `break`:

```
//excerpt from UpdateDialogueWithText() function
//start by trying to fill the first blank line
//iterate through lines
for (int i = 0; i < lines.Length; i++) {

        //check for blank
        if (String.IsNullOrEmpty(lines[i])) {

                //set text
                lines[i] = theText;

                //toggle flag
                isTextPlaced = true;

                //break
                break;
        }
}
```

However, if no empty line is found, we proceed to eliminate our oldest line to make room for the new line. This involves looping through the `lines` array and setting the contents of each line equal to the line that follows it. Hence, the first line is overwritten by the second line, the second line by the third, and so on. In the end, our topmost line is removed, while our other lines have moved up by one space. We then place the new line of text at the last index position, effectively inserting it at the bottom of our dialogue box.

```
//excerpt from UpdateDialogueWithText() function
//if no blank lines are available
if (isTextPlaced == false) {

        //reduce index of existing lines by 1
        for (int j = 0; j < lines.Length - 1; j++) {

                //set current line equal to following line
                lines[j] = lines[j + 1];
        }
```

```
     //update last line with provided text
     lines[lines.Length - 1] = theText;
}
```

Once this process is complete, our new line of text is certain to have found a home in our dialogue box. After all the conditions of our scrolling text effect are handled, we make a final call to `UpdateText()` to finish our `UpdateDialogueWithText()` function. This ensures that the manipulations we made to the `lines` array are reflected visually on screen:

```
//excerpt from UpdateDialogueWithText() function
     //update text
     UpdateText();

} //end function
```

Thanks to the `UpdateText()` and `UpdateDialogueWithText()` functions, our scrolling text effect works. However, there is one more condition that we need to consider. Suppose we create a dialogue box at one time in our game and everything works fine. Sometime later, we use the dialogue box again, only to find that the old text is still there. Since we want to reuse our dialogue box many times, it is important that we have a fresh start when we need it. To correct this situation, we can write a function that clears our `lines` array:

```
private void ClearLines() {

     //clear lines
     for (int i = 0; i < lines.Length; i++) {
          lines[i] = "";
     }
}
```

Quite simply, our `ClearLines()` function loops through all of the items in our `lines` array and sets each of them to an empty string. Note that, if you display an empty string in your dialogue box, the player will not see anything. Hence, this function effectively clears the dialogue box.

Importantly, we must think about when it is necessary to clear our dialogue box. If we are updating an existing dialogue box, there is no need to clear it. However, whenever we create a brand new dialogue box via `CreateDialogueWithText()`, we want to have a fresh start. Furthermore, we should update our existing `CreateDialogueWithText()` function to incorporate our `lines` array. Moreover, our `UpdateText()` function now handles some of the responsibilities previously assigned to `CreateDialogueWithText()`. Hence, we can call `UpdateText()` inside `CreateDialogueWithText()` instead of duplicating the same code. Thus, we make the following updates to our `CreateDialogueWithText()` function:

```
public void CreateDialogueWithText(string[] theText) {

     //clear lines
     ClearLines();
```

```
//iterate through lines
for (int i = 0; i < theText.Length; i++) {

        //set line text
        lines[i] = theText[i];
}

//update text
UpdateText();
}
```

Our revised CreateDialogueWithText() function calls ClearLines() to reset the dialogue box text. After, it uses the provided text argument to fill the lines array. Last, it calls UpdateText() to ensure the text is displayed on screen.

At this point, all functionality has been built into our Dialogue script. For clarity, the entire example Dialogue script from this chapter is provided:

```
//Dialogue script
public class Dialogue : MonoBehaviour {

        //store text lines
        public string[] lines;

        //open a new dialogue box with given text
        public void CreateDialogueWithText(string[] theText) {

                //clear lines
                ClearLines();

                //iterate through lines
                for (int i = 0; i < theText.Length; i++) {

                        //set line text
                        lines[i] = theText[i];
                }

                //update text
                UpdateText();
        }

        //update text in dialogue box
        public void UpdateDialogueWithText(string theText) {

                //whether text has been placed on line
                bool isTextPlaced = false;

                //start by trying to fill the first blank line
                //iterate through lines
                for (int i = 0; i < lines.Length; i++) {

                        //check for blank
                        if (String.IsNullOrEmpty(lines[i])) {

                                //set text
                                lines[i] = theText;
```

```
                    //toggle flag
                    isTextPlaced = true;

                    //break
                    break;
                }
            }

        //if no blank lines are available
        if (isTextPlaced == false) {

                //reduce index of existing lines by 1
                for (int j = 0; j < lines.Length - 1; j++) {

                        //set current line equal to following line
                        lines[j] = lines[j + 1];
                }

                //update last line with provided text
                lines[lines.Length - 1] = theText;
        }

        //update text
        UpdateText();
    }

    //update text
    private void UpdateText() {

        //retrieve text
        Text txt = gameObject.GetComponentInChildren<Text>();

        //clear text
        txt.text = "";

        //iterate through lines
        for (int i = 0; i < lines.Length; i++) {

                //add text
                txt.text += lines[i];

                //add line break
                txt.text += "\n";
        }
    }

    //clear text
    private void ClearLines() {

        //clear lines
        for (int i = 0; i < lines.Length; i++) {
                lines[i] = "";
        }
    }

    //show
    public void Show() {
```

```
                //set alpha to visible
                gameObject.GetComponent<CanvasGroup>().alpha = 0.8f;
        }

        //hide
        public void Hide() {

                //set alpha to invisible
                gameObject.GetComponent<CanvasGroup>().alpha = 0.0f;
        }

        //hide on key press
        public IEnumerator HideOnInput() {

                //whether dialogue is dismissed
                bool isDismissed = false;

                //while not dismissed
                while (isDismissed == false) {

                        //check input
                        if (Input.GetKeyUp(KeyCode.Space)) {

                                //hide
                                Hide();

                                //toggle flag
                                isDismissed = true;
                        }

                        //keep waiting
                        yield return 0;
                }
        }

        //hide after delay
        public IEnumerator HideAfterDelay(float theDelay) {

                //handle delay
                yield return new WaitForSeconds(theDelay);

                //hide
                Hide();
        }
} //end class
```

Take the opportunity to put your scrolling dialogue box into action. Update the "Knight" case in your UserCollision script to the following:

```
//UserCollision script
//excerpt from OnTriggerEnter2D() function
case "Knight":

        //retrieve dialogue
        Dialogue dialogue = GameObject.FindWithTag("Dialogue").
          GetComponent<Dialogue>();
```

```
//create dialogue text
dialogue.CreateDialogueWithText(
    new string[] {
        "I am the Red Knight.",
        "Your quest is about to begin!",
        "Entering the Dungeon in 3"…"
    });

//show
dialogue.Show();

//hide
StartCoroutine(dialogue.HideAfterDelay(4.0f));

//delay
yield return new WaitForSeconds(1.0f);

//update dialogue text
dialogue.UpdateDialogueWithText("2...");

//delay
yield return new WaitForSeconds(1.0f);

//update dialogue text
dialogue.UpdateDialogueWithText("1...");

//delay
yield return new WaitForSeconds(1.0f);

//update dialogue text
dialogue.UpdateDialogueWithText("Go!");

//delay
yield return new WaitForSeconds(1.0f);

//switch to dungeon scene
StateManager.Instance.SwitchSceneTo("Dungeon");

break;
```

Test your game and watch the Red Knight dramatically countdown Luna's entry into the Dungeon scene! Celebrate by exploring the Dungeon scene before proceeding to the next chapter.

Summary

In this chapter, you opened a world of possibilities for sharing information with the player of your game. Using your well-constructed dialogue box, you can display notifications that are dismissed automatically over time or through user input. You can also choose to open a new dialogue box or continually update an existing one with a scrolling text effect. Thus, you have several options available for sending messages to the player in your game. With this success, you should be able to apply all of these game implementation techniques:

- Implement a dialogue box to notify the player about important information

- Update a dialogue box based on changing game conditions

- Create a dialogue box that can be dismissed automatically or through user input

- Use a scrolling effect to update the dialogue box as new information arrives

- Manage function execution using coroutines

Perhaps you feel that the Red Knight is presumptuous to launch Luna directly into the Dungeon scene with little warning. Or perhaps you would like to create a two-way dialogue between the characters in your game. In the next chapter, we will create opportunities such as these by allowing Luna to make decisions of her own.

References

Microsoft Corporation. 2015a. String.IsNullOrEmpty Method (String) (C# Reference). https://msdn.microsoft.com/library/system.string.isnullorempty.aspx (accessed December 9, 2015).

Microsoft Corporation. 2015b. using Statement (C# Reference). https://msdn.microsoft.com/library/yh598w02.aspx (accessed December 9, 2015).

Unity Technologies. 2015a. Canvas Group. http://docs.unity3d.com/Manual/class-CanvasGroup.html (accessed December 9, 2015).

Unity Technologies. 2015b. Collider2D. http://docs.unity3d.com/ScriptReference/Collider2D.html (accessed December 9, 2015).

Unity Technologies. 2015c. Component.GetComponentInChildren. http://docs.unity3d.com/ScriptReference/Component.GetComponentInChildren.html (accessed December 9, 2015).

Unity Technologies. 2015d. Console. http://docs.unity3d.com/Manual/Console.html (accessed December 9, 2015).

Unity Technologies. 2015e. Coroutines. http://docs.unity3d.com/Manual/Coroutines.html (accessed December 9, 2015).

Unity Technologies. 2015f. Debug.Log. http://docs.unity3d.com/ScriptReference/Debug.Log.html (accessed December 9, 2015).

Unity Technologies. 2015g. Input.GetKey. http://docs.unity3d.com/ScriptReference/Input.GetKey.html (accessed December 9, 2015).

Unity Technologies. 2015h. Input.GetKeyDown. http://docs.unity3d.com/ScriptReference/Input.GetKeyDown.html (accessed December 9, 2015).

Unity Technologies. 2015i. Input.GetKeyUp. http://docs.unity3d.com/ScriptReference/Input.GetKeyUp.html (accessed December 9, 2015).

Unity Technologies. 2015j. KeyCode. http://docs.unity3d.com/ScriptReference/KeyCode.html (accessed December 9, 2015).

Unity Technologies. 2015k. MonoBehaviour.OnTriggerEnter2D(Collider2D). http://docs.unity3d.com/ScriptReference/MonoBehaviour.OnTriggerEnter2D.html (accessed December 9, 2015).

Unity Technologies. 2015l. MonoBehaviour.StartCoroutine. http://docs.unity3d.com/ScriptReference/MonoBehaviour.StartCoroutine.html (accessed December 9, 2015).

Unity Technologies. 2015m. Rigidbody2D. http://docs.unity3d.com/ScriptReference/Rigidbody2D.html (accessed December 9, 2015).

Unity Technologies. 2015n. User Interface (UI). https://unity3d.com/learn/tutorials/topics/user-interface-ui (accessed December 9, 2015).

Unity Technologies. 2015o. WaitForSeconds. http://docs.unity3d.com/ScriptReference/WaitForSeconds.html (accessed December 9, 2015).

3 A Daring Decision

Albeit dramatic, the Red Knight's insistence on launching Luna immediately into the Dungeon scene is not an ideal experience for players. By contrast, giving Luna a choice of whether to enter would be more pleasant. Expanding on what you learned while making a dialogue box in Chapter 2, you can allow Luna to make a decision when she encounters the Red Knight. Furthermore, the ability to make decisions supports many additional features that we may implement in our game, such as character conversations and turn-based interactions.

◗ Goals

By the end of this chapter, you will be able to apply these game implementation techniques:

- Implement a selection box to allow the player to make a choice

- Take actions in the game based on the player's choices

- Manage information flow using delegates and lambda expressions

- Execute an asynchronous callback

▮ Required Files

In this chapter, you will use the following files from the *Software > Chapter_03* folder (https://www.crcpress.com/Learn-to-Implement-Games-with-Code/Quick/p/book/9781498753388):

- The contents of the Challenge folder to create, code, and test your solution
- The contents of the Solution folder to compare your solution to the example solution

▮ Challenge: Present a Choice

Your current challenge is to code a Selection script that presents choices to the player. To accomplish this goal, you can leverage your prior work with the Dialogue script in Chapter 2. Similarly, user interface (UI) elements have been provided to you. Open the *Challenge > Assets > Scenes > Map.unity scene* in Unity. In the Hierarchy, you will find that an object named PnlSelection has been added to the Canvas. As with our other Canvas objects, PnlSelection has RectTransform, Image, and Canvas Group components configured. It has also been given the "Selection" tag. In addition, PnlSelection has several children (Figure 3.1). ImgIndicator is meant to display an icon next to the choice that the player is currently considering. Meanwhile, TxtChoice1, TxtChoice2, and TxtChoice3 present the text for the choices offered to the player. Together, all of these objects compose a selection box that can be presented to the player when a choice needs to be made. Ultimately, your Selection script will control the PnlSelection and its children to ensure that the selection box functions properly.

Start by sorting out the logic behind your selection box. Think about what your selection box should do and how the player will interact with it. For instance, you probably need to create a selection box that presents specific choices for the player. Certainly, you want to do things like show, hide, and

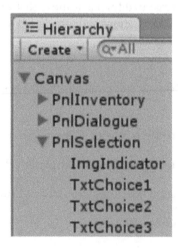

Figure 3.1 The PnlSelection object and its children compose the selection box for your game.

move the selection box. Without these basic features, you won't be able to put everything else into action. The requirements for this challenge are:

1. Create a Selection script to manage the selection box.

2. Permit the choice text to be updated.

3. Allow the visibility of the selection box to be changed.

4. Trigger the selection box when Luna collides with the Red Knight.

Hint: Leverage Your Codebase

You may notice that several of the challenge requirements involve the same features used to make your dialogue box in Chapter 2. It's time to leverage your *codebase*. Your codebase is the collection of all source code and software implementations that you have created. Every time you code something new, you are expanding your codebase. Throughout your coding career, you will amass quite a large collection of successful implementations. The wonderful thing about maintaining your codebase is that you can always refer to it later. For example, the camera movement you coded in Chapter 1 can be applied to many future games that you create. Rather than solving the same problems many times over, you can leverage your codebase to reuse existing code. This allows you to focus on solving new and more complex problems.

Your Selection script is a perfect example of how you can leverage your codebase. As with your dialogue box, you want to be able to change the visibility of your selection box. Again, this is to ensure that you only present a selection box to the player at relevant times during the game, such as when a decision needs to be made. Otherwise, it's best to hide the selection box. The PnlSelection object has a `Canvas Group` component, which is the same component you used to show and hide your dialogue box. Thus, you can easily reuse the `Show()` and `Hide()` functions from your Dialogue script. Just copy those functions over to your Selection script.

There are other ways in which your Dialogue script may be useful to inform the design of your Selection script. While you cannot always directly copy from your codebase, you can often apply what you have already done in new ways. For instance, your selection box needs to be created, updated, and detected in a collision. Your dialogue box also did all of these things. Although these UI elements are not identical, they have many similarities. Keep this in mind as you build your selection box.

Hint: Set and Reset the Selection Box

Imagine that your selection box presents three choices to the player, which are represented by TxtChoice1, TxtChoice2, and TxtChoice3. In addition, the ImgIndicator image is placed next to the first choice by default (Figure 3.2). The player presses a key to cycle through the potential choices. With each key press, the indicator image is repositioned next to the current choice. Once the player confirms a choice, the entire selection box is hidden. At some later time in the game, a whole new selection box is created, and the process repeats.

The preceding paragraph describes the operational logic of your selection box. For the time being, focus on how you will create a selection box with three

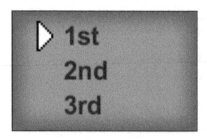

Figure 3.2 By default, the indicator image is placed next to the top choice in your selection box.

choices and an indicator image. Think about what variables you need to store in your Selection script and what functions you need to write.

Once you are able to create a selection box and display it on the screen, think about this: what happens when you want to create another selection box? Like your dialogue box, there is only one selection box in the game, and it is reused every time the player needs to make a choice. When presenting a new selection box, you don't want text from previous choices to be present. Likewise, you don't want the indicator image to be stranded at whatever choice the player last selected. To ensure that you always have a fresh start when creating a selection box, you must find a way to reset the choice text and the indicator image.

Work on your implementation for creating and resetting the selection box. Before proceeding, you should be able to display a selection box with multiple choices and an indicator image. Furthermore, you should be able to create another selection box that doesn't retain any remnants of the previous one.

Hint: Position the Selection Box

By default, your selection box appears in the center of the screen. While this is certainly noticeable to the player, it is not the only way to position the selection box. An alternative way to position your selection box is to place it beside the character who is making a decision. For instance, when Luna encounters the Red Knight, a selection box could be placed above Luna's head. This would better indicate to the player which character is making a decision.

Initially, the concept of positioning the selection box sounds simple. However, things get a bit tricky when working in Unity. This is due to the fact that Unity uses several different coordinate systems, such as screen space, viewport space, and world space (Unity Technologies 2015a). Converting coordinates between various spaces is inevitable when working in Unity. Setting the position for our selection box is one case in which we must convert between coordinate systems in Unity.

Click on the Canvas object in the Hierarchy window and find its `Canvas` component in the Inspector (Figure 3.3). The `Render Mode` is set to `Screen Space - Camera`. Thus, all of our UI elements, including our selection box, are positioned in screen space. Specifically, screen space is measured in pixels (px) with a bottom-left origin point and dimensions equal to the size of the game window (Figure 3.4). So, if our game is played at a resolution of 1024×768 px and our selection box is placed in the center of the screen, it would have a position of (512, 384).

Meanwhile, all of the characters in our game are positioned in world space. Specifically, world space is measured in units (by default, 100 px per unit) with a center origin point and unlimited dimensions (Figure 3.5). So, regardless of resolution, if our selection box is placed in the center of the world, it would have a position of (0, 0).

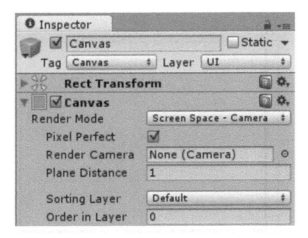

Figure 3.3 The Canvas object's `Render Mode` is set to `Screen Space - Camera`, which means all of its UI elements are positioned in Unity's screen space.

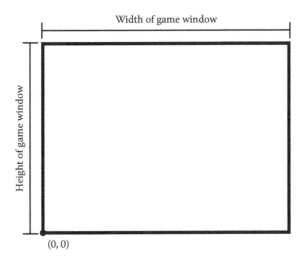

Figure 3.4 In Unity, screen space is measured in pixels with a bottom-left origin point and dimensions equal to the size of the game window.

Since our selection box lives in screen space and our characters live in world space, we have to make a conversion. Suppose our Selection script wants to place our selection box over Luna. To do so, we could convert the selection box's screen space to Luna's world units or vice versa. Fortunately, Unity provides convenient functions to convert between various coordinate systems, such as `WorldToScreenPoint()` (Unity Technologies 2015c) and `ScreenToWorldPoint()` (Unity Technologies 2015b). You can use one of these functions to align the positions of Luna and the selection box in your

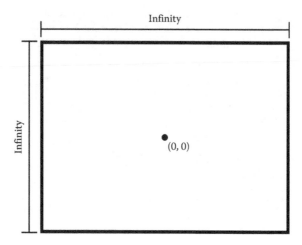

Figure 3.5 In Unity, world space is measured in units with a center origin point and unlimited dimensions.

Selection script. This code demonstrates the basic usage of Unity's coordinate conversion functions:

```
//convert between screen and world space
//retrieve selection box's position (screen space)
Vector3 selectPos = GameObject.FindWithTag("Selection").transform.
  positon;

//retrieve Luna's position (world space)
Vector3 playerPos = GameObject.FindWithTag("Player").transform.
  positon;

//convert screen space to world space
Vector3 worldPos = Camera.main.ScreenToWorldPoint(selectPos);

//convert world space to screen space
Vector3 screenPos = Camera.main.WorldToScreenPoint(playerPos);
```

Recall that Unity objects have a center origin point. Hence, placing the selection box exactly at Luna's position will cause it to cover her. Instead, think about modifying your position calculations to place the selection box above Luna's head.

Hint: Detect the Collision

Return once again to the UserCollision script's `OnTriggerEnter2D()` function. In the "Knight" case, write the necessary code to display a selection box that lets Luna choose whether or not to enter the Dungeon scene. Test your game and move Luna to the Red Knight to make sure your selection box appears as intended. Make any necessary modifications before proceeding to the example solution.

Example Solution: Present a Choice

Your initial challenge entails creating and displaying a selection box to present a number of choices to the player. Let's consider how you could have accomplished this task. Since your Selection script needs to manipulate the choice text and indicator image objects of your PnlSelection, it makes sense to store these as variables:

```
//Selection script
//indicator image
public Image imgIndicator;

//text objects
public GameObject[] txtObjects;
```

Since these are `public` variables, you can assign objects to them in the Unity Inspector window (Figure 3.6).

Before creating a selection box, you want to make sure any previous choices are cleared. Thus, the `ClearText()` function iterates through each of the stored choice text objects, retrieves the `Text` component, and sets it to an empty string:

```
private void ClearText() {

        //iterate through text objects
        foreach (GameObject aTxtObj in txtObjects) {

                //retrieve text
                Text txt = aTxtObj.GetComponent<Text>();
                //update text
                txt.text = "";
        }
}
```

Similarly, you want to reset the indicator image's position when a selection box is created. By default, the indicator always starts next to the topmost choice.

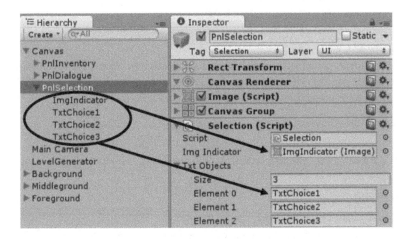

Figure 3.6 The Selection script's public variables are assigned in the Inspector window.

Thus, we can align the y position of the indicator image with the top choice object in the ResetIndicator() function:

```
private void ResetIndicator() {

        //store current position
        Vector3 newPos = imgIndicator.transform.position;

        //update y to match top choice
        newPos.y = txtObjects[0].transform.position.y;

        //update indicator position
        imgIndicator.transform.position = newPos;
}
```

With these functions in place, you can create a new selection box. The CreateSelection() function accepts a List (Microsoft Corporation 2015e) of strings that carries the choice text. Right away, any existing choice text is cleared and the indicator image is reset. Subsequently, a loop iterates through the provided strings and assigns them to the available choice text slots. Thus, a new selection box is created with this function:

```
public void CreateSelection(List<string> theText) {

        //reset indicator
        ResetIndicator();

        //clear text
        ClearText();

        //iterate through text objects
        for (int i = 0; i < theText.Count; i++) {

                //retrieve text
                Text txt = txtObjects[i].GetComponent<Text>();

                //update text
                txt.text = theText[i];
        }
}
```

Of course, we must remember to display our selection box. As previously mentioned, you can directly reuse the Dialogue script's Show() and Hide() functions to manage the visibility of your selection box:

```
public void Show() {

        //set alpha to visible
        gameObject.GetComponent<CanvasGroup>().alpha = 0.8f;
}

public void Hide() {

        //set alpha to invisible
        gameObject.GetComponent<CanvasGroup>().alpha = 0.0f;
}
```

One final step involves positioning the selection box over Luna. See the `PositionAt()` function:

```
public void PositionAt(GameObject theObject, float theBuffer =
    10.0f) {

        //retrieve position
        Vector3 worldPos = theObject.transform.position;

        //offset for object height
        worldPos.y += theObject.GetComponent<Renderer>().bounds.
          size.y / 2;

        //convert position
        Vector3 screenPos = Camera.main.WorldToScreenPoint(worldPos);

        //retrieve canvas scale factor
        float scaleFactor = gameObject.transform.parent.
          GetComponent<Canvas>().scaleFactor;

        //offset for window height
        screenPos.y += scaleFactor * gameObject.
          GetComponent<RectTransform>().rect.size.y / 2;

        //add additional buffer between objects
        screenPos.y += scaleFactor * theBuffer;

        //set position in converted coordinates
        gameObject.transform.position = screenPos;
}
```

The `PositionAt()` function accepts a `GameObject` representing the character that the selection box should be placed over. It also receives an optional buffer distance argument to add extra space between the selection box and character:

```
//excerpt from PositionAt() function
public void PositionAt(GameObject theObject, float theBuffer =
    10.0f) {
```

Next, the character's world position is stored. Its y value is offset in consideration of the character's center origin point. This prepares the selection box to be placed above the character's head:

```
//excerpt from PositionAt() function
//retrieve position
Vector3 worldPos = theObject.transform.position;

//offset for object height
worldPos.y += theObject.GetComponent<Renderer>().bounds.size.y / 2;
```

Then, the character's world position is converted into screen coordinates:

```
//excerpt from PositionAt() function
//convert position
Vector3 screenPos = Camera.main.WorldToScreenPoint(worldPos);
```

Conveniently, our Canvas-based UI automatically scales with the screen size. However, we need to adjust for this fact when positioning our selection box. Just like our UI, the position of our selection box needs to scale regardless of the resolution at which the game is played. We can determine the scale of our Canvas by its scaleFactor property (Unity Technologies 2015d). Subsequently, we calculate the position of our selection box, factoring in the center origin point and buffer, all adjusted by the scaleFactor:

```
//excerpt from PositionAt() function
//retrieve canvas scale factor
float scaleFactor = gameObject.transform.parent.
GetComponent<Canvas>().scaleFactor;

//offset for window height
screenPos.y += scaleFactor * gameObject.
GetComponent<RectTransform>().rect.size.y / 2;

//add additional buffer between objects
screenPos.y += scaleFactor * theBuffer;
```

Last, we set the selection box's position to physically move it on screen:

```
//set position in converted coordinates
gameObject.transform.position = screenPos;
```

To review, the PositionAt() function converts a character's position from world coordinates to screen coordinates. As usual, the position of the selection box is offset for the center origin point of the character and the box itself. Then, based on the scale of the UI, the selection box's final position is adjusted before being set.

To see your selection box in action, remember to incorporate it into your game via the UserCollision script. In this example, the Dialogue script is used to display the Red Knight's message to Luna, while the Selection script presents the potential choices to her. Note that user input is disabled in the UserMove script as well. This prevents our player from running around in the middle of making a decision, which could cause problems to arise:

```
//UserCollision script
//excerpt from OnTriggerEnter2D() function
case "Knight":

        //disable input
        userMove.SetUserInputEnabled(false);

        //retrieve dialogue
        Dialogue dialogue = GameObject.FindWithTag("Dialogue").
          GetComponent<Dialogue>();

        //update dialogue text
        dialogue.CreateDialogueWithText(new string[] {
                "Do you dare to enter the dungeon?",
                "Make your choice..."
        });
```

```
//show
dialogue.Show();

//hide on input
StartCoroutine(dialogue.HideOnInput());

//retrieve selection
Selection selection = GameObject.FindWithTag("Selection").
  GetComponent<Selection>();

//create selection text
List<string> txtSelection = new List<string>() {
      "Yes",
      "No",
      "Cancel"
};

//create selection
selection.CreateSelection(txtSelection);

//position selection
selection.PositionAt(gameObject);

//show selection
selection.Show();

break;
```

Test your game and move Luna over to the Red Knight. You have suc-ceeded in making your selection box appear on screen! However, a major chal-lenge still remains. You must implement the functionality of your selection box, such that the player can make a choice and trigger subsequent events in your game.

▐ Challenge: Make a Choice

You want the player to interact with the selection box once it is presented. For example, the player scrolls through the list of choices by pressing a key. Along the way, the indicator image is updated to show the current selection. Eventually, the final choice is confirmed through a key press. Your Selection script should imple-ment user interaction similar to this.

In addition, your game should respond to the player's choices. Based on the choice the player makes, your game needs to take certain actions. This requires passing information through multiple scripts, such as Selection and UserCollision. Coroutines are once again useful to apply in this case. You may also need to learn a few new techniques to get the job done.

After you complete this challenge, you will be able to present a selection box, allow the player to make a choice, and act upon the player's choice. The require-ments for this challenge are:

1. Let the player scroll through the potential choices in the selection box.

2. Allow the player to confirm one specific choice in the selection box.

3. Act upon the player's choice by taking the necessary actions in your game.

4. Manage the flow of information between your selection box and other areas of the game using techniques such as coroutines, delegates, and lambda expressions.

5. Ensure that the Selection script remains independent of any other scripts.

Hint: Manage Information Flow with Delegates and Lambda Expressions

Our game is composed of many scripts that are mostly independent of one another. For instance, our Selection script is only responsible for creating a selection box, while our CamFollow script is only responsible for moving the camera. If we maintain the independence of these scripts, they can easily be reused in future games. By contrast, the UserCollision script is dependent on many different scripts and has responsibilities that are quite specific to the current game we are making. Thus, it is unlikely that this script can be reused in another project. When making a game, we try to make most scripts independent. In general coding terms, we seek to apply the principles of *coupling* and *cohesion* (Quick 2015). However, it is impractical for all scripts to be independent of one another. Instead, we allow only a select few scripts that are specific to the operations of our current game to depend upon other scripts.

As we embark on implementing our selection box, the concept of independence becomes very important. This is true, because your Selection script allows the player to make a choice that impacts other areas of the game. Thus, information inevitably needs to be passed through multiple scripts. As you code your Selection script, you should make an effort to maintain its independence. Yet, when the need arises to introduce some dependence in your scripts, make sure to limit it to appropriate scripts, such as UserCollision. Your efforts to manage the independence of your scripts will be well worth it in the end, since your codebase will contain implementations that are easily applied to new endeavors.

You've already seen how powerful coroutines can help you manage timing and states in your game. Let's consider two more coding techniques that may be new to you: delegates and lambda expressions. These can be used to manage the flow of information through our game, while helping to maintain the independence of our scripts.

Delegates for Asynchronous Callback

A *delegate* stores a reference to a function (Microsoft Corporation 2015b, 2015c). Delegates can refer to specific, named functions in our code, or be used as anonymous placeholders. Generally speaking, delegates help us pass information through our game in the form of functions. In a sense, delegates are variables that store entire functions, rather than raw data such as numbers. To declare a delegate, use the `delegate` keyword, followed by a return type, function name, parentheses containing any arguments, and a semicolon. Once a delegate is declared in this manner, it can be used later in your code. The declaration format for a delegate is presented in the following text, along with a few examples:

```
//format for declaring a delegate
delegate RETURNTYPE FUNCTIONNAME(ARGUMENTS...);

//example delegates
//no return type and no arguments
delegate void ExampleDelegate();

//one return type and one argument
delegate bool ExampleDelegate(int argument1);

//no return type and two arguments
delegate void ExampleDelegate(bool argument1, int argument2);
```

One way to use a delegate is to pass it as an argument into a function. Later on, that function executes the delegate in order to return information back to the original caller. This technique is called *asynchronous callback* (Microsoft Corporation 2015f). Our current challenge is one in which an asynchronous callback would be helpful to us. Why? Consider that we are trying to keep our scripts independent of one another despite the fact that they sometimes need to share information. Using a delegate, we can pass information between scripts without requiring them to directly reference each other. Furthermore, delegates allow us to pass entire functions as arguments to other functions. Moreover, our game employs multiple coroutines to manage precise states and timing. Thus, an asynchronous callback gives us more control over the timing of events in our game. Of course, while there are many other ways to use delegates, we will focus only on this particular application in our game.

To create an asynchronous callback, write a function that accepts the delegate as an argument. Then, be sure to call the delegate at some point during the execution of that function. Here is an example:

```
//create a delegate
delegate void CallbackDelegate();

//create callback function
//receive the delegate as an argument
void CallbackFunction(CallbackDelegate theDelegate) {

        //call the delegate to complete the callback
        theDelegate();
}
```

Lambda Expressions for Asynchronous Callback

A *lambda expression* allows you to write a succinct anonymous function (Microsoft Corporation 2015d). Stated another way, a lambda expression let's you create a function without declaring an access level, name, return type, arguments, and so on. Thus, lambda expressions can act as a fast, temporary alternative to declaring a function. Commonly, lambda expressions are used to write local functions that become arguments sent to or values returned from other functions. Similarly, lambda expressions can be used to create local delegates in our code. Hence, a major benefit of lambda expressions is that they allow us to quickly create simple functions right when we need them. Lambda expressions require a unique declaration syntax:

```
//format for declaring a lambda expression
PARAMETERS => EXPRESSION

//example lambda expression
//double the player's points
points => points * 2
```

Ironically enough, => is called the *lambda operator* (Microsoft Corporation 2015a). It is used to separate the *parameters* on the left side from the *expression* on the right side. Think of the parameters as what goes into the function, and the expression as the result of the function. For instance, consider the lambda expression of points => points * 2. This suggests that the parameter, points, becomes the expression, points * 2. In other words, "the points are doubled."

In our game, we can use lambda functions along with delegates to support asynchronous callback. Here is a basic example of how a lambda expression can be used in an asynchronous callback:

```
//use a lambda expression in an asynchronous callback
//create a delegate
delegate int PointsDelegate(int thePoints);

//create callback function
void PointsFunction(int thePoints, PointsDelegate theDelegate) {

    //double the points
    thePoints = thePoints * 2;

    //call the delegate
    theDelegate(thePoints);
}

//pass a lambda expression into PointsFunction()
//set the points variable equal to the result of callback
int points = 1;
PointsFunction(value => points = value);
Debug.Log(points); //prints 2
```

Note that lambda expressions can be applied in a wide variety of ways for many different purposes. We are only exploring a single usage in the context of our current challenge.

Asynchronous Callback Example

Conveniently, lambda expressions go hand-in-hand with delegates to form a powerful combination. Let's consider an example asynchronous callback

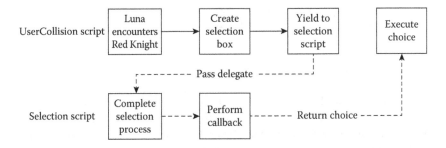

Figure 3.7 A process map depicts an asynchronous callback applied to the flow of information between the Selection and UserCollision scripts.

implementation in the context of our Selection and UserCollision scripts. Suppose you have these goals for the implementation:

1. The Selection script handles the player's decision process independent of the UserCollision script.

2. Once the player makes a decision, the UserCollision triggers the subsequent events.

Since we want to keep the Selection script independent of UserCollision, yet also need to inform UserCollision once the Selection script has completed its work, we are in an excellent position to apply the asynchronous callback technique. This implementation is summarized as a process map in Figure 3.7.

In code, we can implement an asynchronous callback by incorporating a delegate into the Selection script and a lambda expression into the UserCollision script. First, a delegate is declared in the Selection script. The delegate accepts and returns integers that represent the player's choice:

```
//Selection script
//delegate accepts/returns int representing choice
public delegate int SelectedChoice(int theChoice);
```

Second, assume that a coroutine in the Selection script manages the player's decision process. It accepts the delegate as an argument. Once complete, it makes a callback to the delegate and provides the player's final choice as an argument:

```
//Selection script
public IEnumerator MakeChoice(SelectedChoice theChoice) {

    //store the player's choice
    int finalChoice = 0;

    /*
    The choice management code would be placed here.
    For example, the player can cycle through the
    different choices before selecting one.
    */

    /*
```

```
        Eventually, the player would confirm a final choice.
        A callback to the delegate is made and the coroutine
        is ended.
        */
        theChoice(finalChoice);
}
```

Third, assume that UserCollision detects a collision and tells Selection to create a selection box for the player. It then sets up an integer variable to receive the player's choice. Meanwhile, a lambda expression is passed as an argument to the Selection script's MakeChoice() function:

```
//UserCollision script
//excerpt from OnTriggerEnter2D() function
/*
Note: Before using yield return statements,
remember to convert OnTriggerEnter2D() into
a coroutine by returning IEnumerator
instead of void in the function definition.
*/
//assume a collision was detected between Luna and the Red Knight
//assume the selection box was created

//store the choice made by the player
int choice = 0;

//let the Selection script determine the player's choice
//pass a lambda expression as the delegate argument
yield return StartCoroutine(
        selection.MakeChoice(value => choice = value)
        );

/*
Once our script reaches this point, the
Selection script has finished and the choice
variable has been set equal to the player's
final choice. Thus, UserCollision can take
further action based on the value stored in
the choice variable.
*/
```

Ultimately, this process yields a choice variable in the UserCollision script that equals the final decision the player made in the Selection script. For clarity, let's review how this process works:

1. A delegate called SelectedChoice() is defined in the Selection script. It anonymously represents a function that receives an int argument and returns an int value:

   ```
   public delegate int SelectedChoice(int theChoice);
   ```

2. The Selection script's MakeChoice() coroutine accepts the SelectedChoice() delegate in an argument named theChoice:

   ```
   public IEnumerator MakeChoice(SelectedChoice theChoice) {
           //Function code omitted
   }
   ```

3. The UserCollision script sets up an int variable named `choice` to store the player's final choice:

```
int choice = 0;
```

4. When it is time for the player to make a choice, `OnTriggerEnter2D()` yields to the Selection script's `MakeChoice()` coroutine. A lambda expression is passed as a delegate argument into `MakeChoice()`. This lambda expression specifies that `choice` should equal the result of the callback:

```
yield return StartCoroutine(
    selection.MakeChoice(value => choice = value)
    );
```

5. Once the player makes a decision, `MakeChoice()` performs the callback. The delegate is provided with the player's final choice as an argument:

```
theChoice(finalChoice);
```

6. Thus, when `MakeChoice()` executes the callback, the UserCollision script's `choice` variable is set equal to the final choice made by the player in the Selection script. From this point forward, UserCollision can proceed to use the player's choice to take further action.

Through this somewhat complex process, we provide the UserCollision script with timely information about the player's choice. Thankfully, the Selection script need not reference the UserCollision script at all. Instead, an asynchronous callback allows our UserCollision script to wait until the Selection script is finished and then continue with updated information later. This is but one example of how independence and information flow in our scripts can be improved using delegates and lambda expressions. See if you can expand upon this example as you develop a solution for your current challenge.

Hint: Implement the Selection Process

Consider using coroutines to manage the selection process. When a selection box is presented to the player, our game has to wait until a final choice is confirmed. We don't know exactly when the player will choose, but we need to be prepared to take action when a choice is made. Thus, coroutines can support the presentation and handling of user input for our selection box.

In the *Hint: Manage Information Flow with Delegates and Lambda Expressions* section, you saw an overview of how coroutines and an asynchronous callback combined to implement the selection box.

Let's dive deeper into the details behind our implementation. Notice that your selection box is created from the UserCollision script. Meanwhile, the delegate in your Selection script can be used to execute an asynchronous callback. Hence, UserCollision is able to receive the player's choice once the Selection script's job is finished. Thereafter, UserCollision must take action based on the player's choice.

Essentially, our Selection script controls the presentation of a selection box onscreen, as well as the user input required for the player to make a choice. Since there are two primary responsibilities, it makes sense to use two coroutines. This keeps our code cleaner and divides the responsibilities in our script logically among different functions. To begin, we make a coroutine that keeps track of the overall presentation of the selection box:

```
public IEnumerator StartSelection(SelectedChoice
    theSelectedChoice) {

        //whether selection is dismissed
        bool isDismissed = false;

        //while not dismissed
        while (isDismissed == false) {

            /*
            Yield to another coroutine that
            handles user input and confirms
            the player's choice.
            */
            //hide
            Hide();

            //toggle flag
            isDismissed = true;
        }
}
```

As we are accustomed to, the StartSelection() coroutine uses a Boolean flag and while loop to prolong its execution until the required conditions are met. Once complete, the selection box is hidden and the coroutine ends. As suggested, we should yield to another coroutine for handling user input. Unlike other coroutines we've seen in the past, this one accepts a delegate argument. Note that this argument can be passed through as an argument into another coroutine. Be sure to leverage what you know about delegates and lambda expressions to execute this step. Following this, we can make another coroutine that focuses on user input and receives the passed-through delegate:

```
public IEnumerator WaitForChoice(SelectedChoice theSelectedChoice) {

        //while choice has not been made
        bool isChoiceSelected = false;
        while (isChoiceSelected == false) {

            /*
            Place code to check for user input
            in this section. Allow the player
            to cycle through the different
            choices and update the indicator
            image to show the current choice.
            In addition, allow the player to
            confirm a final choice. Recall that
            you need to end the coroutine and
```

```
                execute the callback once the player
                confirms a final choice.
                */

                //keep waiting
                yield return 0;
        }
}
```

In typical coroutine fashion, WaitForChoice() uses a Boolean flag and while loop to manage its execution. It also receives the delegate passed to it from StartSelection(). Near the bottom, yield return 0 is applied to pause the coroutine as it waits for the player to confirm a choice.

While this provides a basic shell for your coroutine, you need to expand WaitForChoice(). All of the necessary user input elements can be incorporated into this coroutine. You want the player to be able to scroll through the potential choices and confirm a final choice. Additionally, you need to keep track of the player's choice and execute the callback when the coroutine ends. Importantly, the callback is what notifies UserCollision that the selection is complete and provides it with the choice that was made.

Hint: Execute the Choice

From the preceding hints, you should have a framework in mind for how to implement your selection box. Remember to fully consider your logic before trying to implement a solution. It may take some effort to finalize your implementation. Test and retest your solution until you have it functioning well.

For a final reminder, make sure to execute the player's choice once it is made. Recall that your UserCollision script receives the player's final choice after the Selection script finishes. Therefore, you should add code in your UserCollision script that acts upon the player's choice. For instance, you might allow Luna a choice of whether or not to enter the Dungeon scene. If she agrees, load the scene. If not, allow her to continue exploring the world map.

Example Solution: Make a Choice

Let's review a complete example solution. In the Selection script, a delegate is added to facilitate passing the player's choice to the UserCollision script:

```
//Selection script
//delegate
//delegate accepts/returns int representing choice
public delegate int SelectedChoice(int theChoice);
```

A coroutine named StartSelection() manages the overall selection process, including display:

```
//Selection script
public IEnumerator StartSelection(int theNumChoices, SelectedChoice
    theChoice) {

        //whether selection is dismissed
        bool isDismissed = false;
```

```
//while not dismissed
while (isDismissed == false) {

        //wait for choice to be made
        yield return StartCoroutine(
                WaitForChoice(theNumChoices, value =>
                    theChoice(value))
                );

        //hide
        Hide();

        //toggle flag
        isDismissed = true;
    }
}
```

The `StartSelection()` coroutine begins after a new selection box is created. Once the entire selection process finishes, it hides the selection box. `StartSelection()` accepts the number of choices and the `SelectedChoice()` delegate as arguments. During the selection process, it pauses and passes these values forward to a coroutine named `WaitForChoice()`, which handles the player's user input:

```
//Selection script
public IEnumerator WaitForChoice(int theNumChoices, SelectedChoice
    theChoice) {

        //store current selection
        int currentChoice = 0;

        //while choice has not been made
        bool isChoiceSelected = false;
        while (isChoiceSelected == false) {

                //check input
                //select current option
                if (Input.GetKeyUp(KeyCode.Space)) {

                        //toggle flag
                        isChoiceSelected = true;

                        //return choice
                        theChoice(currentChoice);
                }

                //move upward through options
                else if (
                        theNumChoices > 1 &&
                        Input.GetKeyDown(KeyCode.UpArrow)
                        ) {

                        //update choice
                        currentChoice--;

                        //check bounds on current choice
                        //exceeds min
```

```
                    if (currentChoice < 0) {

                            //wrap to last choice
                            currentChoice = theNumChoices - 1;
                    }
            }

            //move downward through options
            else if (
                    theNumChoices > 1 &&
                    Input.GetKeyDown(KeyCode.DownArrow)
                    ) {

                    //update choice
                    currentChoice++;
                    //check bounds on current choice
                    //exceeds max
                    if (currentChoice >= theNumChoices) {

                            //wrap to first choice
                            currentChoice = 0;
                    }
            }

            //store indicator position
            Vector3 newPos = imgIndicator.transform.position;

            //update y to match current choice
            newPos.y = txtObjects[currentChoice].transform.
              position.y;

            //update indicator position
            imgIndicator.transform.position = newPos;

            //keep waiting
            yield return 0;
    }
}
```

The WaitForChoice() coroutine also accepts the number of choices and SelectedChoice() delegate as arguments. It stores the player's current choice in a local variable named currentChoice. A Boolean flag named isChoiceSelected and the while loop are used to control the coroutine's execution. If no choice is made during a given frame, the coroutine pauses:

```
//Selection script
//excerpt from WaitForChoice() coroutine
public IEnumerator WaitForChoice(int theNumChoices, SelectedChoice
theChoice) {

    //store current selection
    int currentChoice = 0;

    //while input has not been received
    bool isChoiceSelected = false;
```

```
        while (isChoiceSelected == false) {

                /*
                User input code omitted.
                */

                //keep waiting
                yield return 0;
        }
}
```

Meanwhile, several user input checks are made inside the `while` loop via an `if` statement. We check whether the player has finalized a choice by pressing the spacebar. If so, `isChoiceSelected` is toggled to end the coroutine. In addition, an asynchronous callback is executed on the `SelectedChoice` delegate to return the player's choice to the UserCollision script:

```
//Selection script
//excerpt from WaitForChoice() coroutine
//check input
//select current option
if (Input.GetKeyUp(KeyCode.Space)) {

        //toggle flag
        isChoiceSelected = true;

        //return choice
        theChoice(currentChoice);
}
```

However, if the player has not yet finalized a choice, the up arrow can be used to cycle through the potential options, assuming more than one exists:

```
//Selection script
//excerpt from WaitForChoice() coroutine
//move upward through options
else if (
        theNumChoices > 1 &&
        Input.GetKeyDown(KeyCode.UpArrow)
        ) {

        //update choice
        currentChoice--;

        //check bounds on current choice
        //exceeds min
        if (currentChoice < 0) {

                //wrap to last choice
                currentChoice = theNumChoices - 1;
        }
}
```

Recall that our initial iteration of the Selection script stored the potential choices in an array named `txtObjects`. The `theNumChoices` variable passed into our function represents the total number of choices available to the player. Since this is an integer value, it aligns with the index values in our `txtObjects` array. Hence, no matter what text is specified, we can use integer values to generically represent the player's choice. This makes it easy to reuse our selection box over and over again. By default, our `currentChoice` variable starts at index 0, which is the top option in our selection box. To move upward, we subtract one. Of course, if we go too far, we will arrive at an invalid index value. Therefore, if the player tries to move upward past the top choice, we reset the `currentChoice` equal to the last index value (`theNumChoices - 1`). This creates a pleasant looping effect and lets the player continually cycle through all of the options. A nearly identical process is applied to allow the player to cycle downward through the choices:

```
//Selection script
//excerpt from WaitForChoice() coroutine
//move downward through options
else if (
        theNumChoices > 1 &&
        Input.GetKeyDown(KeyCode.DownArrow)
        ) {

        //update choice
        currentChoice++;

        //check bounds on current choice
        //exceeds max
        if (currentChoice >= theNumChoices) {

                //wrap to first choice
                currentChoice = 0;
        }
}
```

Lastly, we must remember to update the indicator image as the player cycles through the choices. To accomplish this, we retrieve the y position of the current choice from the `txtObjects` array and adjust the position of the indicator image to match:

```
//Selection script
//excerpt from WaitForChoice() function
//store indicator position
Vector3 newPos = imgIndicator.transform.position;

//update y to match current choice
newPos.y = txtObjects[currentChoice].transform.position.y;

//update indicator position
imgIndicator.transform.position = newPos;
```

With the `StartSelection()` and `WaitForChoice()` coroutines, your Selection script is complete. For comparison with your final solution, the entire Selection script from this chapter is presented:

```
//Selection script
public class Selection : MonoBehaviour {
```

```
//indicator image
public Image imgIndicator;

//text objects
public GameObject[] txtObjects;

//delegate accepts/returns int representing choice
public delegate int SelectedChoice(int theChoice);

//create a selection box with given choices
public void CreateSelection(List<string> theText) {

        //reset indicator
        ResetIndicator();

        //clear text
        ClearText();

        //iterate through text objects
        for (int i = 0; i < theText.Count; i++) {

                //retrieve text
                Text txt = txtObjects[i].GetComponent<Text>();

                //update text
                txt.text = theText[i];
        }
}

//show
public void Show() {

        //set alpha to visible
        gameObject.GetComponent<CanvasGroup>().alpha = 0.8f;
}

//hide
public void Hide() {

        //set alpha to invisible
        gameObject.GetComponent<CanvasGroup>().alpha = 0.0f;
}

//clear all text objects
private void ClearText() {

        //iterate through text objects
        foreach (GameObject aTxtObj in txtObjects) {

                //retrieve text
                Text txt = aTxtObj.GetComponent<Text>();

                //update text
                txt.text = "";
        }
}
```

```csharp
//reset indicator
private void ResetIndicator() {

    //store current position
    Vector3 newPos = imgIndicator.transform.position;

        //update y to match top choice
    newPos.y = txtObjects[0].transform.position.y;

        //update indicator position
    imgIndicator.transform.position = newPos;
}

//position selection above object with buffer (in pixels)
public void PositionAt(GameObject theObject, float
  theBuffer = 10.0f) {

    //retrieve position
    Vector3 worldPos = theObject.transform.position;

    //offset for object height
    worldPos.y += theObject.GetComponent<Renderer>().
      bounds.size.y / 2;

    //convert position
    Vector3 screenPos = Camera.main.
      WorldToScreenPoint(worldPos);

    //retrieve canvas scale factor
    float scaleFactor = gameObject.transform.parent.
      GetComponent<Canvas>().scaleFactor;

    //offset for window height
    screenPos.y += scaleFactor * gameObject.
      GetComponent<RectTransform>().rect.size.y / 2;

    //add additional buffer between objects
    screenPos.y += scaleFactor * theBuffer;

    //set position in converted coordinates
    gameObject.transform.position = screenPos;
}

//start selection process
public IEnumerator StartSelection(int theNumChoices,
  SelectedChoice theChoice) {

    //whether selection is dismissed
    bool isDismissed = false;

    //while not dismissed
    while (isDismissed == false) {

        //wait for choice to be made
        yield return StartCoroutine(
            WaitForChoice(theNumChoices, value =>
              theChoice(value))
            );
```

```
            //hide
            Hide();

            //toggle flag
            isDismissed = true;
        }
    }

    //wait for user to select among choices
    public IEnumerator WaitForChoice(int theNumChoices,
      SelectedChoice theChoice) {

        //store current selection
        int currentChoice = 0;

        //while choice has not been made
        bool isChoiceSelected = false;
        while (isChoiceSelected == false) {

            //check input
            //select current option
            if (Input.GetKeyUp(KeyCode.Space)) {

                //toggle flag
                isChoiceSelected = true;

                //return choice
                theChoice(currentChoice);
            }

            //move upward through options
            else if (
                theNumChoices > 1 &&
                Input.GetKeyDown(KeyCode.UpArrow)
                ) {

                //update choice
                currentChoice--;

                //check bounds on current choice
                //exceeds min
                if (currentChoice < 0) {

                    //wrap to last choice
                    currentChoice = theNumChoices - 1;
                }
            }

            //move downward through options
            else if (
                theNumChoices > 1 &&
                Input.GetKeyDown(KeyCode.DownArrow)
                ) {

                //update choice
                currentChoice++;
```

```
                    //check bounds on current choice
                    //exceeds max
                    if (currentChoice >= theNumChoices) {

                            //wrap to first choice
                            currentChoice = 0;
                    }
            }

            //store indicator position
            Vector3 newPos = imgIndicator.transform.
              position;

            //update y to match current choice
            newPos.y = txtObjects[currentChoice].transform.
              position.y;

            //update indicator position
            imgIndicator.transform.position = newPos;

            //keep waiting
            yield return 0;
        }
    }

} //end class
```

Let's turn to our implementation of the selection box in the UserCollision script. To see the selection box in action, we incorporate it into Luna's collision with the Red Knight. The code modified from our previous iteration is in bold:

```
//UserCollision script
//excerpt from OnTriggerEnter2D() function
case "Knight":

    //disable input
    userMove.SetUserInputEnabled(false);

    //retrieve dialogue
    Dialogue dialogue = GameObject.FindWithTag("Dialogue").
      GetComponent<Dialogue>();

    //update dialogue text
    dialogue.CreateDialogueWithText(new string[] {
        "Do you dare to enter the dungeon?",
        "Change your choice using the UP and DOWN ARROW
          keys.",
        "Press SPACE to confirm your choice."
    });

    //show
    dialogue.Show();

    //hide on input
    StartCoroutine(dialogue.HideOnInput());
```

```
//retrieve selection
Selection selection = GameObject.FindWithTag("Selection").
  GetComponent<Selection>();

//create selection text
List<string> txtSelection = new List<string>() {
      "Yes",
      "No",
      "Cancel"
};

//create selection
selection.CreateSelection(txtSelection);

//position selection
selection.PositionAt(gameObject);

//show selection
selection.Show();

//make choice
int choice = 2;
yield return StartCoroutine(
            selection.StartSelection(
                txtSelection.Count,
                value => choice = value
            )
      );

//check choice
//yes
if (choice == 0) {

      //switch to dungeon scene
      StateManager.Instance.SwitchSceneTo("Dungeon");
}

//no
else if (choice == 1 || choice == 2) {

      //enable input
      userMove.SetUserInputEnabled(true);
}

break;
```

Notably, the choice variable is created to receive the player's final choice from the Selection script. The OnTriggerEnter2D() function then yields to the Selection script, passing it the number of choices available and a lambda expression that captures the player's final choice. Once the selection is complete, OnTriggerEnter2D() checks the result. If the player chose "Yes" (index 0), the StateManager script is told to load the Dungeon scene. However, if the player chose "No" (index 1) or "Cancel" (index 2), the selection box is dismissed without consequence. Instead, Luna's UserMove input is enabled to allow her to continue navigating the world map. She is free to initiate the conversation with the Red Knight once again on a subsequent collision. Test your game and take pleasure in Luna's ability to decide whether or not she will enter the Dungeon scene.

Summary

You have succeeded in implementing a versatile selection box. With the new-found ability to offer choices to your characters, the possibilities are limitless for your game. You can easily reuse your selection box to create a variety of discussions and interactions among your characters. Having completed this chapter's challenges, you should now be able to apply all of these game implementation techniques:

- Implement a selection box to allow the player to make a choice

- Take actions in the game based on the player's choices

- Manage information flow using delegates and lambda expressions

- Execute an asynchronous callback

You've come a long way in your use of game implementation techniques. It's time to add even more interactivity to your game. In the next chapter, your characters will square off with one another in a friendly, team-based competition. Furthermore, Luna will encounter her greatest challenge yet in the form of a dreaded dragon.

References

Microsoft Corporation. 2015a. => Operator (C# Reference). https://msdn.microsoft.com/library/bb311046.aspx (accessed December 14, 2015).

Microsoft Corporation. 2015b. Delegates (C# Programming Guide). https://msdn.microsoft.com/library/ms173171.aspx (accessed December 14, 2015).

Microsoft Corporation. 2015c. Delegates Tutorial. https://msdn.microsoft.com/library/aa288459.aspx (accessed December 14, 2015).

Microsoft Corporation. 2015d. Lambda Expressions (C# Programming Guide). https://msdn.microsoft.com/library/bb397687.aspx (accessed December 14, 2015).

Microsoft Corporation. 2015e. List<T> Class. https://msdn.microsoft.com/library/6sh2ey19.aspx (accessed December 14, 2015).

Microsoft Corporation. 2015f. Using Delegates (C# Programming Guide). https://msdn.microsoft.com/library/ms173172.aspx (accessed December 14, 2015).

Quick, J. M. 2015. *Learn to Code with Games*. Boca Raton, FL: CRC Press. ISBN: 9781498704687

Unity Technologies. 2015a. Camera. http://docs.unity3d.com/ScriptReference/Camera.html (accessed December 14, 2015).

Unity Technologies. 2015b. Camera.ScreenToWorldPoint. http://docs.unity3d.com/ScriptReference/Camera.ScreenToWorldPoint.html (accessed December 14, 2015).

Unity Technologies. 2015c. Camera.WorldToScreenPoint. http://docs.unity3d.com/ScriptReference/Camera.WorldToScreenPoint.html (accessed December 14, 2015).

Unity Technologies. 2015d. Canvas.scaleFactor. http://docs.unity3d.com/460/Documentation/ScriptReference/Canvas-scaleFactor.html (accessed December 14, 2015).

4 Face the Dragon

After venturing into the dungeon, Luna explored its myriad passages. She dodged the drakes who gave chase as she searched for her missing friends in room after room. Little did she know that she was about to encounter the most fearsome foe of all. Indeed, the Green Dragon (Figure 4.1) lay just around the corner. Rather playful for a dragon, his plan is to present a new type of challenge. Can Luna best the Green Dragon in a game of wits? Luna's future is to be determined by you. In this chapter, you will implement a turn-based interaction system that allows your characters to compete with one another.

Goals

By the end of this chapter, you will be able to apply these game implementation techniques:

- Implement a turn-based interaction system

- Allow player-controlled and non-player-controlled characters to interact

- Manage multiple independent scripts using a singleton instance

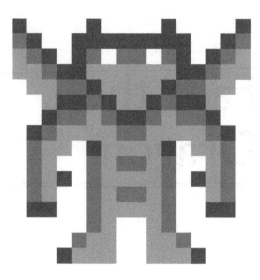

Figure 4.1 The dreaded but playful Green Dragon and his team of drakes will challenge Luna and her friends to a game of wits.

- Design a system that handles an entire interaction sequence between multiple characters

- Use visual indicators to communicate the interactions that take place within a system

▌ Required Files

In this chapter, you will use the following files from the *Software > Chapter_04* folder (https://www.crcpress.com/Learn-to-Implement-Games-with-Code/Quick/p/book/9781498753388):

- The contents of the Challenge folder to create, code, and test your solution

- The contents of the Solution folder to compare your solution to the example solution

▌ Challenge: Prepare the Interaction

Open the *Challenge > Assets > Scenes > Interaction.unity scene* in Unity. This is a new scene that has been added to our game. To simplify things, we will only focus on preparing the Interaction scene in this chapter. Don't worry, everything you've done in previous chapters is safe and sound. We will reincorporate your previous work in a later chapter. For now, let's focus on implementing a turn-based interaction system. The interaction system composes the single largest feature in your game. Therefore, it is useful to build and test this system in phases. Gradually, you will work toward a full implementation of the interaction system.

Start by imagining how your Interaction scene will look to the player when it is complete. A scene is loaded that presents the heroes (Luna's team) and the opponents (Green Dragon's team). Each character takes a turn in order, starting with Luna. On her turn, a selection box allows her to choose an offensive action. Next, another selection box allows her to choose which opponent to target. Then, a defensive action is generated for the targeted opponent. Subsequently, a win–loss result is determined based on the characters' actions in comparison to one another. If Luna wins, the opponent is eliminated. If the opponent wins, Luna is eliminated. This completes Luna's turn. Each character on each team takes a turn in sequence until an entire team is eliminated. The team with characters remaining is victorious. Along the way, a log of every major event is recorded in the dialogue box to inform the player. In Figure 4.2, a process map summarizes the interaction sequence.

Ultimately, you will implement an interaction system similar to what was described. Needless to say, there is quite a bit of activity happening in your interaction system. Thus, it is especially important to break the implementation down into manageable pieces. For this initial challenge, you will focus on setting the stage for your interaction to take place. This requires a combination of leveraging what you have already created, as well as writing new code. Indeed, you already possess the beginnings of your interaction system. For instance, the interaction system will leverage your dialogue and selection boxes. Therefore, the PnlDialogue and PnlSelection objects, as well as the Dialogue and Selection scripts, are present in the Interaction scene. Beyond these, it is your responsibility to create objects and code scripts to further the implementation of your interaction system. A few important things to consider are, how you will generate

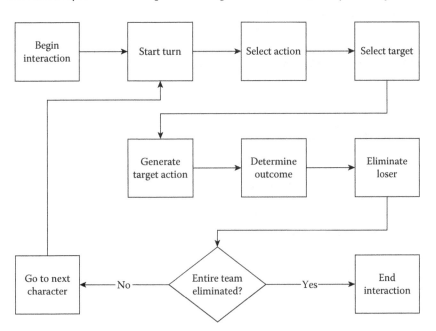

Figure 4.2 A process map visualizes the operations of the turn-based interaction system.

the Interaction scene, start an interaction between characters, and keep track of the characters throughout the interaction. Be sure to think through a logical solution to these aspects of your interaction system before trying to code them. The requirements for this challenge are:

1. Create an InteractionSystem script that implements a singleton instance to manage all aspects of character interaction throughout the game

2. Create a CharacterData script that tracks information about characters who participate in an interaction

3. Create an InteractionGenerator script that prepares the Interaction scene

Hint: Manage All Interactions

Currently, you have independent scripts controlling your dialogue box, selection box, and other game features. However, with your InteractionSystem, you are introducing one script to manage all aspects related to character interaction. This is a case where the singleton design pattern (Quick 2015) is applicable. You can create a singleton instance of your interaction system that will persist throughout the entire duration of your game. It can be used to manage the turn-based gameplay of the Interaction scene, as well as the dialogue and selection boxes you present to the player. The following code snippet demonstrates how to implement a singleton in Unity (Quick 2015):

```
//Unity implementation of singleton design pattern

//create the private singleton instance
private static SingletonScript _Instance;

//create a public accessor to return the instance
public static SingletonScript Instance {

    //create instance via getter
    get {

        //if no instance
        if (_Instance == null) {

            //create game object
            GameObject SingletonObj = new GameObject();
            SingletonObj.name = "Singleton";

            //create instance
            _Instance = SingletonObj.AddComponent
                <SingletonScript>();
        }

        //return the instance
        return _Instance;
    }
}
//awake
void Awake() {
```

```
//prevent destruction
DontDestroyOnLoad(this);
}
```

Let's briefly review the `SingletonScript` example to consider how the singleton design pattern is applied in Unity. First, a `private static _Instance` variable of the `SingletonScript` is declared. Next, a `public static` accessor function (Microsoft Corporation 2015a) allows the instance to be retrieved by other scripts through a call to `SingletonScript.Instance`. Specifically, a `get` accessor supports lazy loading by ensuring that the singleton instance is only created after it is called. Whenever your code attempts to retrieve the singleton instance, a check is made to determine whether the instance already exits. If not, the `_Instance` variable is assigned to a newly created `GameObject` with the `SingletonScript` attached. Last, the `_Instance` variable is returned. Hence, any time another script calls `SingletonScript.Instance`, it is provided access to the singleton instance of our script. In addition, note that the Unity `Awake()` function (Unity Technologies 2015a) is present. Inside this function, we call `DontDestroyOnLoad()` on the `SingletonScript` to ensure that our singleton instance persists throughout the duration of our game. This covers the basic implementation of the Unity singleton. For a more extensive discussion of the singleton design pattern in Unity, see Quick (2015).

After you apply the singleton design pattern to your InteractionSystem script, think about what should be managed by this system. For example, your InteractionSystem can take full control over your dialogue and selection boxes by including them as variables in the singleton instance. Subsequently, instead of calling to those user interface (UI) elements directly in your code, you can access them through your singleton instance. Thus, any existing or future calls to these elements should be routed through your InteractionSystem singleton. That way, your InteractionSystem singleton provides consistent and convenient access to all features related to character interaction in your game.

Hint: Keep Track of the Characters

Keeping track of the characters involved in an interaction is an important task. The idea is to define certain unique information about each character. For example, suppose you want to print a message such as "Luna's turn" to your dialogue box when Luna takes a turn. Your dialogue box knows nothing of the characters—it merely prints whatever message you tell it to. Meanwhile, your interaction system is designed to support any characters who are present in the interaction, so it won't store specifics about individual characters. However, to print something like "Luna's turn" in the dialogue box (Dialogue script) requires us to know whose turn it is (InteractionSystem script), and have some information about that character. This is where a CharacterData script would be helpful. This script can be attached to each character. It stores unique information, such as a character's name. Thereafter, other scripts can reference the CharacterData as needed. For instance, on Luna's turn, the InteractionSystem could retrieve her name from the CharacterData script and pass it to the Dialogue script to present the "Luna's turn" message in the dialogue box.

Besides a name, think about what information would be useful to store in your CharacterData script. Store any necessary information as variables in your script. For now, add what you think will be useful. As you build your interaction system, you are likely to discover unforeseen information that would be best kept in the CharacterData script. Later, you can revisit this script and revise it.

Once you have created your CharacterData script, you need to attach it to all of your characters. Go to the *Assets > Prefabs > Characters* folder (Figure 4.3). For each character prefab, go to the Inspector window and select Add Component > Scripts > Character Data (Figure 4.4). This attaches a CharacterData script to

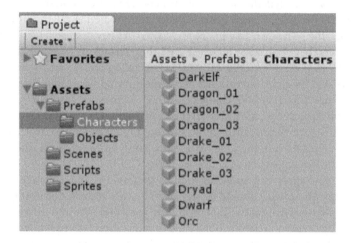

Figure 4.3 You can find prefabs for all of the game's characters in the *Assets > Prefabs > Characters* folder.

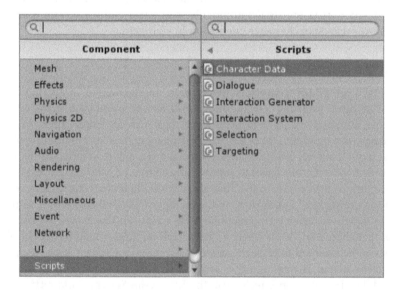

Figure 4.4 Attach your CharacterData script to every character in the *Assets > Prefabs > Characters* folder.

4. Face the Dragon

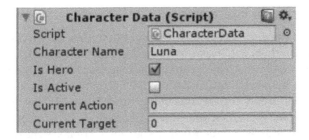

Character Data (Script)	
Script	CharacterData
Character Name	Luna
Is Hero	☑
Is Active	☐
Current Action	0
Current Target	0

Figure 4.5 Use the Inspector window to set values in the CharacterData script for every character. For example, the DarkElf prefab is used to create our Luna character.

the character. Afterward, fill in information for each character in the Inspector window. For example, Figure 4.5 shows Luna's name being defined in the CharacterData script. When you are finished, all of your character prefabs should have CharacterData associated with them.

Hint: Start an Interaction

Head back over to your InteractionSystem script. Think about the first thing the player will see upon entering the Interaction scene. Surely, you need to present characters from Luna's team of heroes and the Green Dragon's team of opponents. Therefore, it makes sense to store all of the characters who will participate in the interaction. You can create a collection to store the characters in your InteractionSystem script:

```
//store the characters
public List<GameObject> allCharacters;
```

In this sample code, the characters are stored in a `List` with the `GameObject` type. Our characters come from prefabs, which are of the `GameObject` type. Hence, this is an appropriate storage method.

Furthermore, we want to present status messages and choices to the player during an interaction. Recall that our InteractionSystem singleton is in full control over our dialogue and selection boxes. If you haven't done so already, you should store these variables in your Interaction System:

```
//dialogue box in scene
public Dialogue dialogue;

//selection box in scene
public Selection selection;
```

Having declared variables for your characters, dialogue box, and selection box in the InteractionSystem script, remember to initialize them as part of your singleton instance. Moreover, with your variables in place, you are prepared to initiate an interaction between characters. Write a `CreateInteraction()` function that adds all of the characters to your Interaction scene and prints a message to let the player know that the game has begun!

Hint: Generate an Interaction

Your Map and Dungeon scenes make use of the LevelGenerator script. This script sets the stage for the scene. It spawns the background tiles and characters, generates random positions for objects on the tile map, and so on. In similar fashion, you can create an InteractionGenerator script that prepares the requisite items for your Interaction scene. For the time being, think of your InteractionGenerator script as a way for you to test your interaction system. Accordingly, your script should allow you to determine whether your interaction system is functioning properly.

Thus far, your interaction system only requires a cast of characters who will participate. Therefore, you can store a group of heroes (Luna's team) and opponents (Green Dragon's team) in your InteractionGenerator script. From there, you can also make a call to your interaction system's `CreateInteraction()` function. Hence, your InteractionGenerator serves the purpose of storing characters and initiating an interaction. Create an InteractionGenerator script to do just that. Remember to add a `GameObject` to your scene and attach this script. Thereafter, test your Interaction scene to ensure you have completed the initial phase of this implementation.

Example Solution: Prepare the Interaction

The initial phase of your interaction system sets the stage for the Interaction scene. Your InteractionSystem should contain variables to store the characters, dialogue box, and selection box:

```
//InteractionSystem script
//dialogue box in scene
public Dialogue dialogue;

//selection box in scene
public Selection selection;

//store interaction characters
public List<GameObject> allCharacters;
```

In addition, your InteractionSystem implements the singleton design pattern. Notice that the `dialogue`, `selection`, and `allCharacters` variables are initialized when the singleton instance is created:

```
//InteractionSystem script
//singleton instance
private static InteractionSystem _Instance;

//singleton accessor
//access InteractionSystem.Instance from other classes
public static InteractionSystem Instance {

    //create instance via getter
    get {

        //if no instance
        if (_Instance == null) {
```

```
            //create game object
            GameObject InteractionSystemObj = new GameObject();
            InteractionSystemObj.name = "InteractionSystem";

            //create instance
            _Instance = InteractionSystemObj.AddComponent
              <InteractionSystem>();

            //retrieve scene objects
            _Instance.dialogue = GameObject.
              FindWithTag("Dialogue").GetComponent<Dialogue>();
            _Instance.selection = GameObject.
              FindWithTag("Selection").GetComponent<Selection>();

            //init
            _Instance.allCharacters = new List<GameObject>();
        }

        //return the instance
        return _Instance;
    }
}

//awake
void Awake() {

    //prevent destruction
    DontDestroyOnLoad(this);
}
```

Meanwhile, your `CharacterData` script should store essential information about your characters in relation to the interaction system. While your script may vary at this point, here is a suggested set of variables:

```
//CharacterData script
public class CharacterData : MonoBehaviour {

    //character's name
    public string characterName;

    //whether the character is a hero
    public bool isHero;

    //whether the character is active in the current interaction
    public bool isActive;

    //currently selected action
    public int currentAction;

    //currently selected target
    public int currentTarget;
}
```

Although tiny, your `CharacterData` script stores important information. The `characterName` variable can be used to present messages that use the character's actual names, such as "Luna wins!" The `isHero` Boolean indicates whether a character is on Luna's team or the Green Dragon's team. This is useful, since we may need to handle characters differently based on their team.

The isActive Boolean is essential for our interaction system, because it indicates whether a character is currently active in the interaction. Since victory in our interaction system is based on a process of elimination, we can use this variable to track the characters are and are not participating at a given moment. For instance, we can skip the turns of characters who have already been eliminated and determine the victors once an entire team of characters is eliminated. Continuing, the currentAction and currentTarget variables store the action that a character takes and the target that the character chooses on a given turn. Later on, we may need to refer back to these values to determine the outcomes of a given turn. With these variables, your CharacterData script is complete. Remember to add it to all of your character prefabs and initialize the variable values in the Inspector window.

Further, your InteractionSystem script's CreateInteraction() function prepares an interaction to take place by adding the characters to the scene. Notice that it leverages the CharacterData script as well:

```
//InteractionSystem script
public void CreateInteraction(List<GameObject> theCharacters) {

    //reset characters
    allCharacters.Clear();

    //create container
    GameObject container = new GameObject();
    container.name = "Characters";

    //for all characters
    foreach (GameObject aChar in theCharacters) {

        //clone
        GameObject newChar = Instantiate<GameObject>(aChar);

        //parent
        newChar.transform.parent = container.transform;

        //activate
        CharacterData charData = newChar.GetComponent
          <CharacterData>();
        charData.isActive = true;

        //add to collection
        allCharacters.Add(newChar);
    }
}
```

Here, the CreateInteraction() function receives a collection of character prefabs as an argument. It starts by clearing the allCharacters collection:

```
//InteractionSystem script
//excerpt from CreateInteraction() function
public void CreateInteraction(List<GameObject> theCharacters) {

    //clear characters
    allCharacters.Clear();
```

Similar to the dialogue and selection boxes, our interaction system will be reused throughout the game. Thus, we need to clear `allCharacters` to remove any characters that may be left over from a previous interaction. Next, a `GameObject` named "Characters" is added to the scene to serve as a container for the characters:

```
//InteractionSystem script
//excerpt from CreateInteraction() function
    //create container
    GameObject container = new GameObject();
    container.name = "Characters";
```

Then, a loop iterates through the character prefabs that were passed into the function. Each prefab is cloned using the `Instantiate()` function (Unity Technologies 2015b) and placed as a child in the "Characters" container. Conveniently, the CharacterData script is retrieved and the `isActive` flag is set to `true`. Since this is a brand new interaction and no characters have been eliminated yet, we make sure all of them are activated. Last, each character is added to the `allCharacters` collection, which allows them to be tracked throughout the interaction:

```
//InteractionSystem script
//excerpt from CreateInteraction() function

    //for all characters
    foreach (GameObject aChar in theCharacters) {

        //clone
        GameObject newChar = Instantiate<GameObject>(aChar);

        //parent
        newChar.transform.parent = container.transform;

        //activate
        CharacterData charData = newChar.GetComponent
          <CharacterData>();
        charData.isActive = true;

        //add to collection
        allCharacters.Add(newChar);
    }
}
```

Thus, upon completion, `CreateInteraction()` has incorporated all of the active characters into the Interaction scene.

Finally, to prepare our Interaction scene for testing, we create the InteractionGenerator script. Remember to add a `GameObject` to your scene with this script attached:

```
//InteractionGenerator script
public class InteractionGenerator : MonoBehaviour {

    //store character prefabs
    public GameObject[] heroPrefabs;
    public GameObject[] opponentPrefabs;
```

```
//init
void Start() {

    //store all characters
    List<GameObject> allChars = new List<GameObject>();

    //add characters to interaction
    //heroes
    allChars.AddRange(heroPrefabs);

    //opponents
    allChars.AddRange(opponentPrefabs);

    //create interaction

    InteractionSystem.Instance.CreateInteraction(allChars);
    }
}
```

The InteractionGenerator script uses two arrays to store the character prefabs from Luna's team (heroPrefabs) and the Green Dragon's team (opponentPrefabs):

```
//InteractionGenerator script
//store character prefabs
public GameObject[] heroPrefabs;
public GameObject[] opponentPrefabs;
```

You can assign characters to these arrays by dragging them from the *Assets > Prefabs > Characters* folder to the Inspector window (Figure 4.6).

Inside Start(), a local collection of characters is created. The hero and opponent prefabs are added to this collection using the AddRange()

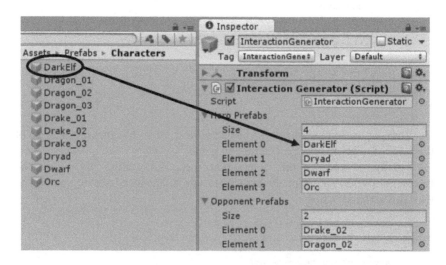

Figure 4.6 Assign characters to teams by dragging prefabs from *Assets > Prefabs > Characters* into your InteractionGenerator script.

4. Face the Dragon

command (Microsoft Corporation 2015f). After this, the entire collection of characters is passed to the InteractionSystem script's `CreateInteraction()` function:

```
//InteractionGenerator script
//excerpt from Start() function

//store all characters
List<GameObject> allChars = new List<GameObject>();

//add characters to interaction
//heroes
allChars.AddRange(heroPrefabs);

//opponents
allChars.AddRange(opponentPrefabs);

//create interaction
InteractionSystem.Instance.CreateInteraction(allChars);
```

Hence, the InteractionGenerator script sets up the Interaction scene and initiates an interaction between characters.

It's time to test your interaction system. Play your game to see that the Characters GameObject is added to the Hierarchy and contains all of the provided characters (Figure 4.7). Additionally, the individual characters carry CharacterData scripts with the `isActive` flag set to `true` (Figure 4.8).

Frankly, the Interaction scene is not that exciting at the moment. However, the foundation for bigger and better things is in place. Let's make our interaction system a little more interesting by implementing turns in the next phase of development.

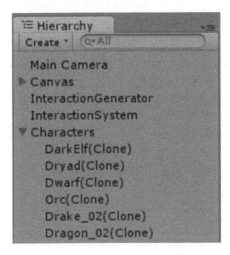

Figure 4.7 When you test the interaction scene, you should see that a Characters GameObject is added to the Hierarchy that contains all of the participating characters.

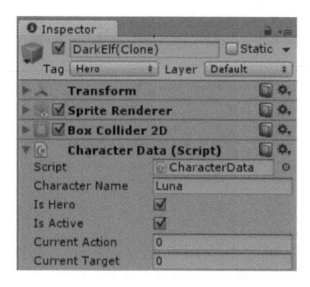

Figure 4.8 The CharacterData script's `isActive` variable has been set to `true` for all characters added to your Interaction scene by the `CreateInteraction()` function. For example, Luna's CharacterData script is shown.

▮ Challenge: Implement Turns

Needless to say, turns are a core component of your turn-based interaction system. You want each character on each team to take a turn in sequence. During a turn, a character needs to select an action and a target. After each character takes a turn, your interaction system passes the turn to the next character. Once all characters have had a turn, the process begins anew. In this challenge, you will implement turns like this in your interaction system.

By the way, we need to determine what actions our characters can take on their turns. For demonstration purposes, we will implement the Star–Sun–Moon (SSM) game. SSM is strikingly similar to the traditional rock–paper–scissors game. On a given turn, a character can choose to play either star, sun, or moon. Simultaneously, the character and the targeted opponent reveal their moves. Star beats sun, sun beats moon, and moon beats star (Figure 4.9). A draw occurs if both characters play the same move. Thus, to implement SSM,

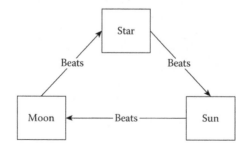

Figure 4.9 The balanced counter system of the Star–Sun–Moon game is depicted.

we must allow characters to choose either star, sun, or moon as their turn action. The requirements for this challenge are:

1. On a turn, a character should be able to choose a star, sun, or moon action.

2. On a turn, a character should be able to choose a target from the active opponents.

3. Each character on each team should take a turn before returning back to the first character and repeating the process.

Although we are implementing the SSM game in this chapter, note that your interaction system could be used in many different ways. For instance, you could create a more complex system in which every character has a unique set of moves. Thus, you may want to revisit it later on to create a different style of turn-based gameplay. Thankfully, the foundational interaction system you create in this chapter will be easy to expand and modify for future games.

Hint: Choose an Action

On a character's turn, we know that an action must be selected. In our SSM game, there are three potential actions: star, sun, or moon. Since these values are used for all characters in our game, you should store them in your InteractionSystem script for easy reference. For example, you could create an `enum` (Microsoft Corporation 2015c) or use `const` variables (Microsoft Corporation 2015b) to store the possible actions.

Afterward, write a coroutine named `TurnAction()` in your InteractionSystem script that allows the player to select from the available choices. Recall that the actual process of making a choice is handled by the Selection script. Thus, the responsibility of `TurnAction()` is to pass the potential choices into the Selection script. Furthermore, `TurnAction()` can receive the final choice made by the player in the Selection script. You successfully completed a similar process when you implemented an asynchronous callback in Chapter 3. Revisit your prior implementation and leverage your codebase to implement the `TurnAction()` function.

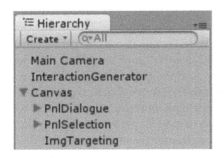

Figure 4.10 In the Hierarchy window, the ImgTargeting object has been added as a child to the Canvas.

Hint: Choose a Target

Besides an action, a character must also select a target to complete a full turn. In the Hierarchy of your Unity project, you will find that an ImgTargeting object has been added to your Canvas (Figure 4.10). ImgTargeting contains an image of a downward pointing arrow. It has also been given the "Targeting" tag. Similar to the ImgIndicator object in PnlSelection, ImgTargeting can be used to indicate what target the player is currently selecting. For instance, you can place the arrow above the head of the character who the player is targeting (Figure 4.11). When the choice is changed, move the arrow above the next character. This provides the player with a clear visual indication of the chosen target.

Figure 4.11 The indicator image is placed above the head of the character who the player is currently targeting.

Of course, before the visuals can be implemented, you must code the underlying process. Create a Targeting script and attach it to ImgTargeting. For the time being, the code inside your Targeting script should be quite similar to your Selection script. However, there are a few differences. Instead of selecting among a fixed set of actions, your Targeting script is selecting among the active opponents involved in the interaction. Thus, each time a character needs to choose a target, you should identify all of the active characters on the opposing team. Thereafter, the player should only be allowed to choose from among active characters when selecting a target. For now, implement the code underlying the targeting process in your Targeting script. At a later phase, we will update the Targeting script to include the visual indicator.

Before we proceed, return to the InteractionSystem script. Make sure to store the Targeting script in your InteractionSystem, just as you have done with Dialogue and Selection. Then, create a `TurnTarget()` function that allows a character to select from among the active opponents during a turn. Think about referring to your CharacterData script to determine which characters are active and which are opponents relative to the character who is taking a turn. This function should be quite similar to `TurnAction()`, with the exception that a choice is being made from among several characters, rather than actions.

Hint: Focus on a Single Turn

It's time to focus on what needs to happen to complete a single turn. Essentially, on a character's turn, we know that an action and a target need to be selected. Your InteractionSystem script's `TurnAction()` and `TurnTarget()` functions take care of these choices. However, we don't know exactly when input will be received from the player. Thus, we need the ability to listen for certain activities throughout the turn. After the player acts, we should trigger subsequent events. Hopefully, this process sounds quite familiar to you. Indeed, we have used coroutines throughout our game to model interactions such as this. Once again, coroutines are an invaluable resource for the implementation of our interaction system.

Write a coroutine named `StartTurn()` in your InteractionSystem script that represents one character's turn. Surely, you must include a way to keep track of which character is taking the turn. In addition, you should build in the capacity to wait until an action and a target are selected before continuing. In the past, we've done this by yielding one coroutine to another. Hence, by coordinating your `StartTurn()`, `TurnAction()`, and `TurnTarget()` coroutines, you can implement a complete turn sequence for a single character. Once you have a turn working for one character, you can reuse it for all of the characters.

Hint: Focus on the Entire Interaction

With one turn settled, let's consider the scope of an entire interaction. Not only one, but all of the characters need to take turns. Create yet another coroutine in your InteractionSystem script called `StartInteraction()` to manage the overall interaction process. Recall that all of the characters are stored in your InteractionSystem script's `allCharacters` collection. Hence, your `StartInteraction()` coroutine can keep track of which character is currently taking a turn. After that, it can iterate through every character and offer each one a turn by yielding to the `StartTurn()` coroutine. Once all of the characters have had a turn, `StartInteraction()` can return to the first character. Write your `StartInteraction()` function to execute this turn-based process.

To see this process at work, call `StartInteraction()` right after `CreateInteraction()` in your InteractionGenerator script's `Start()` function. Then proceed to complete turns for each of the characters by making the necessary choices. At present, this cycle continues indefinitely. Eventually, you will implement win–loss conditions that end the interaction once one of the teams is victorious.

Hint: Generate Opponent Turns

Most of our focus thus far has been on characters that the player controls. However, the player only controls Luna's team. We must also consider what happens when the characters on the Green Dragon's team take their turns. When it comes to selecting an action and a target, no input from the player is required. Instead, these choices can be generated on behalf of the non-player characters (NPCs). For instance, you could implement any artificial intelligence (AI) of your choice, including a simple random selection among the available choices. Yet, after an NPC selects a target from Luna's team, the player needs to be able to select a defense action on behalf of the targeted character. Thus, your `TurnAction()` function comes into play even when an NPC takes a turn.

The major point is that you need to be aware of how you will handle turns for different characters. Recall that your CharacterData script stores information about which team a character is on using the `isHero` flag. Thus, when a turn begins, you can check the character's team. Depending on the team, you may choose to implement a different turn process.

Example Solution: Implement Turns

In this example solution, we'll consider one way that you may have implemented turns in your interaction system. This is a multifaceted process, so we'll break it down piece by piece. In the InteractionSystem script, the potential SSM game actions are stored in an enum:

```
//InteractionSystem script
//define actions for characters
public enum Actions {
     Star = 0,
     Sun = 1,
     Moon = 2
}
```

Meanwhile, the TurnAction() coroutine allows the player to select an action in the SSM game:

```
//InteractionSystem script
//determine action for character's turn
public IEnumerator TurnAction(GameObject theObject) {

     //retrieve character data
     CharacterData charData = theObject.GetComponent
       <CharacterData>();

     //create selection
     List<string> txtSelection = new List<string>();
     txtSelection.AddRange(Enum.GetNames(typeof(Actions)));
     selection.CreateSelection(txtSelection);

     //select action
     yield return StartCoroutine(
         selection.StartSelection(
         txtSelection.Count,
         value => charData.currentAction = value)
         );
}
```

TurnAction() receives a GameObject argument that represents the character who is taking a turn. That character's CharacterData script is stored in a local variable:

```
//InteractionSystem script
//excerpt from TurnAction() function
public IEnumerator TurnAction(GameObject theObject) {

     //retrieve character data
     CharacterData charData = theObject.GetComponent
       <CharacterData>();
```

A List called txtSelection is created to store the possible action choices as strings. The SSM game actions from the Actions enum are converted to strings using the Enum.GetNames() (Microsoft Corporation 2015d) and typeof() (Microsoft Corporation 2015g) functions. Once these actions are added to the txtSelection List, they are fed into the Selection script's CreateSelection() box to generate a new selection box:

```
//InteractionSystem script
//excerpt from TurnAction() function
```

```
//create selection
    List<string> txtSelection = new List<string>();
    txtSelection.AddRange(Enum.GetNames(typeof(Actions)));
    selection.CreateSelection(txtSelection);
```

Lastly, `TurnAction()` yields to the Selection script's `StartSelection()` coroutine. A lambda expression is passed in that sets the CharacterData script's `currentAction` variable to the ultimate choice made by the player. Hence, an asynchronous callback is used to capture the character's action after it has taken place in the Selection script:

```
//InteractionSystem script
//excerpt from TurnAction() function
    //select action
    yield return StartCoroutine(
        selection.StartSelection(
        txtSelection.Count,
        value => charData.currentAction = value)
        );
}
```

To facilitate target selection, a Targeting script is created and added to the ImgTargeting object in the scene. Since the Targeting script is nearly identical to our Selection script at this phase, only the code is presented here. Refer to the *Example Solution: Make a Choice* section in Chapter 3 for additional details:

```
//Targeting script
public class Targeting : MonoBehaviour {

    //delegate accepts/returns int representing choice
    public delegate int SelectedChoice(int theChoice);

    //show
    public void Show() {

        //set alpha to visible
        gameObject.GetComponent<CanvasGroup>().alpha = 1.0f;
    }

    //hide
    public void Hide() {

        //set alpha to invisible
        gameObject.GetComponent<CanvasGroup>().alpha = 0.0f;
        }

        //start a new target selection
        public IEnumerator StartTargeting(int theNumChoices,
          SelectedChoice theChoice) {

            //show
            Show();

            //whether dismissed
            bool isDismissed = false;
```

```
        //while not dismissed
        while (isDismissed == false) {

            //wait for choice to be made
            yield return StartCoroutine(
                WaitForChoice(
                theNumChoices,
                value => theChoice(value),
                theTargets)
                );

            //hide
            Hide();

            //toggle flag
            isDismissed = true;
        }
    }

    //wait for user to select among choices
    public IEnumerator WaitForChoice(int theNumChoices,
      SelectedChoice theChoice, List<GameObject> theTargets) {

        //store current selection
        int currentChoice = 0;

        //while input has not been received
        bool isChoiceSelected = false;
        while (isChoiceSelected == false) {

            //check input
            //select current option
            if (Input.GetKeyUp(KeyCode.Space)) {

                //toggle flag
                isChoiceSelected = true;
                //return choice
                theChoice(currentChoice);
            }

            //move right through options
            else if (
                theNumChoices > 1 &&
                Input.GetKeyDown(KeyCode.RightArrow)
                ) {

                //update choice
                currentChoice++;

                //check bounds on current choice
                //exceeds max
                if (currentChoice >= theNumChoices) {
                //wrap to first choice
                currentChoice = 0;
                }
            }
        }

        //move left through options
```

```
          else if (
              theNumChoices > 1 &&
              Input.GetKeyDown(KeyCode.LeftArrow)
              ) {

              //update choice
              currentChoice--;

              //check bounds on current choice
              //exceeds min
              if (currentChoice < 0) {

              //wrap to last choice
              currentChoice = theNumChoices - 1;
              }
          }

          //keep waiting
          yield return 0;
      }
  }

} //end class
```

Just like our dialogue and selection boxes, our target indicator is managed by the InteractionSystem script. Thus, it is stored in a variable and initialized in our singleton accessor:

```
//InteractionSystem script
//store the Targeting script as a variable
public Targeting targeting;

//excerpt from singleton accessor
//initialize the targeting variable
//place code after initialization of dialogue and selection
  variables
_Instance.targeting = GameObject.FindWithTag("Targeting").
  GetComponent<Targeting>();
```

Recall that our targeting system depends upon the team that a character is on and whether the opponents are active in the current interaction. For convenience, a FindCharacters() function is used:

```
//InteractionSystem script
public List<GameObject> FindCharacters(bool theIsActive, bool
  theIsHero) {

    //store characters
    List<GameObject> chars = new List<GameObject>();

    //check all characters
    for (int i = 0; i < allCharacters.Count; i++) {

        //retrieve character data
        CharacterData charData = allCharacters[i].GetComponent
          <CharacterData>();

        //whether character is active
        bool isActive = charData.isActive;
```

```
            //whether current character is hero
            bool isHero = charData.isHero;

            //if matching active and matching type
            if (isActive == theIsActive && isHero == theIsHero) {

                //add character
                chars.Add(allCharacters[i]);
            }
        }

    //return
    return chars;
}
```

FindCharacters() receives arguments indicating whether we want to include active characters and whether the characters are heroes (on Luna's team). A temporary List called chars stores the potential targets. The function iterates through all of the characters in the interaction and checks their CharacterData scripts to see if they match the arguments passed in. If so, the characters are added to chars. Once complete, chars returns only the desired characters to the caller. Hence, this function can be utilized any time we need to distinguish between active and inactive characters or select among characters who are on Luna's or the Green Dragon's team.

Also, in the InteractionSystem script, the TurnTarget() coroutine leverages the Targeting script and FindCharacters() function to allow a character to choose a target:

```
//InteractionSystem script
public IEnumerator TurnTarget(GameObject theObject) {

    //retrieve character data
    CharacterData charData = theObject.
      GetComponent<CharacterData>();

    //find potential targets
    List<GameObject> targets = FindCharacters(true, false);

    //select target
    yield return StartCoroutine(
        targeting.StartTargeting(
        targets.Count,
        value => charData.currentTarget = value)
        );
}
```

TurnTarget() receives a GameObject argument that represents the character who is taking a turn. That character's CharacterData script is stored in a local variable:

```
//InteractionSystem script
//excerpt from TurnTarget() function
public IEnumerator TurnTarget(GameObject theObject) {

    //retrieve character data
    CharacterData charData = theObject.GetComponent<CharacterData>();
```

A List called `targets` is created to store the possible target choices. The `FindCharacters()` function is called with a request to locate active characters who are not heroes (on the Green Dragon's team). The requested characters are returned to the `targets List`:

```
//InteractionSystem script
//excerpt from TurnTarget() function
    //find potential targets
    List<GameObject> targets = FindCharacters(true, false);
```

Last, `TurnTarget()` yields to the Targeting script's `StartTargeting()` coroutine. A lambda expression sets the CharacterData script's `currentTarget` variable to the final choice made by the player. Once again, an asynchronous callback lets us capture the character's target after it has been determined by the Targeting script:

```
//InteractionSystem script
//excerpt from TurnTarget() function
    //select target
    yield return StartCoroutine(
        targeting.StartTargeting(
        targets.Count,
        value => charData.currentTarget = value)
        );
}
```

At this point, we have implemented the ability for a character to select an action and a target. Accordingly, the `StartTurn()` coroutine manages a complete turn for a single character:

```
//InteractionSystem script
public IEnumerator StartTurn(GameObject theObject) {

    //retrieve character data
    CharacterData charData = theObject.
      GetComponent<CharacterData>();

    //if hero
    if (charData.isHero == true) {

        //select action
        yield return StartCoroutine(TurnAction(theObject));

        //select target
        yield return StartCoroutine(TurnTarget(theObject));

        //generate random opponent action
        GameObject theOpponent = FindCharacters(true, false)
          [charData.currentTarget];

        theOpponent.GetComponent<CharacterData>().currentAction =
          UnityEngine.Random.Range(0, Enum.
          GetValues(typeof(Actions)).Length);
    }
```

```
    //if opponent
    else if (charData.isHero == false) {

        //generate random action
        charData.currentAction = UnityEngine.Random.Range(0, Enum.
          GetValues(typeof(Actions)).Length);

        //find potential targets
        List<GameObject> targets = FindCharacters(true, true);

        //generate random target
        charData.currentTarget = UnityEngine.Random.Range(0,
          targets.Count);

        //allow player to select defense action
        GameObject theHero = FindCharacters(true, true)[charData.
          currentTarget];
        yield return StartCoroutine(TurnAction(theHero));
        );
    }
}
```

The StartTurn() coroutine receives a GameObject argument representing the character who is taking a turn. It retrieves the CharacterData script to determine whether the character is a hero (Luna's team) or not (Green Dragon's team):

```
//InteractionSystem script
//excerpt from StartTurn() function
public IEnumerator StartTurn(GameObject theObject) {

    //retrieve character data
    CharacterData charData = theObject.GetComponent
      <CharacterData>();
```

If the character is a hero (Luna's team), the player is allowed to select an action and a target by yielding to the TurnAction() and TurnTarget() coroutines. Once a target is selected, Unity's Random.Range() function (Unity Technologies 2015c) is used in coordination with Enum.GetValues() (Microsoft Corporation 2015e) and the Actions enum to generate a random defense action on behalf of the NPC:

```
//InteractionSystem script
//excerpt from StartTurn() function
    //if hero
    if (charData.isHero == true) {

        //select action
        yield return StartCoroutine(TurnAction(theObject));

        //select target
        yield return StartCoroutine(TurnTarget(theObject));

        //generate random opponent action
        GameObject theOpponent = FindCharacters(true, false)
          [charData.currentTarget];
```

```
theOpponent.GetComponent<CharacterData>().currentAction =
  UnityEngine.Random.Range(0, Enum.GetValues(typeof(Actions)).
  Length);
}
```

On the other hand, if the character is not a hero (the Green Dragon's team), a random action and a target are generated on behalf of the NPC. After this, the player is allowed to select a defense action for the targeted character on Luna's team:

```
//InteractionSystem script
//excerpt from StartTurn() function
    //if opponent
    else if (charData.isHero == false) {

        //generate random action
        charData.currentAction = UnityEngine.Random.Range(0, Enum.
          GetValues(typeof(Actions)).Length);

        //find potential targets
        List<GameObject> targets = FindCharacters(true, true);

        //generate random target
        charData.currentTarget = UnityEngine.Random.
          Range(0, targets.Count);

        //allow player to select defense action
        GameObject theHero = FindCharacters(true, true)[charData.
          currentTarget];
        yield return StartCoroutine(TurnAction(theHero));
        );
    }
}
```

Thus, our `StartTurn()` function handles the entire turn of a single character, regardless of which team it belongs to. Turning toward the interaction as a whole, a global Boolean flag named `_isComplete` is added to the InteractionSystem script:

```
//InteractionSystem script
//whether interaction is complete
private bool _isComplete;
```

Initially, `_isComplete` is set to `false` inside the `CreateInteraction()` function:

```
//InteractionSystem script
//excerpt from CreateInteraction() function
public void CreateInteraction(List<GameObject> theCharacters) {

    //start interaction
    _isComplete = false;

    /*
    Code omitted.
    */
}
```

Thereafter, `StartInteraction()` manages the turns for all characters:

```
//InteractionSystem script
public IEnumerator StartInteraction() {

    //store current character index
    int currentChar = 0;

    //while interaction is not complete
    while (_isComplete == false) {

        //retrieve character data
        CharacterData charData = allCharacters[currentChar].
          GetComponent<CharacterData>();

        //if character is active
        if (charData.isActive == true) {

            //start turn
            yield return StartCoroutine(
            StartTurn(allCharacters[currentChar])
            );
        }

        //increment index
        currentChar++;

        //check bounds on index
        if (currentChar >= allCharacters.Count) {

            //reset index
            currentChar = 0;
        }
    }
}
```

The `StartInteraction()` coroutine counts from the first character (index 0) by setting an `int` variable called `currentChar` to 0. As long as the interaction is ongoing (`_isComplete` is `false`), a `while` loop is executed:

```
//InteractionSystem script
//excerpt from StartInteraction() coroutine
public IEnumerator StartInteraction() {

    //store current character index
    int currentChar = 0;

    //while interaction is not complete
    while (_isComplete == false) {

        /*
        Code omitted.
        */
    }
```

Inside the while loop, the current character is retrieved from allCharacters using the currentChar index value. Then, the

CharacterData script is retrieved. If the character is active, the coroutine yields to `StartTurn()`, which allows the character to complete a turn:

```
//InteractionSystem script
//excerpt from StartInteraction() coroutine
    //retrieve character data
    CharacterData charData = allCharacters[currentChar].
      GetComponent<CharacterData>();

    //if character is active
    if (charData.isActive == true) {

        //start turn
        yield return StartCoroutine(
        StartTurn(allCharacters[currentChar])
        );
    }
```

After this, `currentChar` is incremented by one to pass the turn to the character at the next index value. Last, a bounds check is made to ensure that we don't try to access a character who does not exist. If we exceed the total number of characters, we return back to the first character at index 0:

```
//InteractionSystem script
//excerpt from StartInteraction() coroutine
        //increment index
        currentChar++;

        //check bounds on index
        if (currentChar >= allCharacters.Count) {

            //reset index
            currentChar = 0;
        }
    }
}
```

Effectively, the `StartInteraction()` coroutine ensures that each character takes a turn in sequence throughout the course of the interaction. At this point, we only need to call the `StartInteraction()` function from our InteractionGenerator script:

```
//InteractionGenerator script
//excerpt from Start() function
//start interaction
StartCoroutine(InteractionSystem.Instance.StartInteraction());
```

Make sure to place this line at the bottom of the `Start()` function, below your call to `CreateInteraction()`. What this does is kick off the entire interaction process that you just coded. Therefore, you can see it in action.

Note that printing messages to the Unity console window via `Debug.Log()` would be extremely helpful in testing the operations of your interaction system. Basically, you can print a message for every major event, such as when a character starts a turn, selects an action, chooses a target, and so on.

As of this phase, you should be able to take turns with all of the characters over and over again to infinity. Our next phase of implementation will focus on putting conditions in place to determine which team wins the game.

▮ Challenge: Determine the Interaction Result

The latest iteration of your interaction system allows all of the characters to take a turn. However, upon completing a turn, nothing of consequence happens. That's because we haven't coded any outcomes into our game based on the choices the characters make. In this challenge, you will ensure that every choice made in the interaction system has an outcome. Further, you will determine who wins the SSM game, thus completing an entire interaction between the teams. The requirements for this challenge are:

1. Whenever two characters select actions, their choices should be compared to determine a win, lose, or draw outcome

2. Whenever a character experiences a losing outcome, that character should be eliminated from the interaction

3. A team should be declared the winner once all of the characters on the opposing team have been eliminated

Hint: Determine Outcomes

Two characters compare actions in each round of the SSM game. There are three potential outcomes for each round: win, lose, or draw. Similar to the three actions that characters can take, you should store the three outcomes in your InteractionSystem script. For consistency, you may store the outcome values the same way as your actions.

After storing the potential outcomes, write a `CompareActions()` function that determines the result of a round. Ideally, you can determine the result of a round regardless of which characters are interacting. All you need to know is what action each character took. From there, you should be able to identify whether the result is a win, lose, or draw. Remember the rules of SSM when making your comparisons: star beats sun, sun beats moon, and moon beats star (Figure 4.9).

Hint: Apply Outcomes

After determining the outcome for a round of the SSM game, you need to apply the result to the characters. For example, if Luna bests the Green Dragon in a round of play, the Green Dragon needs to be eliminated from the rest of the game. You are already able to determine the outcome of a round using your `CompareActions()` function. Accordingly, write another function called `ApplyActionToTarget()` that applies the outcome of the round to the necessary character(s). This function should take both characters involved in the round into consideration. Based on the outcome of the round (win, lose, or draw), you can apply the effects to the characters. Be sure to leverage the data stored in your CharacterData script when writing this function. It contains useful information such as the action taken, selected target, and whether the character is active.

When writing your `ApplyActionToTarget()` function, it may be helpful to take the perspective of the character whose turn it is. Ask yourself what happens for each outcome relative to this character. If the character wins, the targeted opponent should be eliminated. In contrast, if the character loses, she is eliminated. For a draw, neither character is eliminated. Your coding job becomes easier by taking a specific perspective like this. Ideally, your `ApplyActionToTarget()` function can be reused for any character on any team.

In addition, think about when to call your `ApplyActionToTarget()` function. Clearly, you should incorporate it into each character's turn. The previous iteration of your InteractionSystem script allowed a character to choose an action and target each turn. In this iteration, you should also apply the action to the target by calling to your `ApplyActionToTarget()` function as part of a character's turn.

Hint: Manage the Interaction State

Another factor that you need to be aware of is the overall interaction state. Your characters are capable of challenging and eliminating one another in the SSM game. However, without managing the overall interaction state in your code, the game will never end. You know that one team is declared victorious once all members of the opposing team have been eliminated. You just need to formalize this rule in your code. The CharacterData script attached to each character uses the `isActive` flag to indicate whether a character is or is not active in the interaction. Thus, you can tell if a team has lost when all of its members' `isActive` flags are set to `false`. Write a `CheckInteraction()` function in your InteractionSystem script that checks the win–loss conditions for the participating teams.

Furthermore, think about where in your InteractionSystem script you should call the `CheckInteraction()` function. You want to regularly check the overall interaction state, since the SSM game could end after any character's turn. Also, you need to specifically trigger the end of the game to prevent additional characters from taking inconsequential turns.

Example Solution: Determine the Interaction Result

With a few additions to your InteractionSystem script, your characters can play through the complete SSM game. Similar to your actions, your outcomes could be stored nicely in an enum:

```
//InteractionSystem script
//define outcomes for interactions
public enum Outcomes {
    Win = 0,
    Lose = 1,
    Draw = 2
}
```

The `CompareActions()` function is used to determine the outcome of any given round:

```
//InteractionSystem script
public int CompareActions(int theFirstAction, int
theSecondAction) {

    //store result
    int outcome = (int)Outcomes.Lose;

    //draw
    if (theFirstAction == theSecondAction) {

        //return
        return (int)Outcomes.Draw;
    }

    //possible win states
    else if (

        //star beats sun
        (theFirstAction == (int)Actions.Star &&
        theSecondAction == (int)Actions.Sun) ||

        //sun beats moon
        (theFirstAction == (int)Actions.Sun &&
        theSecondAction == (int)Actions.Moon) ||

        //moon beats star
        (theFirstAction == (int)Actions.Moon &&
        theSecondAction == (int)Actions.Star)
        ) {

        //return
        return (int)Outcomes.Win;
    }

    //return
    return outcome;
}
```

Conveniently, `CompareActions()` receives two integer arguments that represent actions taken by the competing characters. Technically speaking, our actions and outcomes are represented by integer values. However, this function demonstrates the accessibility gained by storing our data in an `enum`. Rather than using raw integer values such as 0, 1, and 2 to represent our actions and outcomes, we refer to them by their enum names, such as `Actions.Star` and `Outcomes.Win`. By default, the result is stored in an integer called outcome as `Outcomes.Lose`:

```
//InteractionSystem script
//excerpt from CompareActions() function
public int CompareActions(int theFirstAction, int
  theSecondAction) {

    //store result
    int outcome = (int)Outcomes.Lose;
```

Next, an `if` statement checks whether both of the characters' actions are the same. If so, the outcome is returned as `Outcomes.Draw`:

```
//InteractionSystem script
//excerpt from CompareActions() function
//draw
    if (theFirstAction == theSecondAction) {

        //return
        return (int)Outcomes.Draw;
    }
```

Then, the possible win conditions are evaluated. If any of them occurred, the outcome is set to `Outcomes.Win`:

```
//InteractionSystem script
//excerpt from CompareActions() function
//possible win states
    else if (

        //star beats sun
        (theFirstAction == (int)Actions.Star &&
        theSecondAction == (int)Actions.Sun) ||

        //sun beats moon
        (theFirstAction == (int)Actions.Sun &&
        theSecondAction == (int)Actions.Moon) ||

        //moon beats star
        (theFirstAction == (int)Actions.Moon &&
        theSecondAction == (int)Actions.Star)

        ) {

        //return
        return (int)Outcomes.Win;
    }
```

Last, if the outcome was neither returned as win nor draw, the unaltered lose outcome variable is returned:

```
//InteractionSystem script
//excerpt from CompareActions() function
        //return
        return outcome;
}
```

With these few checks, the `CompareActions()` function will always determine the outcome of an SSM round. The returned result represents the outcome of the round from the perspective of the character whose action was provided as the first argument relative to the character whose action was provided in the second argument.

Continuing, the `ApplyActionToTarget()` function works hand in hand with `CompareAction()` to apply the outcome of an SSM round to the characters:

```
//InteractionSystem script
public void ApplyActionToTarget(GameObject theActor, GameObject
theTarget) {
```

```
    //retrieve character data
    CharacterData actorData = theActor.GetComponent
      <CharacterData>();
    CharacterData targetData = theTarget.GetComponent
      <CharacterData>();

    //determine result
    int actorOutcome = CompareActions(actorData.currentAction,
      targetData.currentAction);

    //check result
    switch (actorOutcome) {

        //win
        case (int)Outcomes.Win:
        //deactivate target
        targetData.isActive = false;

        break;

    //lose
    case (int)Outcomes.Lose:

        //deactivate actor
        actorData.isActive = false;

        break;

    //draw
    case (int)Outcomes.Draw:
        break;

        //default
        default:
            Debug.Log("[InteractionSystem] Error: Outcome not
              recognized");
            break;
    }
}
```

ApplyActionToTarget() accepts two GameObject arguments that represent the character whose turn it is (theActor) and the character who is being targeted (theTarget). The CharacterData scripts from both characters are retrieved and stored in local variables:

```
//InteractionSystem script
//excerpt from ApplyActionToTarget() function
public void ApplyActionToTarget(GameObject theActor, GameObject
theTarget) {

    //retrieve character data
    CharacterData actorData = theActor.GetComponent
      <CharacterData>();
    CharacterData targetData = theTarget.GetComponent
      <CharacterData>();
```

Meanwhile, a local integer named actorOutcome stores the result of the two character's actions, as returned by the CompareActions() function.

The character's actions are passed into `CompareActions()` from the `currentAction` variable in their respective CharacterData scripts:

```
//InteractionSystem script
//excerpt from ApplyActionToTarget() function
    //determine result
    int actorOutcome = CompareActions(actorData.currentAction,
      targetData.currentAction);
```

To complete the function, a `switch` statement is used to check the potential outcomes from the perspective of `theActor`. Hence, `theTarget` is deactivated if `theActor` wins, `theActor` is deactivated if `theTarget` wins, or neither character is affected in case of a draw:

```
//InteractionSystem script
//excerpt from ApplyActionToTarget() function
    //check result
    switch (actorOutcome) {

        //win
        case (int)Outcomes.Win:

            //deactivate target
            targetData.isActive = false;

            break;

        //lose
        case (int)Outcomes.Lose:

            //deactivate actor
            actorData.isActive = false;

            break;

        //draw
        case (int)Outcomes.Draw:
            break;

        //default
        default:
        Debug.Log("[InteractionSystem] Error: Outcome not
          recognized");
        break;
    }
}
```

Although the `ApplyActionToTarget()` function is written, you must incorporate it into your turn process for it to take effect. To do so, place calls to `ApplyActionToTarget()` in your existing `StartTurn()` coroutine. One call applies to the hero characters on Luna's team, whereas the other applies to members of the Green Dragon's team. Both calls are placed at the end of their respective characters' turns, after they have finished choosing an action and a target:

```
//InteractionSystem script
//excerpt from StartTurn() coroutine
```

```
public IEnumerator StartTurn(GameObject theObject) {

    //retrieve character data
    CharacterData charData = theObject.GetComponent
      <CharacterData>();

    //if hero
    if (charData.isHero == true) {

        /*
        Code omitted.
        */

            //apply action
            ApplyActionToTarget(theObject, theOpponent);
    }

    //if opponent
    else if (charData.isHero == false) {

        /*
        Code omitted.
        */

            //apply action
            ApplyActionToTarget(theObject, theHero);
    }
}
```

Moreover, the CheckInteraction() function tracks the overall state of the SSM game:

```
//InteractionSystem script
public void CheckInteraction() {

    //check active characters
    List<GameObject> activeOpponents = FindCharacters(true, false);
    List<GameObject> activeHeroes = FindCharacters(true, true);

        //if no opponents remain
        if (activeOpponents.Count <= 0) {

        //heroes win
        Debug.Log("Luna's team wins!");

        //end interaction
        _isComplete = true;
    }

    //if no heroes remain
    else if (activeHeroes.Count <= 0) {

        //heroes lose
        Debug.Log("Green Dragon's team wins!");

        //end interaction
        _isComplete = true;
    }
}
```

In CheckInteraction(), our existing FindCharacters() function is used to retrieve the active characters on both teams:

```
//InteractionSystem script
//excerpt from CheckInteraction() function
public void CheckInteraction() {

    //check active characters
    List<GameObject> activeOpponents = FindCharacters(true, false);
    List<GameObject> activeHeroes = FindCharacters(true, true);
```

If the Green Dragon's team is left without any active characters, Luna's team is declared the winner and the _isComplete flag is set to true:

```
//InteractionSystem script
//excerpt from CheckInteraction() function
    //if no opponents remain
    if (activeOpponents.Count <= 0) {

        //heroes win
        Debug.Log("Luna's team wins!");

        //end interaction
        _isComplete = true;
    }
```

Conversely, if Luna's team is left without any active characters, the Green Dragon's team wins:

```
//InteractionSystem script
//excerpt from CheckInteraction() function
    //if no heroes remain
    else if (activeHeroes.Count <= 0) {

        //heroes lose
        Debug.Log("Green Dragon's team wins!");

        //end interaction
        _isComplete = true;
    }
}
```

On a final note, recall that a call to the CheckInteraction() function needs to be placed wisely in your InteractionSystem code. Since the SSM game can potentially end after any character's turn, it makes sense to check the status of the game at the end of each turn. You can do so by placing a call to CheckInteraction() inside your existing StartInteraction() coroutine:

```
//InteractionSystem script
//excerpt from StartInteraction() coroutine
public IEnumerator StartInteraction() {

    /*
    Code omitted.
    */
```

```
            //if character is active
            if (charData.isActive == true) {

                //start turn
                yield return StartCoroutine(
                    StartTurn(allCharacters[currentChar])
                    );

                //check interaction
                CheckInteraction();
            }

        /*
        Code omitted.
        */
    }
```

Prior to testing your latest iteration of the interaction system, it is again recommended that you add Debug.Log() messages to your newly written functions. These will help you witness the activity of your interaction system in the Console window. Indeed, your interaction system is fully functional at this point. However, the visuals leave much to be desired. Therefore, our final iteration of the interaction system will focus on cleaning up the visual aspects of the Interaction scene to provide a pleasant presentation to the player.

▌ Challenge: Visualize the Interaction

Although our interaction system is technically complete and fully functional, the overall player experience can be improved greatly by using visuals. Currently, all of the characters are clumped in the middle of the screen and the Console window messages are your only indication that the interaction system is working. Let's make some minor adjustments to introduce visual cues that inform the player on the status of the interaction. After completing this challenge, your interaction system will be complete. The requirements for this challenge are:

1. The characters should be positioned on screen in a way that clearly indicates their team membership and turn order.

2. Any time a choice of action is given to the player, the Selection script should show the selection box above the corresponding character.

3. Any time a choice of target is given to the player, the Targeting script should show the indicator image above the targeted character.

4. All major events during the interaction should be logged in the dialogue box.

Hint: Position the Characters

Instead of piling up all of the characters in the center of the screen, it makes sense to lay them out in a sensible presentation to the player. When your characters

Figure 4.12 The characters are arranged in the Interaction scene according to team and turn order.

are cloned from prefabs in the `CreateInteraction()` function, they default to a position of (0, 0), which is why they all appear in the center of the screen. However, you may choose to give the characters a different position after they have been cloned.

Think about how you would like to present the characters. A potential option is to group the characters by team, with Luna's team at the bottom of the screen and the Green Dragon's team at the top. Further, the characters within each team could be arranged in turn order from left to right. This scenario is depicted in Figure 4.12. Of course, you are free to come up with any suitable arrangement of characters. When you have decided on an arrangement, update your `CreateInteraction()` function to execute it.

Hint: Show the Actions

In Chapter 3, you created a selection box. It was used to present Luna's choice of whether or not to enter the Dungeon scene when she encountered the Red Knight. Thus, you already have experience in creating, showing, and positioning your selection box. In the Interaction scene, the player is presented with a choice of three SSM actions any time a character on Luna's team takes a turn. Indeed, your `TurnAction()` function already creates a selection box and uses an asynchronous callback to retrieve the player's choice. However, it does not yet present the selection box on screen or position the selection box over the character who is making a choice. Update your `TurnAction()` function to make full use of your selection box by showing it on screen and positioning it over the corresponding character.

Hint: Indicate the Target

As mentioned earlier, we would return to update our Targeting script. Previously, we focused only on its logical functionality in code. Yet, we also want to provide a visual cue to the player while a target is being selected. The downward pointing arrow image in our ImgTargeting object should be placed above the head of the currently selected target. As the player cycles through the potential targets, the indicator should be updated to represent the current choice. Indeed, this behavior is quite similar to the indicator image in your Selection script. However, the Targeting script's indicator image is oriented differently and needs to be placed above specific characters in the interaction, rather than beside a list of choices. Update your Targeting script to ensure that, any time the player is choosing a target on behalf of a character on Luna's team, the indicator image shows the player's current target choice.

Hint: Log the Events

A critical visual addition to your interaction system is the dialogue box. In Chapter 2, you coded the ability to present messages and update them over time in your dialogue box. However, your interaction system currently does not utilize these features. Think about what important events the player needs to know about during the course of the interaction. Some examples include:

- A character beings a turn, chooses an action, or selects a target

- Two characters face off in a round, and an outcome is determined

- A character is eliminated from the game

- A team wins the game

You may choose to update the player about other events as well. Remember to leverage the information stored in your CharacterData script, such as the character names, to present readable information to the player. Work through your InteractionSystem script to incorporate the dialogue box. Once you have completed this step, test your game. Not only should you see an array of characters, action choices in a selection box, and an indicator image above targets, but the moment-by-moment details of the entire interaction are presented in your dialogue box!

Example Solution: Visualize the Interaction

The final phase of implementation for your interaction system involved adding visuals to the Interaction scene. To better position your characters on screen, you can add code to the end of your `CreateInteraction()` function:

```
//InteractionSystem script
//excerpt from CreateInteraction() function
public void CreateInteraction(List<GameObject> theCharacters) {

    /*
    Code omitted.
    */
```

```
    //retrieve teams
    List<GameObject> allHeroes = FindCharacters(true, true);
    List<GameObject> allOpponents = FindCharacters(true, false);

    //position teams
    //heroes
    for (int i = 0; i < allHeroes.Count; i++) {

        //centered at bottom of screen
        Vector3 pos = Vector3.zero;
        float w = allHeroes[i].GetComponent<Renderer>().bounds.
          size.x;
        float h = allHeroes[i].GetComponent<Renderer>().bounds.
          size.y;
        pos.x = w / 2 + i * w - (w * (float)allHeroes.Count / 2);
        pos.y = -Camera.main.orthographicSize + 3 * h;
        allHeroes[i].transform.position = pos;
    }

    //opponents
    for (int j = 0; j < allOpponents.Count; j++) {

        //centered at top of screen
        Vector3 pos = Vector3.zero;
        float w = allOpponents[j].GetComponent<Renderer>().bounds.
          size.x;
        float h = allOpponents[j].GetComponent<Renderer>().bounds.
          size.y;
        pos.x = w / 2 + j * w - (w * (float)allOpponents.Count / 2);
        pos.y = Camera.main.orthographicSize - 3 * h;
        allOpponents[j].transform.position = pos;
    }
}
```

This code is placed inside CreateInteraction(), after all of the characters have been cloned. Local List variables are created to store Luna's team (allHeroes) and the Green Dragon's team (allOpponents), as returned by the FindCharacters() function:

```
//InteractionSystem script
//excerpt from CreateInteraction() function
    //retrieve teams
    List<GameObject> allHeroes = FindCharacters(true, true);
    List<GameObject> allOpponents = FindCharacters(true, false);
```

A for loop iterates through all of the characters on Luna's team. The characters are positioned from left to right near the top of the screen:

```
//InteractionSystem script
//excerpt from CreateInteraction() function
    //heroes
    for (int i = 0; i < allHeroes.Count; i++) {
    //centered at bottom of screen
    Vector3 pos = Vector3.zero;
    float w = allHeroes[i].GetComponent<Renderer>().bounds.size.x;
    float h = allHeroes[i].GetComponent<Renderer>().bounds.size.y;
    pos.x = w / 2 + i * w - (w * (float)allHeroes.Count / 2);
```

```
pos.y = -Camera.main.orthographicSize + 3 * h;
allHeroes[i].transform.position = pos;
}
```

Note that specific position calculations may be adjusted to your liking. In nearly identical fashion, the characters on the Green Dragon's team are positioned toward the bottom of the screen:

```
//InteractionSystem script
//excerpt from CreateInteraction() function
    //opponents
    for (int j = 0; j < allOpponents.Count; j++) {

        //centered at top of screen
        Vector3 pos = Vector3.zero;
        float w = allOpponents[j].GetComponent<Renderer>().bounds.
            size.x;
        float h = allOpponents[j].GetComponent<Renderer>().bounds.
            size.y;
        pos.x = w / 2 + j * w - (w * (float)allOpponents.Count / 2);
        pos.y = Camera.main.orthographicSize - 3 * h;
        allOpponents[j].transform.position = pos;
    }
```

Another visual improvement to your Interaction scene involves presenting the selection box whenever a player-controlled character chooses an action. This can be accomplished with a simple update to your TurnAction() function:

```
//InteractionSystem script
//TurnAction() function
public IEnumerator TurnAction(GameObject theObject) {

    //retrieve character data
    CharacterData charData = theObject.GetComponent<CharacterData>();

    //update dialogue
    dialogue.CreateDialogueWithText(charData.characterName +
        ": Choose your action.");

    //create selection
    List<string> txtSelection = new List<string>();
    txtSelection.AddRange(Enum.GetNames(typeof(Actions)));
    selection.CreateSelection(txtSelection);

    //position selection
    selection.PositionAt(theObject);

    //show selection
    selection.Show();

    //select action
    yield return StartCoroutine(
        selection.StartSelection(
        txtSelection.Count,
        value => charData.currentAction = value)
        );
}
```

By placing calls to your Selection script's PositionAt() and Show() functions inside TurnAction(), you are able to present the selection box whenever a player-controlled character needs to choose an action. Similarly, you want to present the target indicator image whenever a player-controlled character needs to select a target. This requires a few updates to your Targeting script. To start, store the indicator image in your Targeting script as a variable. Remember to assign your ImgTargeting object to this variable in the Inspector window:

```
//Targeting script
//indicator image
public Image imgIndicator;
```

Next, update your StartTargeting() coroutine to accept a GameObject collection that represents the potential target characters. This collection is passed into the WaitForChoice() coroutine:

```
//Targeting script
public IEnumerator StartTargeting(int theNumChoices, SelectedChoice
theChoice, List<GameObject> theTargets) {

    //show
    Show();

    //whether is dismissed
    bool isDismissed = false;

    //while not dismissed
    while (isDismissed == false) {

        //wait for choice to be made
        yield return StartCoroutine(
            WaitForChoice(
            theNumChoices,
            value => theChoice(value),
            theTargets)
            );

        //hide
        Hide();

        //toggle flag
        isDismissed = true;
    }
}
```

Accordingly, the WaitForChoice() coroutine should also accept the potential targets as an argument. Furthermore, the indicator image position is perpetually updated based on the character who the player is currently targeting:

```
//Targeting script
//excerpt from WaitForChoice() coroutine
public IEnumerator WaitForChoice(int theNumChoices, SelectedChoice
theChoice, List<GameObject> theTargets) {

    //store current selection
    int currentChoice = 0;
```

```
//while input has not been received
bool isChoiceSelected = false;
while (isChoiceSelected == false) {

    /*
    Code omitted.
    */

    //calculate indicator position relative to target
    Vector3 targetPos = theTargets[currentChoice].transform.
        position;
    float targetHeight = theTargets[currentChoice].
        GetComponent<Renderer>().bounds.size.y;

    //convert to screen coordinates
    Vector3 newPos =
        Camera.main.WorldToScreenPoint(new Vector3(
            targetPos.x,
            targetPos.y + targetHeight,
            0));

    //update position
    Vector3 indicatorPos = imgIndicator.transform.position;
    indicatorPos.x = newPos.x;
    indicatorPos.y = newPos.y;
    imgIndicator.transform.position = indicatorPos;

    //keep waiting
    yield return 0;
    }
}
```

Let's discuss how the indicator image is positioned. Based on the current selection, we retrieve the position and height of the targeted character in the Interaction scene:

```
//Targeting script
//excerpt from WaitForChoice() coroutine
            //calculate indicator position relative to target
            Vector3 targetPos = theTargets[currentChoice].
                transform.position;
            float targetHeight = theTargets[currentChoice].
                GetComponent<Renderer>().bounds.size.y;
```

Recall that our UI elements, including the indicator image, are positioned in Unity's screen space, whereas our characters are positioned in world space. Thus, we must convert the target character's position from world space to screen space. The demonstrated calculation centers the x coordinate on the character. Meanwhile, the character's height is added to the y coordinate to find a point just above the character's head:

```
//Targeting script
//excerpt from WaitForChoice() coroutine
            Vector3 newPos =
                Camera.main.WorldToScreenPoint(new Vector3(
                targetPos.x,
                targetPos.y + targetHeight,
                0));
```

With the calculations complete, the indicator image's position is updated to physically move it on screen:

```
//Targeting script
//excerpt from WaitForChoice() coroutine
            Vector3 indicatorPos = imgIndicator.transform.position;
            indicatorPos.x = newPos.x;
            indicatorPos.y = newPos.y;
            imgIndicator.transform.position = indicatorPos;
```

Thus, the Targeting script is complete and the indicator image always appears above the currently selected target. For clarity, the entire Targeting script is presented:

```
//Targeting script
public class Targeting : MonoBehaviour {

    //indicator image
    public Image imgIndicator;

    //delegate accepts/returns int representing choice
    public delegate int SelectedChoice(int theChoice);

    //show
    public void Show() {

        //set alpha to visible
        gameObject.GetComponent<CanvasGroup>().alpha = 1.0f;
    }

    //hide
    public void Hide() {

        //set alpha to invisible
        gameObject.GetComponent<CanvasGroup>().alpha = 0.0f;
    }

    //start a new target selection
    public IEnumerator StartTargeting(int theNumChoices,
        SelectedChoice theChoice, List<GameObject> theTargets) {

        //show
        Show();

        //whether dialogue is dismissed
        bool isDismissed = false;

        //while not dismissed
        while (isDismissed == false) {

            //wait for choice to be made
            yield return StartCoroutine(
            WaitForChoice(
            theNumChoices,
            value => theChoice(value),
            theTargets)
            );
```

```
        //hide
        Hide();

        //toggle flag
        isDismissed = true;
    }
}

//wait for user to select among choices
public IEnumerator WaitForChoice(int theNumChoices,
    SelectedChoice theChoice, List<GameObject> theTargets) {

    //store current selection
    int currentChoice = 0;

    //while input has not been received
    bool isChoiceSelected = false;
    while (isChoiceSelected == false) {

        //check input
        //select current option
        if (Input.GetKeyUp(KeyCode.Space)) {

            //toggle flag
            isChoiceSelected = true;

            //return choice
            theChoice(currentChoice);
        }

        //move forward through options
        else if (theNumChoices > 1 &&
            (Input.GetKeyDown(KeyCode.W) ||
            Input.GetKeyDown(KeyCode.UpArrow) ||
            Input.GetKeyDown(KeyCode.D) ||
            Input.GetKeyDown(KeyCode.RightArrow))
            ) {

            //update choice
            currentChoice++;

            //check bounds on current choice
            //exceeds max
            if (currentChoice >= theNumChoices) {

                //wrap to first choice
                currentChoice = 0;
            }
        }

        //move backward through options
        else if (theNumChoices > 1 &&
            (Input.GetKeyDown(KeyCode.S) ||
            Input.GetKeyDown(KeyCode.DownArrow) ||
            Input.GetKeyDown(KeyCode.A) ||
            Input.GetKeyDown(KeyCode.LeftArrow))
            ) {

            //update choice
            currentChoice--;
```

```
            //check bounds on current choice
            //exceeds min
            if (currentChoice < 0) {

                //wrap to last choice
                currentChoice = theNumChoices - 1;
            }
        }

        //calculate indicator position relative to target
        Vector3 targetPos = theTargets[currentChoice].transform.
          position;
        float targetHeight = theTargets[currentChoice].
          GetComponent<Renderer>().bounds.size.y;

        //convert to screen coordinates
        Vector3 newPos =
            Camera.main.WorldToScreenPoint(new Vector3(
                targetPos.x,
                targetPos.y + targetHeight,
                0));

        //update position
        Vector3 indicatorPos = imgIndicator.transform.position;
        indicatorPos.x = newPos.x;
        indicatorPos.y = newPos.y;
        imgIndicator.transform.position = indicatorPos;

        //keep waiting
        yield return 0;
    }
}

} //end class
```

Moving on, the final visual improvement to the interaction system involves utilizing your dialogue box. Since you may have implemented the dialogue box in a variety of places, a sample of suggested applications is provided. For instance, you could kick off a new SSM game with a message to the player:

```
//InteractionSystem script
//excerpt from CreateInteraction() function
    public void CreateInteraction(List<GameObject> theCharacters) {

    //create dialogue
    dialogue.CreateDialogueWithText(
        "The heroes have been challenged!"
        );

    //show dialogue
    dialogue.Show();

    /*
    Code omitted.
    */
}
```

Similarly, you could announce the start of a new turn:

```
//InteractionSystem script
//excerpt from StartTurn() function
public IEnumerator StartTurn(GameObject theObject) {

    //retrieve character data
    CharacterData charData = theObject.GetComponent<CharacterData>();

    //update dialogue
    //example: "Luna's turn!"
    dialogue.UpdateDialogueWithText(
        charData.characterName +
        "'s turn!"
        );
```

In addition, you might mention a character by name when it is time to select an action:

```
//InteractionSystem script
//excerpt from TurnAction() function
public IEnumerator TurnAction(GameObject theObject) {

    //retrieve character data
    CharacterData charData = theObject.GetComponent<CharacterData>();

    //update dialogue
    //example: "Luna: Choose your action."
    dialogue.UpdateDialogueWithText(
        charData.characterName +
        ": Choose your action."
        );
```

Similarly, you could update the dialogue box when it is time to select a target:

```
//InteractionSystem script
//excerpt from TurnTarget() function
public IEnumerator TurnTarget(GameObject theObject) {

    //retrieve character data
    CharacterData charData = theObject.GetComponent<CharacterData>();

    //update dialogue
    //example: "Luna: Choose your target."
    dialogue.UpdateDialogueWithText(
        charData.characterName +
        ": Choose your target."
        );
```

Furthermore, it would be useful to print a message for each outcome in the ApplyActionToTarget() function. Here is an example message that could be used for the win outcome:

```
//InteractionSystem script
//excerpt from ApplyActionToTarget() function
public void ApplyActionToTarget(GameObject theActor, GameObject
theTarget) {
```

```
/*
Code omitted.
*/

//check result
switch (actorOutcome) {

    //win
    case (int)Outcomes.Win:

        //deactivate target
        targetData.isActive = false;

        //set target color
        theTarget.GetComponent<SpriteRenderer>().color =
          fadeColor;

        //create dialogue
        //example: "Luna's Star beats Green Dragon's Sun!"
        dialogue.UpdateDialogueWithText(
            actorData.characterName + "'s " +
            Enum.GetName(typeof(Actions),
            actorData.currentAction) +
            " beats " +
            targetData.characterName + "'s " +
            Enum.GetName(typeof(Actions),
            targetData.currentAction) +
            "!"
            );

        break;
```

Moreover, allow the winning team to celebrate by printing a message at the conclusion of the interaction:

```
//InteractionSystem script
//CheckInteraction() function
public void CheckInteraction() {

    //check active characters
    List<GameObject> activeOpponents = FindCharacters(true, false);
    List<GameObject> activeHeroes = FindCharacters(true, true);

    //if no opponents remain
    if (activeOpponents.Count <= 0) {

        //create dialogue
        dialogue.UpdateDialogueWithText("Heroes win!");

        //end interaction
        _isComplete = true;
    }

    //if no heroes remain
    else if (activeHeroes.Count <= 0) {

        //create dialogue
        dialogue.UpdateDialogueWithText("Dragons win!");
```

```
        //end interaction
        _isComplete = true;
    }
}
```

These are but a few examples of how your dialogue box could keep the player updated on the action in your Interaction scene. Finally, the entire example InteractionSystem script is presented for comparison with your solution:

```
//InteractionSystem script
public class InteractionSystem : MonoBehaviour {

    //dialogue box in scene
    public Dialogue dialogue;

    //selection box in scene
    public Selection selection;

    //targeting indicator in scene
    public Targeting targeting;

    //interaction characters
    public List<GameObject> allCharacters;

    //whether interaction is complete
    private bool _isComplete;

    //define actions for characters
    /*
    Note: In the Star-Sun-Moon game, each character
    takes a turn by challenging one opponent. Both
    characters reveal their moves at the same time.
    Star beats Sun, Sun beats Moon, and Moon beats Star.
    Any character who loses a match is eliminated. The
    winning team is the first to eliminate all opponents.
    */
    public enum Actions {
        Star = 0,
        Sun = 1,
        Moon = 2
    }

    //define outcomes for interactions
    /*
    Note: Each interaction between two characters in
    the Star-Sun-Moon game has three possible outcomes:
    Win, Lose, or Draw.
    */
    public enum Outcomes {
        Win = 0,
        Lose = 1,
        Draw = 2
    }

    //singleton instance
    private static InteractionSystem _Instance;
```

```
//singleton accessor
//access InteractionSystem.Instance from other classes
public static InteractionSystem Instance {

    //create instance via getter
    get {

        //if no instance
        if (_Instance == null) {

            //create game object
            GameObject InteractionSystemObj = new
              GameObject();
            InteractionSystemObj.name = "InteractionSystem";

            //create instance
            _Instance = InteractionSystemObj.AddComponent
              <InteractionSystem>();

            //retrieve scene objects
            _Instance.dialogue = GameObject.FindWithTag
              ("Dialogue").GetComponent<Dialogue>();
            _Instance.selection = GameObject.FindWithTag
              ("Selection").GetComponent<Selection>();
            _Instance.targeting = GameObject.FindWithTag
              ("Targeting").GetComponent<Targeting>();

            //init
            _Instance.allCharacters = new List<GameObject>();
        }

        //return the instance
        return _Instance;
    }
}

//awake
void Awake() {

    //prevent destruction
    DontDestroyOnLoad(this);
}

//start a new interaction between characters
public void CreateInteraction(List<GameObject> theCharacters) {

    //show canvas

GameObject.FindWithTag("Canvas").GetComponent<CanvasGroup>().
  alpha = 1.0f;

    //create dialogue
    dialogue.CreateDialogueWithText(
        "The heroes have been challenged to a game of
          Star-Sun-Moon!"
        );

    //show dialogue
    dialogue.Show();
```

```
//toggle flag
_isComplete = false;

//reset characters
allCharacters.Clear();

//create container
GameObject container = new GameObject();
container.name = "Characters";

//for all characters
foreach (GameObject aChar in theCharacters) {

    //clone
    GameObject newChar = Instantiate<GameObject>(aChar);

    //parent
    newChar.transform.parent = container.transform;

    //activate
    CharacterData charData = newChar.GetComponent
      <CharacterData>();
    charData.isActive = true;

    //add to collection
    allCharacters.Add(newChar);
}

//retrieve teams
List<GameObject> allHeroes = FindCharacters(true, true);
List<GameObject> allOpponents = FindCharacters(true,
  false);

//position teams
//heroes
for (int i = 0; i < allHeroes.Count; i++) {

    //centered at bottom of screen
    Vector3 pos = Vector3.zero;
    float w = allHeroes[i].GetComponent<Renderer>().bounds.
      size.x;
    float h = allHeroes[i].GetComponent<Renderer>().bounds.
      size.y;
    pos.x = w / 2 + i * w - (w * (float)allHeroes.
      Count / 2);
    pos.y = -Camera.main.orthographicSize + 3 * h;
    allHeroes[i].transform.position = pos;
}

//opponents
for (int j = 0; j < allOpponents.Count; j++) {

    //centered at top of screen
    Vector3 pos = Vector3.zero;
    float w = allOpponents[j].GetComponent<Renderer>().
      bounds.size.x;
    float h = allOpponents[j].GetComponent<Renderer>().
      bounds.size.y;
```

```csharp
            pos.x = w / 2 + j * w - (w * (float)allOpponents.
              Count / 2);
            pos.y = Camera.main.orthographicSize - 3 * h;
            allOpponents[j].transform.position = pos;
        }
    }

    //start an interaction between characters
    public IEnumerator StartInteraction() {

        //store current character index
        int currentChar = 0;

        //while interaction is not complete
        while (_isComplete == false) {

            //retrieve character data
            CharacterData charData = allCharacters[currentChar].
              GetComponent<CharacterData>();

            //if character is active
            if (charData.isActive == true) {

            //start turn
            yield return StartCoroutine(
                StartTurn(allCharacters[currentChar])
                );

                //check interaction
                CheckInteraction();
            }

            //increment index
            currentChar++;

            //check bounds on index
            if (currentChar >= allCharacters.Count) {

                //reset index
                currentChar = 0;
            }
        }
    }

    //start a new turn for a character
    public IEnumerator StartTurn(GameObject theObject) {

        //retrieve character data
        CharacterData charData = theObject.GetComponent
          <CharacterData>();

        //update dialogue
        dialogue.UpdateDialogueWithText(
            charData.characterName +
            "'s turn!"
            );

        //if hero
        if (charData.isHero == true) {
```

```
        //select action
        yield return StartCoroutine(TurnAction(theObject));

        //select target
        yield return StartCoroutine(TurnTarget(theObject));

        //generate random opponent action
        GameObject theOpponent = FindCharacters(true, false)
          [charData.currentTarget];
        theOpponent.GetComponent<CharacterData>().currentAction
          = UnityEngine.Random.Range(0, Enum.GetValues
          (typeof(Actions)).Length);

        //apply action
        ApplyActionToTarget(theObject, theOpponent);
    }

    //if opponent
    else if (charData.isHero == false) {

        //generate random action
        charData.currentAction = UnityEngine.Random.Range(0,
          Enum.GetValues(typeof(Actions)).Length);

        //find potential targets
        List<GameObject> targets = FindCharacters(true, true);

        //generate random target
        charData.currentTarget = UnityEngine.Random.Range(0,
          targets.Count);

        //allow player to select defense action
        GameObject theHero = FindCharacters(true, true)
          [charData.currentTarget];
        yield return StartCoroutine(
        TurnAction(theHero)
        );

        //apply action
        ApplyActionToTarget(theObject, theHero);
    }
}

//determine action for character's turn
public IEnumerator TurnAction(GameObject theObject) {

    //retrieve character data
    CharacterData charData = theObject.GetComponent
      <CharacterData>();

    //update dialogue
    dialogue.UpdateDialogueWithText(
        charData.characterName +
        ": Choose your action."
        );

    //create selection
    List<string> txtSelection = new List<string>();
```

```
txtSelection.AddRange(Enum.GetNames(typeof(Actions)));
selection.CreateSelection(txtSelection);

//position selection
selection.PositionAt(theObject);

//show selection
selection.Show();

//select action
yield return StartCoroutine(
    selection.StartSelection(
    txtSelection.Count,
    value => charData.currentAction = value)
);
}

//determine target for character's turn
public IEnumerator TurnTarget(GameObject theObject) {

    //retrieve character data
    CharacterData charData = theObject.GetComponent
      <CharacterData>();

    //update dialogue
    dialogue.UpdateDialogueWithText(
        charData.characterName +
        ": Choose your target."
        );

    //find potential targets
    List<GameObject> targets = FindCharacters(true, false);

    //select target
    yield return StartCoroutine(
        targeting.StartTargeting(
        targets.Count,
        value => charData.currentTarget = value,
        targets)
        );
}

//apply action to target
public void ApplyActionToTarget(GameObject theActor, GameObject
  theTarget) {

    //retrieve character data
    CharacterData actorData = theActor.GetComponent
      <CharacterData>();
    CharacterData targetData = theTarget.GetComponent
      <CharacterData>();

    //determine result
    int actorOutcome = CompareActions(actorData.currentAction,
      targetData.currentAction);

    //check result
    switch (actorOutcome) {
```

```
//win
case (int)Outcomes.Win:

    //deactivate target
    targetData.isActive = false;

    //create dialogue
    dialogue.UpdateDialogueWithText(
        actorData.characterName + "'s " +
        Enum.GetName(typeof(Actions), actorData.
          currentAction) +
        " beats " +
        targetData.characterName + "'s " +
        Enum.GetName(typeof(Actions), targetData.
          currentAction) +
        "!"
        );
    break;

//lose
case (int)Outcomes.Lose:

    //deactivate actor
    actorData.isActive = false;

    //create dialogue
    dialogue.UpdateDialogueWithText(
        targetData.characterName + "'s" +
        Enum.GetName(typeof(Actions), targetData.
          currentAction) +
        " beats " +
        actorData.characterName + "'s " +
        Enum.GetName(typeof(Actions), actorData.
          currentAction) +
        "!"
        );
    break;

//draw
case (int)Outcomes.Draw:

    //create dialogue
        dialogue.UpdateDialogueWithText(
            actorData.characterName + "'s " +
            Enum.GetName(typeof(Actions), actorData.
              currentAction) +
            " ties " +
            targetData.characterName + "'s" +
            Enum.GetName(typeof(Actions), targetData.
              currentAction) +
            "."
            );
        break;

//default
default:
    Debug.Log("[InteractionSystem] Error: Outcome not
      recognized");
```

```
                    break;
        }
}

//compare actions and determine winner
public int CompareActions(int theFirstAction, int
  theSecondAction) {

    //store result
    int outcome = (int)Outcomes.Lose;

    //draw
    if (theFirstAction == theSecondAction) {

        //return
        return (int)Outcomes.Draw;
    }

    //possible win states
    else if (

        //star beats sun
        (theFirstAction == (int)Actions.Star &&
        theSecondAction == (int)Actions.Sun) ||

        //sun beats moon
        (theFirstAction == (int)Actions.Sun &&
        theSecondAction == (int)Actions.Moon) ||

        //moon beats star
        (theFirstAction == (int)Actions.Moon &&
        theSecondAction == (int)Actions.Star)

        ) {

        //return
        return (int)Outcomes.Win;
    }

    //return
    return outcome;
}

//check for end of interaction
public void CheckInteraction() {

    //check active characters
    List<GameObject> activeOpponents = FindCharacters(true,
      false);
    List<GameObject> activeHeroes = FindCharacters(true, true);

    //if no opponents remain
    if (activeOpponents.Count <= 0) {

        //create dialogue
        dialogue.UpdateDialogueWithText("Heroes win!");

        //end interaction
```

```
            _isComplete = true;
        }

        //if no heroes remain
        else if (activeHeroes.Count <= 0) {

            //create dialogue
            dialogue.UpdateDialogueWithText("Dragons win!");

            //end interaction
            _isComplete = true;
        }
    }

    //find characters
    public List<GameObject> FindCharacters(bool theIsActive, bool
      theIsHero) {

        //store active characters
        List<GameObject> chars = new List<GameObject>();

        //check all characters
        for (int i = 0; i < allCharacters.Count; i++) {

            //retrieve character data
            CharacterData charData = allCharacters[i].GetComponent
              <CharacterData>();

            //whether character is active
            bool isActive = charData.isActive;

            //whether current character is hero
            bool isHero = charData.isHero;

            //if matching active and matching type
            if (isActive == theIsActive && isHero == theIsHero) {

                //add character
                chars.Add(allCharacters[i]);
            }
        }

        //return
        return chars;
    }

} //end class
```

At long last, you have successfully completed your interaction system and added a new dimension to your game. Play through the Interaction scene and see how many games of SSM you can help Luna's team win over the Green Dragon's team. Meanwhile, look for opportunities to further refine and expand your interaction system. For example, you might add WaitForSeconds() calls at various points to create a smoother flow of action. Right now, the system instantly moves from state to state without any delay, which doesn't allow the player to fully appreciate the action. Of course, this sort of polishing can also be done endlessly, so don't get carried away either. We'll continually refine our game as we work through subsequent challenges. You have already succeeded in implementing the raw functionality of the interaction system, which is the most important part.

Summary

Creating a turn-based interaction system adds tremendous value and depth to your game. Your interaction system allows a wide variety of character encounters to take place. Furthermore, your Interaction scene becomes one of the most important pieces of your game. With the latest series of challenges complete, you should be able to apply all of these game implementation techniques:

- Implement a turn-based interaction system

- Allow player-controlled and non-player-controlled characters to interact

- Manage multiple independent scripts using a singleton instance

- Design a system that handles an entire interaction sequence between multiple characters

- Use visual indicators to communicate the interactions that take place within a system

What good is an interaction system without characters? Soon, you will formally introduce Luna's friends—Lily, Pink Beard, and Larg—into your game. These are the heroes who will join Luna on her quest. She needs their help to defeat the dragons of the world. Thus, the next chapter will focus on the friendship and formation of an epic group of heroes.

References

Microsoft Corporation. 2015a. Accessors. https://msdn.microsoft.com/library/aa287786 (accessed December 17, 2015).

Microsoft Corporation. 2015b. const (C# Reference). https://msdn.microsoft.com/library/e6w8fe1b.aspx (accessed December 17, 2015).

Microsoft Corporation. 2015c. enum (C# Reference). https://msdn.microsoft.com/library/sbbt4032.aspx (accessed December 17, 2015).

Microsoft Corporation. 2015d. Enum.GetNames Method (Type). https://msdn.microsoft.com/library/system.enum.getnames.aspx (accessed December 17, 2015).

Microsoft Corporation. 2015e. Enum.GetValues Method (Type). https://msdn.microsoft.com/library/system.enum.getvalues.aspx (accessed December 17, 2015).

Microsoft Corporation. 2015f. List<T>.AddRange Method (IEnumerable<T>). https://msdn.microsoft.com/library/z883w3dc (accessed December 17, 2015).

Microsoft Corporation. 2015g. typeof (C# Reference). https://msdn.microsoft.com/library/58918ffs.aspx (accessed December 17, 2015).

Microsoft Corporation. 2015h. bool (C# Reference). https://msdn.microsoft.com/library/c8f5xwh7.aspx (accessed December 31, 2015).

Quick, J. M. 2015. *Learn to Code with Games*. Boca Raton, FL: CRC Press. ISBN: 9781498704687.

Unity Technologies. 2015a. Input. http://docs.unity3d.com/ScriptReference/Input.html (accessed December 31, 2015).

Unity Technologies. 2015b. MonoBehaviour.Awake(). http://docs.unity3d.com/ScriptReference/MonoBehaviour.Awake.html (accessed December 17, 2015).

Unity Technologies. 2015c. Object.Instantiate. http://docs.unity3d.com/ScriptReference/Object.Instantiate.html (accessed December 17, 2015).

Unity Technologies. 2015d. Random.Range. http://docs.unity3d.com/ScriptReference/Random.Range.html (accessed December 17, 2015).

5 A Group of Heroes

Drakes and dragons weren't the only things on Luna's mind as she explored the depths of the dungeon. She was also on the lookout for her missing friends. If only she could find them, these heroes would surely join her on her quest.

Let's introduce Luna's friends (Figure 5.1). Lily is a Dryad with skin made of bark and hair made of leaves. Finely attuned to nature, Lily is a protector of the forest from whence she came. Pink Beard is a flamboyant Dwarf, known for his bright pink whiskers and the large sunglasses that he wears all times of day and night. Larg is an Orc who was exiled by his brutish kin and forced to leave his homeland. Although he didn't inherit the poor temperament typically associated with Orcs, he's physically strong as any.

Previously, you built an interaction system that allows teams of characters to play a game with one another. Obviously, we need to introduce more characters into our game for the interaction system to be fully utilized. Furthermore, placing multiple characters under the player's control will add depth to our game. In this chapter, you will focus on managing an entire group of heroes. Thus, you will grant Luna the capacity to find friends who will join her on her quest.

Figure 5.1 Luna's friends—(from left to right) Lily, Pink Beard, and Larg—are ready to join her on her quest.

Goals

By the end of this chapter, you will be able to apply these game implementation techniques:

- Manage a group of characters

- Add characters to a group based on collisions

- Swap the group leader based on user input

- Move multiple characters relative to one another

Required Files

In this chapter, you will use the following files from the *Software > Chapter_05* folder (https://www.crcpress.com/Learn-to-Implement-Games-with-Code/Quick/p/book/9781498753388):

- The contents of the Challenge folder to create, code, and test your solution

- The contents of the Solution folder to compare your solution to the example solution

Challenge: Swap the Leader

There are many potential ways to handle groups of characters. In this chapter, you will implement two different methods. As the foundation for any method, you need to come up with a way to add characters to Luna's group, such as through collision detection. Furthermore, you also need to manage Luna's group throughout the game, which can be accomplished by coding a Group script. For example, you'll certainly need to store the characters in a collection of some sort.

Open the *Challenge > Assets > Scenes > Map.unity scene* in Unity. Similar to last chapter's interaction system, it will be especially helpful for you to focus on the task at hand during this chapter. Thus, we will only work in the Map scene. For convenience, find the Heroes GameObject added to the Middleground inside the Hierarchy window. As you can see, it has children objects that represent Luna's friends (Figure 5.2). All of these objects have been given the "Hero" tag. Press the play button in the Unity editor to see that these characters are positioned in a neat row very close to Luna's starting position (Figure 5.3). While you probably wouldn't do this in the final version of your game, lining up the characters in your scene is a great way to make your life easier during the development process. Every time you change your code, you can rapidly run Luna over her friends to test whether your implementation is functioning properly. Of course, once everything is working, you can remove the test characters from the scene to make way for proper game design. This is a great way to save time and iterate rapidly toward a successful implementation. Remember to apply such techniques in your future projects.

Your first specific challenge entails creating a *swap the leader* version of your group. In this version, only the player's chosen character is displayed on the screen at a given time. By default, the player sees and controls Luna throughout the game. However, Luna may encounter friends during gameplay and add them to her group. Although several characters are contained within the group,

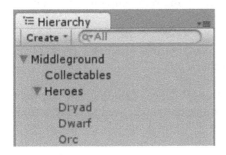

Figure 5.2 In the Hierarchy window, a Heroes object has been added as a child to the Middleground. It contains objects that represent Luna's friends.

only the leader is shown at a given time. With the press of a key, the player can choose to swap the leader, thus revealing a different hero. For instance, the player might choose to swap from Luna to Lily. Likewise, the entire group of characters can be cycled through by the player. Once the last character is reached, we return back to Luna and start the cycle over again. This system keeps things simple, because your code still only has to deal with one character on screen at a time. Yet, it also adds value to the player by

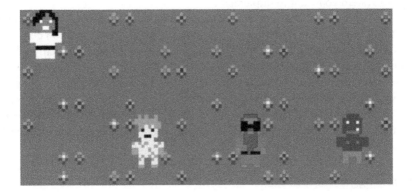

Figure 5.3 Test the game in Unity to see that the heroes are conveniently lined up close to Luna's starting position.

allowing any chosen character from the group to be displayed. The requirements for the swap the leader challenge are:

1. Create a Group script that manages the group of heroes.

2. When Luna collides with another hero, add that character to the group.

3. Allow the player to cycle through the group of characters and choose which one remains visible on screen.

Hint: Detect Collisions

Before you can add more heroes to Luna's group, you need to implement some mechanism to trigger the encounter between Luna and the heroes. It is suggested that you use collisions to accomplish this feat. Consistent with how you coded Luna's encounter with the Red Knight, you can expand your UserCollision script to include hero collisions. Recall that each of the heroes in your scene carries the "Hero" tag. Thus, you can check the "Hero" tag inside the `OnTriggerEnter2D()` function in your UserCollision script. When coding your collisions, remember to think about two things:

1. Leverage your codebase, which contains past examples of how you implemented collisions between characters

2. Consider the specific context of this challenge, including how you want the group to function and what information you need to retrieve from the characters

Hint: Store Group Data

You can create a Group script to manage your group of heroes. One thing you will undoubtedly want to do is to store information about the heroes who are in Luna's group. For instance, you could use a collection such as a `List` to keep track of who is in the group. The exact information that you store depends on the type of system you want to implement.

Think about your current challenge. You only need to display one character at a time on the screen, but must allow the player to swap the visual on demand. When Luna collides with another hero, you can potentially access any of the components attached to that character's `GameObject`. Thus, you have access to everything you need and can choose to pass any necessary information to your Group script. Ask yourself what you need to know about the characters in order to implement this version of your group. Once you've decided, begin coding your Group script. In addition, remember to attach your Group script to an appropriate object in the scene, so you can test it.

Hint: Toggle the Leader

Besides storing information about your characters, your Group script should implement a mechanism for switching the lead character. You've already handled user input several times before. Furthermore, you've cycled through collections before, such as the choices in your Selection script. Therefore, your Group script can receive a key press from the player and use it to cycle through the characters in Luna's group, while updating which character is visible on screen along the way. Implement this behavior in your Group script before proceeding to the example solution.

Example Solution: Swap the Leader

Recall that the objectives of this challenge were to detect collisions between Luna and the other heroes, add the heroes to Luna's group, and allow the player to swap which hero appears on screen at a given time. To manage the group of heroes, create a brand new script named "Group." Although you could potentially handle this script in several ways, the example Group script was designed to be attached to the Player prefab in our Unity project (Figure 5.4).

Begin your Group script by storing and initializing a collection of sprites that represent the hero characters:

```
//Group script
//the member sprites
public List<Sprite> members;

//excerpt from Start() function
void Start() {

    //init
    members = new List<Sprite>();
}
```

Why store a collection of the `Sprite` type? Well, our Player prefab, as well as all of our hero prefabs, have `SpriteRenderer` components. These components contain a `Sprite` variable that stores the image for each character. Since all that

Figure 5.4 Create a new script named "Group" and attach it to the Player prefab in the *Assets > Prefabs > Characters* folder.

we need to implement our "swap-the-leader" mechanism is a visual representation of each character, taking the Sprite is enough.

In addition, we need to keep track of which character is currently selected. This is a prerequisite to allowing the player to select a different character through user input. Enter the _currentMember variable, which represents the index position of the current character from our members List:

```
//Group script
//the member sprites
public List<Sprite> members;

//index of current member selected in group
private int _currentMember;
```

Since our script is attached to Luna and she is present in the group at the beginning of the game, the Start() function immediately adds her Sprite to the members List. Accordingly, the _currentMember index is initialized to 0 to represent Luna, our first group member:

```
//Group script
//excerpt from Start() function
void Start() {

        //init List
        members = new List<Sprite>();

        //add player sprite
        members.Add(gameObject.GetComponent<SpriteRenderer>().
          sprite);

        //start at first member
        _currentMember = 0;
}
```

With the foundation for swapping group members set, let's turn to the ToggleMember() function:

```
//Group script
//ToggleMember() function
private void ToggleMember() {

        //increment current index
        _currentMember++;

        //verify that index is within bounds
        if (_currentMember > members.Count - 1) {

                //reset
                _currentMember = 0;
        }

        //update the renderer based on the current index
        gameObject.GetComponent<SpriteRenderer>().sprite =
          members[_currentMember];
}
```

The `ToggleMember()` function increments our `_currentMember` index by 1 to change which hero is currently selected. After this, it does a bounds check to ensure that the selected index position is within the range of our members List. With a valid `_currentMember` index ensured, the `SpriteRenderer` of the attached Player GameObject is updated to match the selected `Sprite` from the members List. Effectively, any time `ToggleMember()` is called, the next hero in the group is displayed on screen.

Subsequently, we can check for user input from the player in the `Update()` function. In this sample code, an "E" key press triggers the `ToggleMember()` function:

```
//Group script
void Update() {

        //check for e key press
        if (Input.GetKeyDown(KeyCode.E)) {

                //toggle member
                ToggleMember();
        }
}
```

Thus, any time the player presses the "E" key, the next hero in the group is displayed. This completes our Group script. For clarity, the entire script is presented:

```
//Group script
public class Group : MonoBehaviour {

    //the member sprites
    public List<Sprite> members;

    //index of current member selected in group
    private int _currentMember;

    //init
    void Start() {

        //init
        members = new List<Sprite>();

        //add player sprite
        members.Add(gameObject.GetComponent<SpriteRenderer>().
          sprite);

        //start at first member
        _currentMember = 0;
    }

    //update
    void Update() {

        //check for e key press
        if (Input.GetKeyDown(KeyCode.E)) {
```

```
            //toggle member
            ToggleMember();
        }
    }

    //toggle between group members
    private void ToggleMember() {

        //increment current index
        _currentMember++;

        //verify that index is within bounds
        if (_currentMember > members.Count - 1) {

            //reset
            _currentMember = 0;
        }

        //update the renderer based on the current index
        gameObject.GetComponent<SpriteRenderer>().sprite =
            members[_currentMember];
    }

} //end class
```

Lastly, we must remember to add our heroes to Luna's group. This requires collision detection, which brings us back to our familiar UserCollision script:

```
//UserCollision script
//excerpt from OnTriggerEnter2D() function
//before the switch statement, retrieve the group script
Group group = gameObject.GetComponent<Group>();

//inside the switch statement, detect hero collisions
//hero collision
case "Hero":

    //disable collisions
    theCollider.enabled = false;

    //update group
    Sprite sprite = theCollider.gameObject.
      GetComponent<SpriteRenderer>().sprite;
        group.members.Add(sprite);

    //destroy
    Destroy(theCollider.gameObject);

    break;
```

Quite simply, we retrieve the Group script attached to our Player object inside our OnTriggerEnter2D() function. Then, we add a check for the "Hero" tag to the function's switch statement. When Luna encounters a hero, the hero's collider is immediately disabled. Meanwhile, the hero's Sprite is retrieved from the SpriteRenderer component and added to the members List in our Group script. From this point forward, the hero is part of Luna's group.

Finally, the existing `GameObject` representation of the hero is destroyed to remove it from the scene.

On a side note, don't forget that you already built a fine interaction system with dialogue and selection boxes into your game. Thus, if you fancy printing a message such as "Lily joined your group!" or offering a choice such as "Pink Beard wants to join your group. Would you like to adventure with him?" you could easily incorporate it into your collision checks. Something such as this would add a bit of extra polish to the game and better inform the player on what is happening in real time.

At this point, you can test your scene and run Luna over to Lily, Pink Beard, and Larg. You should see each character disappear from the screen. Press the "E" key to swap the heroes' sprites on screen. Hence, this version of your group is complete. While it's nice to have a group of heroes and player choice built into our game, we'll consider a different way of handling the group next. Although the upcoming version requires more code and logic, it allows all of our characters to remain visible to the player at all times.

▮ Challenge: Follow the Leader

For a different take on our Group script, let's consider a system where all of the heroes follow one another around on the map. Recall that the player controls the Player object in our scene by default, which we see on screen as Luna. The attached UserMove script contains code that lets the player use the arrow keys to move Luna around the screen. Your *follow the leader* Group script should leverage the player's input to make the heroes follow Luna around the screen. For example, suppose you have all four characters in your group: Luna, Lily, Pink Beard, and Larg. When the player moves Luna upward on screen, Lily should follow her, Pink Beard should follow Lily, and Larg should follow Pink Beard. Hence, a chain reaction of movement is led by the player's control of Luna and carried through by the group members who follow her. Your Group script should create a movement pattern such as this among the characters. The requirements for this challenge are:

1. The Group script manages the group of heroes.

2. When Luna collides with another hero, add that character to the group.

3. When the player moves Luna around the game world, the remaining heroes in the group should follow her movement in an orderly fashion.

Importantly, be sure to make a backup copy of your Group script from the previous challenge and save it in a safe place. The revised version of the Group script you will code in this challenge implements a very different set of logic. Therefore, be prepared to make changes to your existing Group script. You may also choose to recreate the Group script from scratch. Just remember to save your existing code somewhere in your codebase, so you can refer back to it in the future.

Hint: Revise Your Code

In the previous challenge, all you needed to do was store the image of each character. After a collision occurred and the image was stored in your Group script, the UserCollision script destroyed the hero GameObject. At a fundamental level, you can apply the same process in the current challenge: detect collisions between Luna and the heroes, and then store the heroes in a collection. However, this challenge is more complex on a technical level. Since you need to move all of the heroes on screen at the same time, you cannot simply delete them upon collision. Likewise, you need access to more than just the image for each hero. Thus, you should revise the foundational elements of your group implementation. Indeed, you still need to store the heroes in your Group script. However, a List of the Sprite type is no longer enough. Think of a better way to store your heroes that suits the current challenge. Meanwhile, revise your UserCollision script as well. Instead of deleting the GameObject for each hero on collision, perhaps you could store it in your Group script. This would give you full access to the heroes, which is needed to implement this version of your group.

Hint: Design the Movement Logic

The major feature of your current implementation is how all of characters follow one another. Before you can code anything, you need to determine exactly how the characters will move on screen. As an example, suppose we want to create an UpdatePos() function in our Group script. This function is called every time the player moves Luna. It controls the movement of every other character in Luna's group. If a given hero is ever too far from the person immediately in front, the hero's position is updated to close the gap. Hence, as the heroes move, they are constantly trying to keep up with the person immediately in front of them. This creates a sort chain or snake-like behavior as the characters run around the screen. This pseudocode describes the logic behind the example UpdatePos() function:

```
//Group script
//example UpdatePos() function
//called whenever the player moves Luna
UpdatePos():
```

   For all heroes:

   - Retrieve hero position

   - Retrieve position of hero immediately in front

   - Calculate distance between heroes

     - If x distance > threshold:

       - Move x position toward hero in front

- If y distance > threshold:

  – Move y position toward hero in front

  ▪ Update position of hero to reflect movement

This logic sets the foundation for creating an `UpdatePos()` function in the Group script. However, it doesn't tell the whole story. There are many potential options for designing the follow movement of your characters. Furthermore, endless fine-tuning and polishing could take place. To get started, solidify the logic behind how you want to make the characters move. Anything that you think will look pleasant to the player is acceptable. You can always refine it along the way. Indeed, you will need to test your movement logic extensively to ensure it works well. The important thing is that you take down your logic, perhaps in pseudocode or a process map, before you try to code it. Then, work toward bringing your design to life in the Group script.

Example Solution: Follow the Leader

Hopefully, you designed a follow movement logic for your heroes and were able to implement it with a degree of success in your Group script. The example solution builds upon the basic logic presented in the *Hint: Design the Movement Logic* section, but also includes several tweaks that make the heroes' movement more pleasant for the player experience. Let's review the solution in its entirety. The implementation begins with setting up the foundational elements in the Group script:

```
//excerpt from Group script
public class Group : MonoBehaviour {

    //group members
    public List<GameObject> members;

    //follow distance between characters
    public float followDist;
```

A `List` of the `GameObject` type, named `members`, is used to store all of the heroes in the group. The `GameObject` type is declared because we must access its `Transform` component to set each hero's position. In addition, a `float` named `"followDist"` is declared to set the distance threshold at which characters follow one another. For easy testing and revision, this variable is set to `public`, which allows it to be initialized via the Inspector window. The remaining initialization takes place in the `Start()` function:

```
//Group script
//Start() function
void Start() {

    //init collection
    members = new List<GameObject>();
```

```
    //add leader
    members.Add(gameObject);
}
```

The members List is initialized. Subsequently, the GameObject to which the Group script is attached is added to members. Recall that our Group script is attached to the Player object, which represents Luna in our scene. Since Luna is present in the group from the start of the game, she is immediately added as the first group member. The only other item in the Group script is the UpdatePos() function, which implements the logic behind how the characters follow one another:

```
//Group script
//UpdatePos() function
//update member positions based on movement
public void UpdatePos(float theSpeed, Vector2 theDir) {

    //update position for each hero in party
    //start at 1 to skip leader
    for (int i = 1; i < members.Count; i++) {

        //get game object
        GameObject theMember = members[i];

        //store current position
        float currentX = theMember.transform.position.x;
        float currentY = theMember.transform.position.y;

        //get next position
        //the position of the character immediately in front in
            line
        float nextX = members[i - 1].transform.position.x;
        float nextY = members[i - 1].transform.position.y;

        //get distance between hero and character being followed
        float distToFollowedX = nextX - currentX;
        float distToFollowedY = nextY - currentY;

        //get distance between hero and leader of group
        float distToLeaderX = members[0].transform.position.x
            - currentX;
        float distToLeaderY = members[0].transform.position.y
            - currentY;

        //store new position
        float newX = currentX;
        float newY = currentY;

        //check whether follow distance is sufficient and
            update movement
        //move only if at least min distance away from both
            followed character and leader
        //x axis
        if (Mathf.Abs(distToFollowedX) >= followDist &&
        Mathf.Abs(distToLeaderX) >= followDist) {

            //positive
            if (distToFollowedX > 0) {
```

```
                //update movement
                newX += theSpeed * Time.deltaTime;
        }

        //negative
        else if (distToFollowedX < 0) {

                //update movement
                newX -= theSpeed * Time.deltaTime;
        }

        //manage snapping to next y position
        //if currently moving on x and not yet at next y
            position
        if (theDir.x != 0 && newY != nextY) {

                //update movement
                newY = nextY;
        }
    }

    //y axis
    if (Mathf.Abs(distToFollowedY) >= followDist &&
            Mathf.Abs(distToLeaderY) >= followDist) {

        //positive
        if (distToFollowedY > 0) {

                //update movement
                newY += theSpeed * Time.deltaTime;
        }

        //negative
        else if (distToFollowedY < 0) {

                //update movement
                newY -= theSpeed * Time.deltaTime;
        }

        //manage snapping to next x position
        //if currently moving on y and not yet at next x
            position
        if (theDir.y != 0 && newX != nextX) {

                //update movement
                newX = nextX;
        }
    }

    //update hero position
    theMember.transform.position =
        new Vector3(
            newX,
            newY,
            gameObject.transform.position.z + i
        );
    }
}
```

Generally speaking, the idea behind the UpdatePos() function is to make each hero follow the person immediately in front. Beyond that, there are a few tweaks in the logic to create a more pleasant player experience, which will be explained. The UpdatePos() function has quite a few elements, so let's break it down.

Recall that the player is controlling the Player object in our scene (Luna). Initially, UpdatePos() receives Luna's most recent speed and direction information as arguments. It then iterates through each hero in the group, excluding Luna, since she is the leader:

```
//Group script
//excerpt from UpdatePos() function
public void UpdatePos(float theSpeed, Vector2 theDir) {

        //update position for each hero in party
        //start at 1 to skip leader
        for (int i = 1; i < members.Count; i++) {

            /*
            Code omitted.
            */
        }
}
```

Inside the loop, a series of local variables is created to store information about the heroes. These are used to make subsequent calculations and checks. For example, the current hero's GameObject and x–y position are stored:

```
//Group script
//excerpt from UpdatePos() function
//retrieve hero object
GameObject theMember = members[i];

//store current position
float currentX = theMember.transform.position.x;
float currentY = theMember.transform.position.y;
```

Similarly, the x–y position of the hero immediately in front is retrieved:

```
//Group script
//excerpt from UpdatePos() function
//get next position
//the position of the hero immediately in front in line
float nextX = members[i - 1].transform.position.x;
float nextY = members[i - 1].transform.position.y;
```

Next, the distance between the current hero and the person immediately in front is calculated. Likewise, the distance between the current hero and the leader (Luna) is calculated:

```
//Group script
//excerpt from UpdatePos() function
```

```
//get distance between hero and character being followed
float distToFollowedX = nextX - currentX;
float distToFollowedY = nextY - currentY;

//get distance between hero and leader of group
float distToLeaderX = members[0].transform.position.x - currentX;
float distToLeaderY = members[0].transform.position.y - currentY;
```

Prior to making any checks, we prepare to store the new x–y position of the hero, if any:

```
//Group script
//excerpt from UpdatePos() function
//store new position
float newX = currentX;
float newY = currentY;
```

With the fundamental variables and calculations made, we proceed to make context-specific considerations. By design, we set a minimum threshold at which a hero begins to follow the person immediately in front. If the threshold is too low, such as 0, the characters hyperactively attempt to follow one another and bunch up in a most unpleasant way. If the threshold is too high, the characters appear a bit dull and unresponsive. Test different `followDist` values in your Group script to experience these phenomena.

Besides the person immediately in front, we also check to see whether the hero is the minimum distance away from the group leader (Luna). This creates a different effect. Suppose the characters are moving in a tight formation, such as a small circle (Figure 5.5). This might cause Luna, who is at the front of the line, to run very close to Larg, who is at the back of the line. Normally, Larg would blindly follow Pink Beard. However, if Larg sees Luna near him, does it make sense for him to follow Pink Beard a longer distance around, just to end up in the same place again? Well, it's your game, so the choice is up to you. However, the heroes are arguably smarter to standby if the leader comes close to them and only

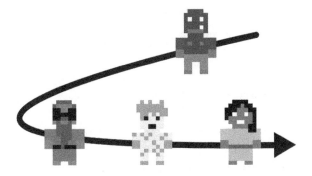

Figure 5.5 If the heroes move in a tight formation, the leader may pass by a hero toward the end of the line. In this case, it makes more sense for the hero to wait, rather than following the person immediately in front. In this diagram, the arrow indicates Luna's movement path. Notice that Larg stays in place, rather than following Pink Beard, as Luna moves past him.

---

start moving again once they are a good distance away. Both of the described distance threshold designs are captured in `if` statements for the x and y axes:

```
//Group script
//excerpt from UpdatePos() function
//check whether follow distance is sufficient and update movement
//move only if at least min distance away from both followed
    character and leader
//x axis
if (Mathf.Abs(distToFollowedX) >= followDist &&
    Mathf.Abs(distToLeaderX) >= followDist) {

/*
    Code omitted.
    */
}

//y axis
if (Mathf.Abs(distToFollowedY) >= followDist &&
    Mathf.Abs(distToLeaderY) >= followDist) {

    /*
    Code omitted.
    */
}
```

As you can see, the `if` statements check whether a given hero's distance to the person in front, as well as the group leader, exceeds the minimum distance threshold. If not, the hero's position won't change, giving the impression that the character is standing still. However, if both thresholds are exceeded, the character's position is updated. Let's pick apart the x axis `if` statement:

```
//Group script
//excerpt from UpdatePos() function
if (Mathf.Abs(distToFollowedX) >= followDist &&
    Mathf.Abs(distToLeaderX) >= followDist) {

    //positive
    if (distToFollowedX > 0) {

        //update movement
        newX += theSpeed * Time.deltaTime;
    }

    //negative
    else if (distToFollowedX < 0) {

        //update movement
        newX -= theSpeed * Time.deltaTime;
    }

    //manage snapping to next y position
    //if currently moving on x and not yet at next y position
    if (theDir.x != 0 && newY != nextY) {

        //update movement
        newY = nextY;
    }
}
```

To begin, we check whether the distance to the hero immediately in front is positive or negative. Recall that left is negative and right is positive in our 2D world. Based on the direction, the newX variable, which represents the hero's new position, is adjusted. The adjustment amount is equal to Luna's speed, which was passed into the function as theSpeed. This ensures that all heroes move at the same speed. This value is multiplied by Time.deltaTime to achieve frame rate independence.

Interestingly, there is yet another player experience tweak found at the very bottom of the if statement:

```
//Group script
//excerpt from UpdatePos() function
    /*
    Code omitted.
    */

    //manage snapping to next y position
    //if currently moving on x and not yet at next y position
    if (theDir.x != 0 && newY != nextY) {

        //update movement
        newY = nextY;
    }
}
```

You can think of this as a *snapping* mechanism. Imagine that our player moved Luna only to the left. By our current code, the next hero in line would follow her only to the left. However, if these characters weren't already aligned on the y axis, their movement may look awkward (Figure 5.6). Likewise, this situation presents itself any time our player moves only on the x axis (left or right) or only on the y axis (up or down).

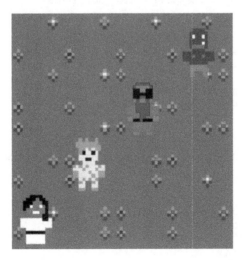

Figure 5.6 By handling x and y axis movements separately, we create a situation where the heroes may not align when moving along a single axis. For example, this image shows the characters moving together horizontally, but misaligned vertically. This situation can be corrected by snapping the heroes into the same x and y positions as needed.

To prevent this from happening, we automatically snap our characters into the same x and y positions in the event they are misaligned. For instance, in the shown x axis `if` statement, we check whether the player is moving Luna on the x axis (`theDir.x != 0`) and whether the hero does not have the same y position as the character being followed (`newY != nextY`). If these conditions are true, we immediately set the hero's y position equal to the character being followed (`newY = nextY`). This causes our characters to look like they are really following one another, rather than awkwardly mirroring one another. To get a better idea of the impact that this code has, try commenting it out of your script and testing your game to witness the ill effects.

That covers the x axis `if` statement. The y axis `if` statement employs identical logic, but is coded to represent vertical movement:

```
//Group script
//excerpt from UpdatePos() function
//y axis
if (Mathf.Abs(distToFollowedY) >= followDist &&
        Mathf.Abs(distToLeaderY) >= followDist) {

        //positive
        if (distToFollowedY > 0) {

                //update movement
                newY += theSpeed * Time.deltaTime;
        }

        //negative
        else if (distToFollowedY < 0) {

                //update movement
                newY -= theSpeed * Time.deltaTime;
        }

        //manage snapping to next x position
        //if currently moving on y and not yet at next x position
        if (theDir.y != 0 && newX != nextX) {

                //update movement
                newX = nextX;
        }
}
```

The very last thing to do in our `UpdatePos()` function is to update the hero's position:

```
//Group script
//excerpt from UpdatePos() function
//update hero position
theMember.transform.position =
        new Vector3(
                newX,
                newY,
                gameObject.transform.position.z + i
        );
```

This code updates the hero's position by setting it equal to a `Vector3` variable composed of the newX and newY coordinates. Interestingly, the z component is incremented by the `for` loop's iterator variable, `i`. This has the effect of making each hero in the group slightly farther away from the camera. Hence, if the heroes overlap one another when walking, we will always see Luna on top, followed by the second hero, then the third, and so on. This is a pleasant effect that gives the player an additional sense of order to the group's movement. Take a moment to appreciate the Group script in its entirety:

```
//Group script
public class Group : MonoBehaviour {

    //group members
    public List<GameObject> members;

    //follow distance between characters
    public float followDist;

    //init
    void Start() {

        //init collection
        members = new List<GameObject>();

        //add leader
        members.Add(gameObject);
    }

    //update member positions based on movement
    public void UpdatePos(float theSpeed, Vector2 theDir) {

        //update position for each hero in party
        //start at 1 to skip leader
        for (int i = 1; i < members.Count; i++) {

            //get hero object
            GameObject theMember = members[i];

            //store current position
            float currentX = theMember.transform.position.x;
            float currentY = theMember.transform.position.y;

            //get next position
            //the position of the character immediately in front in
                line
            float nextX = members[i - 1].transform.position.x;
            float nextY = members[i - 1].transform.position.y;

            //get distance between hero and character being
                followed
            float distToFollowedX = nextX - currentX;
            float distToFollowedY = nextY - currentY;

            //get distance between hero and leader of group
            float distToLeaderX = members[0].transform.position.x
                - currentX;
```

```
float distToLeaderY = members[0].transform.position.y
    - currentY;

//store new position
float newX = currentX;
float newY = currentY;

//check whether follow distance is sufficient and
    update movement
//move only if at least min distance away from both
    followed character and leader
//x axis
if (Mathf.Abs(distToFollowedX) >= followDist &&
    Mathf.Abs(distToLeaderX) >= followDist) {

    //positive
    if (distToFollowedX > 0) {

        //update movement
        newX += theSpeed * Time.deltaTime;
    }

    //negative
    else if (distToFollowedX < 0) {

        //update movement
        newX -= theSpeed * Time.deltaTime;
    }

    //manage snapping to next y position
    //if currently moving on x and not yet at next y
        position
    if (theDir.x != 0 && newY != nextY) {

        //update movement
        newY = nextY;
    }
}

//y axis
if (Mathf.Abs(distToFollowedY) >= followDist &&
    Mathf.Abs(distToLeaderY) >= followDist) {

    //positive
    if (distToFollowedY > 0) {

        //update movement
        newY += theSpeed * Time.deltaTime;
    }

    //negative
    else if (distToFollowedY < 0) {

        //update movement
        newY -= theSpeed * Time.deltaTime;
    }
```

```
                //manage snapping to next x position
                //if currently moving on y and not yet at next x
                    position
                if (theDir.y != 0 && newX != nextX) {

                    //update movement
                    newX = nextX;
                }
            }

            //update hero position
            theMember.transform.position =
                new Vector3(
                    newX,
                    newY,
                    gameObject.transform.position.z + i
                );
        }
    }

} //end class
```

With the Group script complete, only a couple finishing touches are needed to see it in action. Although we have an `UpdatePos()` function coded, we must remember to call it any time the player moves Luna. One reasonable place to call `UpdatePos()` is from the UserMove script, right after Luna's own position is updated:

```
//UserMove script
//Update() function
void Update() {

    //if input enabled
    if (isInputEnabled == true) {

        //check user input
        CheckUserInput();

        //move object
        MoveObject();

        //move group
        Group heroes = gameObject.GetComponent<Group>();
        heroes.UpdatePos(speed, _newDir);
    }
}
```

Since both the Group and UserMove scripts are attached to the Player object in our scene, a call to `GetComponent()` easily retrieves the Group script. The `UpdatePos()` function is called, and the UserMove script's `speed` and `_newDir` (Luna's speed and direction) are passed in as arguments. This ensures that the positions of the heroes in Luna's group are updated every time the player updates Luna's position.

Finally, remember to update your UserCollision script to accommodate your group implementation:

```
//UserCollision script
//excerpt from OnTriggerEnter2D() function
case "Hero":

        //disable collisions
        theCollider.enabled = false;

        //update group
        group.members.Add(theCollider.gameObject);

        break;
```

Once again, in the "Hero" case, we add the hero who Luna collided with to our group. However, we do not destroy the GameObject, since it is still needed to display the hero on screen. Again, feel free to incorporate additional embellishments into your UserCollision script. For instance, you could use your interaction system to present a dialogue box with information regarding Luna's encounter with a given hero.

Test your project and run Luna over to her friends. This time, you will see all of the heroes follow Luna smoothly around the screen, creating a pleasant flow of group movement for the player.

Summary

In this chapter, you succeeded in, not one, but two different implementations of group management. Depending on the context, both of these systems, as well as their variations, will serve you well in the future. Not only have you reunited Luna with her friends, but you've gained the experience necessary to apply these game implementation techniques:

- Manage a group of characters

- Add characters to a group based on collisions

- Swap the group leader based on user input

- Move multiple characters relative to one another

You have an epic quest brewing with Luna, her friends, drakes, and dragons. With so much to entertain the player, we shouldn't expect it all to happen in a single sitting. Thus, in the coming chapter, you will implement a save system that allows the player's accomplishments to persist across play sessions.

6 Save the Day

Although you may not yet have a release-ready game, your implementations have put you on pace to make something great. You have several characters, such as Luna, Lily, the Red Knight, the Green Dragon, and others. You also have multiple scenes, including a world map, dungeon, and turn-based interaction between teams. While your game world is not yet formed, nearly all of the pieces are in place to create your game.

Yet, to best utilize these features in our game world, we need to consider how data flows through the game. For instance, when the player transits from one scene to another, we may want to preserve certain information. Likewise, to determine whether the player has won the game requires leveraging multiple pieces of information from different times and places. Moreover, with everything to do in our world, we shouldn't expect the player to enjoy it all in a single sitting. To address these data-related issues, we will create a data management system. Not only will our data management system allow us to track information as it flows through our game, but it will also let players enjoy our game over multiple sessions.

▌ Goals

By the end of this chapter, you will be able to apply these game implementation techniques:

- Manage the saving and loading of game data

- Allow the game to be saved and continued across multiple play sessions

- Write custom classes and constructor functions

▌ Required Files

In this chapter, you will use the following files from the *Software > Chapter_06* folder (https://www.crcpress.com/Learn-to-Implement-Games-with-Code/Quick/p/book/9781498753388).

- The contents of the Challenge folder to create, code, and test your solution

- The contents of the Solution folder to compare your solution to the example solution

▌ Challenge: Save and Load Game Data

Open the *Challenge > Assets > Scenes > Map.unity scene* in Unity to examine the challenge project. The map scene should look familiar to what you worked with in Chapter 3. Further, recall that Chapter 5 placed Luna's friends immediately on the world map. These heroes have been removed, since they only existed for testing purposes. Instead, the Red Knight is back on the map and offers Luna the choice of whether to enter the Dungeon scene. Test the game now and move Luna over the Red Knight to refresh your memory.

This challenge is all about saving and loading game data. Since we like to keep things simple when pursuing a new implementation, we'll focus on saving and loading a single piece of data. Look at the Hierarchy window and find the PnlInventory object inside the Canvas (Figure 6.1). This object represents Luna's inventory of collectable objects, which appears in the upper-right-hand corner of the screen at all times (Figure 6.2). PnlInventory is driven by the CollectableInventory script, which you should review in full. In essence, the CollectableInventory script stores the number of objects that Luna has collected and allows that number to be incremented or decremented. Whenever Luna collides with a collectable or drake, the UserCollision script commands to the CollectableInventory script to change the number of collectables Luna has in her inventory. See the UserCollision script's `OnTriggerEnter2D()` function and the "Collectable" and "Drake" tags to examine the related code.

Luna's number of collectables is a perfect place for us to demonstrate how to save and load data in our game. Normally, when a player switches to a

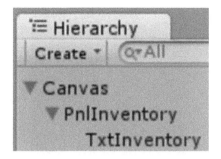

Figure 6.1 Luna's collectable inventory is represented in the Hierarchy by the PnlInventory object.

Figure 6.2 On screen, Luna's number of collectables appears in the upper right-hand corner.

different scene, Unity deletes everything in the present scene. Previously, we used `DontDestroyOnLoad()` to prevent specific objects from being destroyed when the scene switches. However, sometimes we only want to preserve data, such as a number, and not entire objects. Furthermore, we want to allow our player to enjoy our game across multiple sessions. Instead of starting over each time, the player should continue from wherever he or she left off last time. Accordingly, Luna's number of collectables should remain the same across scenes, as well as across play sessions. As a case in point, try running the game now and picking up a collectable. You should see the number in the user interface (UI) increase from 0 to 1 (Figure 6.3). Exit the game and start it again. The number returns to its original value of 0 (Figure 6.4). Of course, we don't want this to happen. Any time the player starts the game, she should carry on with whatever progress has already been made. In this challenge, you will focus on ensuring that Luna's number of collectables persists across scenes and play sessions. In the process, you will implement a reusable and expandable data management system that will serve you well in your development of this game and future projects. The requirements for this challenge are:

1. Create a DataSave script with a custom constructor to store critical game information.

2. Create a DataManager script to handle all saving and loading in your game.

3. Employ your data management system to save and load Luna's collectable inventory.

Hint: Create the Save Data

Think of your DataSave script as a representation of the game state at one moment in time. All information that you need to save about your game state should be stored in the DataSave script. In a sense, the DataSave script is a

Figure 6.3 When you pick up a collect-able object during play, notice that the number of objects in Luna's inventory increases by 1.

Figure 6.4 Without a data management system, the number of collectables in Luna's inventory resets to 0 each time the game is played.

container for raw game data. It needs to store whatever data are necessary to accurately recreate the game state at a later time. Depending on your purpose, the exact variables will change. For the current challenge, you need to create a variable in your DataSave script that stores the number of collectables in Luna's inventory.

Serialization

Serialization is a process by which information is converted into an appropriate format for saving and loading (Microsoft Corporation 2015k). In our case, we will use *binary serialization* (Microsoft Corporation 2015a), which applies binary encoding to prepare our data for compact storage. Hence, we don't directly save the number of collectables in Luna's inventory to a file. Rather, the information is encoded prior to being written to a save file. Later on, during the loading process, we decode the data to produce an exact replica of the original. This is the fundamental process at work whenever data are saved and loaded.

Importantly, any data that you wish to save must be serializable. In Unity, you can mark a script as serializable using the [System.Serializable] tag (Unity Technologies 2015c). Since your DataSave script contains the save data for your game, be sure to mark it as serializable, like so:

```
//DataSave script

//mark class for saving
[System.Serializable]

public class DataSave {

    /*
    Place class code here.
    */
}
```

Effectively, this allows our entire DataSave script to be written to a save file. Any variable stored inside the DataSave script can be restored in the future. Hence, the DataSave script represents our game state frozen at one moment in time. By loading a saved instance of our DataSave script, we are able to recreate a prior state of the game. This is what allows our player to continue the game with previous accomplishments intact, even across multiple play sessions.

MonoBehaviour and Serialization

Open any script you've worked on thus far, other than DataSave. Look to the class definition. You will see that the script inherits from MonoBehaviour, as depicted in this example:

```
//ExampleScript
//most Unity scripts inherit from MonoBehaviour
//cannot be serialized
public class ExampleScript : MonoBehaviour {
}
```

MonoBehaviour is a base class for Unity scripts that gives us access to a variety of features, such as the Start() and Update() functions (Unity Technologies 2015b). Due to the inner workings of the Unity engine, classes that derive from MonoBehaviour cannot be serialized. That's why our DataSave class does not inherit from MonoBehaviour:

```
//DataSave
//does not inherit from MonoBehaviour
//can be serialized
public class DataSave {
}
```

Remember that, whenever you're creating a class to store save data, it should not derive from MonoBehaviour. At the same time, realize that we cannot leverage the features associated with MonoBehaviour in such a script either. Essentially, this restricts us to saving our data in basic C# formats, such as bool, int, and string, as well as a few others (Unity Technologies 2015d). We cannot directly save Unity-specific components such as GameObject, Transform, or SpriteRenderer. Well, technically speaking, we could write a custom serialization script that would allow such things. However, that would require an advanced implementation beyond the scope of this book. For our current game, and likely most projects you'll create, you won't miss not having MonoBehaviour in your save script.

Custom Constructor

On the other hand, a benefit of not inheriting from MonoBehaviour is that you can create a custom constructor function for it. A constructor function is used to create an instance of a script (Microsoft Corporation 2015d). The constructor is automatically called any time the new keyword (Microsoft Corporation 2015j) is used to create an instance of the script. Constructor functions are especially useful for initializing values when a script is created. By default, all C# scripts have a constructor function, even if you don't code one into your script. Conveniently, you can write your own custom constructor that overrides the default one. To do so, create a function that has the same name as the script itself and no return type. Arguments are optional. Furthermore, you can create multiple versions of your constructor that apply different arguments. The process of creating multiple versions of the same function with different arguments is known as *overloading*. The following code presents an example script that demonstrates these concepts:

```
public class ExampleScript {

        //property
        int exampleInt;

        //default constructor
        public ExampleScript() {

                //initialize property
                exampleInt = 0;
        }

        //overloaded constructor
        //accept argument to initialize property
        public ExampleScript(int theValue) {

                //initialize property
                exampleInt = theValue;
        }
}

//example usage of constructor functions
//create a new script the default way
//exampleInt would equal 0
ExampleScript example1 = new ExampleScript();

//create a new script and provide a value
//exampleInt would equal 10
ExampleScript example2 = new ExampleScript(10);
```

By design, Unity's MonoBehaviour scripts do not have constructors. Instead, they can only be added to objects as components. This is what we do every time we use the Add Component button to attach a script to an object in the Unity editor. However, you should create a custom constructor for your DataSave script, which is unencumbered by the limitations of MonoBehaviour. Essentially, whenever you create a new instance of your DataSave script, you are creating a new save file to capture the present state of the game. Thus, your custom constructor function can establish all of the default values for the save file. For instance, you can set the default number of collectables in Luna's inventory.

Hint: Manage the Data

Whereas your DataSave script represents a single instance of a saved game, your DataManager script is the authority over all saving and loading that happens in your game. Hence, you may consider implementing the DataManager as a singleton that persists throughout the lifetime of your game. Any time the player needs to save or load data, place a call to the DataManager instance to make it happen.

There are two major responsibilities that your DataManager script must handle: saving and loading. As discussed in the *Hint: Create the Save Data* section, saving amounts to encoding data into a proper format for storage and writing it to a file. Conversely, loading is the process of decoding data from a save file back into its original format. Since your DataManager script has two primary responsibilities, it makes sense to code two corresponding functions, such as `SaveData()` and `LoadData()`.

Let's review the fundamental code behind the saving and loading process. Before we begin, make sure to place these two import statements at the top of your DataManager script:

```
//required import statements for saving/loading
using System.Runtime.Serialization.Formatters.Binary;
using System.IO;
```

As you may have guessed, the `System.Runtime.Serialization. Formatters.Binary` statement allows us to serialize our data in binary format (Microsoft Corporation 2015m). Meanwhile, `System.IO` lets us access the necessary features to read and write save files (Microsoft Corporation 2015l).

Continuing, these are the basic steps involved in saving data:

1. Create a file path

2. Create the file

3. Serialize the data

4. Close the file stream

These steps are applied in the following code snippet:

```
//save data example

//step 1: create a file path
//name the file and give it an extension
string filename = "save.luna";

//add the name to the save location to make a complete path
string filePath = Application.persistentDataPath + "/" + filename;

//step 2: create the file
//use the file path to create the save file
FileStream fileStream = File.Create(filePath);

//step 3: serialize the data
//create a binary formatter
BinaryFormatter formatter = new BinaryFormatter();
```

```
//use the formatter to serialize the data through the stream
/*
Note: This code assumes that a DataSave named saveData
already exists and contains the necessary data to save.
*/
formatter.Serialize(fileStream, saveData);

//step 4: close the file stream
fileStream.Close();
```

Start by creating a file name. Any valid name approved by your operating system will do, such as a string of alphanumeric characters. Entertainingly, you get to invent your own file extension during this process. The example code uses .luna, which is named after the main character in our game:

```
//step 1: create a file path
//name the file and give it an extension
string filename = "save.luna";
```

In addition to a filename, you also need a complete path to the exact save location for the file. This location will differ across operating systems and individual computers. For example, a Windows path would resemble something like C:\Users\Luna\AppData\LocalLow\LearnToCode. For testing purposes, you may want to find this location on your computer and save a shortcut to it. That way, you can choose to delete any existing save data as necessary. While your implementation is a work-in-progress, you may want to delete the existing save data before each test. Otherwise, old save data that no longer matches your implementation may cause errors. Of course, once everything is working, there is no need to delete the existing data, since your system will handle it appropriately.

Conveniently, Unity allows us to automatically retrieve the proper file location with `Application.persistentDataPath` (Unity Technologies 2015a), regardless of which system we are working with. By putting our save location and filename together with a separating slash in between, we arrive at the complete path:

```
//add the name to the save location to make a complete path
string filePath = Application.persistentDataPath + "/" + filename;
```

Next, we create the file and open a file stream to access it. The `File.Create()` function takes our path as an argument. It then creates the save file or overwrites it if it already exists (Microsoft Corporation 2015e). In addition, it opens a file stream that allows us to read and write data to the file:

```
//step 2: create the file
//use the file path to create the save file
FileStream fileStream = File.Create(filePath);
```

Then, it is time to serialize our data. Since we have opted to use binary serialization, we create a `BinaryFormatter`. Subsequently, we pass our file stream and save data into the `BinaryFormatter.Serialize()` function (Microsoft Corporation 2015c):

```
//step 3: serialize the data
//create a binary formatter
BinaryFormatter formatter = new BinaryFormatter();

//use the formatter to serialize the data through the stream
/*
Note: This code assumes that a DataSave named saveData
already exists and contains the necessary data to save.
*/
formatter.Serialize(fileStream, saveData);
```

Note that the sample code assumes that we already have a DataSave named `saveData` accessible to our script. Recall that our DataSave script is the package of information that represents a single save game. Indeed, it is the information stored in our DataSave script that gets written to our save file. Thus, prior to saving, we would have already created a DataSave with all of the necessary information about our game state.

Lastly, we complete the save process by closing our file stream with `Close()` (Microsoft Corporation 2015i):

```
//step 4: close the file stream
fileStream.Close();
```

Closing our file stream writes any last bits of information to our file and shuts off our access to it. It also releases any computer resources that were occupied while we kept the stream open. Thus, it is important to close our file stream when we are done working with it. This completes the entire save process.

On the other hand, these are the basic steps involved in loading data:

1. Verify the file path

2. Open the file stream

3. Deserialize the data

4. Close the file stream

These steps are applied in the following code snippet:

```
//load data example

//step 1: verify the file path
/*
Note: This code assumes that a complete file path
named filePath already exists.
*/
//check whether file exists
if (File.Exists(filePath)) {

        //step 2: open the file stream
        //open a file stream to the provided file path
        FileStream fileStream = File.Open(filePath, FileMode.Open);
```

```
//step 3: deserialize the data
//create a binary formatter
BinaryFormatter formatter = new BinaryFormatter();

//use the formatter to serialize the data through the stream
/*
Note: This code assumes that a DataSave named saveData
already exists to receive the deserialized data.
*/
saveData = (DataSave)formatter.Deserialize(fileStream);

//step 4: close the file stream
fileStream.Close();
}
```

When loading, we already have a specific save file in mind. We only need to check whether it is valid using the File.Exists() function (Microsoft Corporation 2015f):

```
//step 1: verify the file path
/*
Note: This code assumes that a complete file path
named filePath already exists.
*/
//check whether file exists
if (File.Exists(filePath)) {

    /*
    Code omitted.
    */
}
```

Note that our sample code assumes that a file path named filePath was provided. Given this file path, File.Exists() tells us whether it is valid. We place this code inside an if statement to ensure that we proceed only if the file exists. Accordingly, all of the remaining code in our load example is placed inside the if statement.

For our next step, we open a file stream with File.Open() (Microsoft Corporation 2015g) by providing our file path and setting the FileMode to Open (Microsoft Corporation 2015h):

```
//step 2: open the file stream
//open a file stream to the provided file path
FileStream fileStream = File.Open(filePath, FileMode.Open);
```

Similar to our save process, once the file stream is opened, we can read data from or write data to our file. However, since we are loading data this time around, we deserialize the information in our save file using the Deserialize() function (Microsoft Corporation 2015b):

```
//step 3: deserialize the data
//create a binary formatter
BinaryFormatter formatter = new BinaryFormatter();

//use the formatter to serialize the data through the stream
/*
```

```
Note: This code assumes that a DataSave named saveData
already exists to receive the deserialized data.
*/
saveData = (DataSave)formatter.Deserialize(fileStream);
```

Once again, our sample code assumes that a DataSave named `saveData` already exists. Thus, our deserialized data are stored inside the DataSave, where it can be used to recreate the saved game state.

Last, we close our file stream, since we are finished loading the necessary data. This completes the loading process:

```
//step 4: close the file stream
fileStream.Close();
```

Now that you're familiar with the process of saving and loading data, put your skills to work. Write the `SaveData()` and `LoadData()` functions in your DataManager script.

Hint: Update the Data

The core of your data management system is in place. You have a DataManager script that handles saving and loading, as well as a DataSave script that saves the game state. It's time to put these scripts into action throughout your game. If you created a singleton instance for your DataManager, you can potentially access it from any other script in your game. Thus, you should think about when and why you might need to handle data. Here are a few ideas:

1. Load existing save data when the game is started

2. Update the save data any time it is affected by in-game events

3. Save the game state at logical intervals, such as after each major accomplishment

4. Save the game state prior to exiting the application

Think about when and where you should access your data management system in the context of the current challenge. Remember that you're keeping track of the quantity of collectables in Luna's inventory. This information should be updated as she collects objects during the game. It should also persist across scenes and play sessions. Update some of your existing scripts to leverage your data management system and make sure Luna's collectables are saved successfully.

Example Solution: Save and Load Game Data

Let's review the example solution for this challenge. Your data management system begins with the DataSave script, which stores the game data that we want to save. In our case, we want to store the number of collectables in Luna's inventory. The entire DataSave script is presented:

```
//DataSave script
//mark class for saving
[System.Serializable]
```

```
public class DataSave {

    //number of collectables
    public int numCollectables;

    //custom constructor
    //create new save data
    public DataSave() {

        //initial number of collectables
        numCollectables = 5;
    }

} //end class
```

Primarily, we must remember to apply the [System.Serializable] tag to our DataSave script. From there, an integer named numCollectables is declared to store the number of collectables in Luna's inventory. Via a custom constructor function, the default number of collectables in Luna's inventory is set to 5. For details on serialization, refer back to the *Hint: Create the Save Data* section.

To accompany our DataSave script, the DataManager script handles saving and loading for our game:

```
//DataManager script
//save/load imports
using System.Runtime.Serialization.Formatters.Binary;
using System.IO;

public class DataManager:MonoBehaviour {

    //current save data
    public DataSave currentSave;

    //singleton instance
    private static DataManager _Instance;

    //singleton accessor
    //access StateManager.Instance from other classes
    public static DataManager Instance {

        //create instance via getter
        get {

        //check for existing instance
        //if no instance
        if (_Instance == null) {

            //create game object
            GameObject DataManagerObj = new GameObject();
            DataManagerObj.name = "DataManager";

            //create instance
            _Instance = DataManagerObj.
              AddComponent<DataManager>();
```

```
            //init
            _Instance.currentSave = new DataSave();

            //load
            _Instance.LoadData();
        }

        //return the instance
        return _Instance;
    }
}

//awake
void Awake() {

        //prevent destruction
        DontDestroyOnLoad(this);
}

//save game data
public void SaveData() {

        //create formatter
        BinaryFormatter formatter = new BinaryFormatter();

        //create name for saved file
        string fileName = "save.luna";

        //create path for saved file
        string filePath = Application.persistentDataPath + "/"
          + fileName;

        //create file stream
        FileStream fileStream = File.Create(filePath);

        //serialize data
        formatter.Serialize(fileStream, currentSave);

        //close file stream
        fileStream.Close();
}

//load game data
public void LoadData(string theFileName = "save.luna") {

        //create file path
        string filePath = Application.persistentDataPath + "/"
          + theFileName;

        //if file exists
        if (File.Exists(filePath)) {

                //create formatter
                BinaryFormatter formatter = new BinaryFormatter();

                //open file stream
                FileStream fileStream = File.Open(filePath,
                  FileMode.Open);
```

```
            //deserialize data
            currentSave = (DataSave)formatter.
              Deserialize(fileStream);

            //close file stream
            fileStream.Close();
        }

        //otherwise, create new save data
        else {

            //save
            SaveData();
        }
    }

} //end class
```

Importantly, we must remember to add the necessary imports to the top of our script:

```
//DataManager script
//save/load imports
using System.Runtime.Serialization.Formatters.Binary;
using System.IO;
```

Our DataManager contains a DataSave variable named currentSave. This represents the present game state, which we may update from time to time. It also contains the data that we ultimately save to a file. Furthermore, it receives any data that we load from an existing save file:

```
//DataManager script
public class DataManager:MonoBehaviour {

        //current save data
        public DataSave currentSave;
```

Moreover, the DataManager script implements our familiar singleton instance. This is because we only need a single entity to handle the saving and loading of information for our game. We also need it to be available at all times. Hence, a singleton makes sense. Note that the currentSave DataSave variable is initialized using our custom constructor. In addition, LoadData() is called to update our currentSave with any save data that may already exist:

```
//DataManager script

        //singleton instance
        private static DataManager _Instance;

        //singleton accessor
        //access StateManager.Instance from other classes
        public static DataManager Instance {

                //create instance via getter
                get {
```

```
//check for existing instance
//if no instance
if (_Instance == null) {

        //create game object
        GameObject DataManagerObj = new GameObject();
        DataManagerObj.name = "DataManager";

        //create instance
        _Instance = DataManagerObj.
          AddComponent<DataManager>();

        //init
        _Instance.currentSave = new DataSave();

        //load
        _Instance.LoadData();
    }

    //return the instance
    return _Instance;
    }
}

//awake
void Awake() {

    //prevent destruction
    DontDestroyOnLoad(this);
}
```

At last, we arrive at the SaveData() function, which implements our save process:

```
//save game data
public void SaveData() {

    //create formatter
    BinaryFormatter formatter = new BinaryFormatter();

    //create name for saved file
    string fileName = "save.luna";

    //create path for saved file
    string filePath = Application.persistentDataPath + "/"
      + fileName;

    //create file stream
    FileStream fileStream = File.Create(filePath);

    //serialize data
    formatter.Serialize(fileStream, currentSave);

    //close file stream
    fileStream.Close();
}
```

Likewise, our `LoadData()` function implements our loading process:

```
//load game data
public void LoadData(string theFileName = "save.luna") {

        //create file path
        string filePath = Application.persistentDataPath + "/"
          + theFileName;

        //if file exists
        if (File.Exists(filePath)) {

                //create formatter
                BinaryFormatter formatter = new BinaryFormatter();

                //open file stream
                FileStream fileStream = File.Open(filePath,
                  FileMode.Open);

                //deserialize data
                currentSave = (DataSave)formatter.
                  Deserialize(fileStream);

                //close file stream
                fileStream.Close();
        }

        //otherwise, create new save data
        else {

                //save
                SaveData();
        }
    }

} //end class
```

Recall that we always check whether a file exists prior to trying to load it. As you can see in the `LoadData()` function, if the requested file doesn't exist, we make a call to `SaveData()` instead. Since our `SaveData()` function automatically creates a file if one doesn't exist, all of our bases are covered. Any time `LoadData()` is called, either the existing data are loaded or new data are created. For technical details on the saving and loading processes, refer back to the *Hint: Manage the Data* section.

With our data management system complete, let's focus on how it can be applied in our game. There are many times and places in which you might make calls to your DataManager instance. Thus, consider the following examples as just one way you might handle things.

Currently, our data management system focuses on Luna's collectable inventory. We always want to present the correct number of collectables to the player. Thus, we can add a `LoadItems()` function to our CollectableInventory script:

```
//CollectableInventory script
//LoadItems() function
public void LoadItems() {
```

```
//retrieve number of items
numObjects = DataManager.Instance.currentSave.numCollectables;

//retrieve text
_txtObjects = gameObject.GetComponentInChildren<Text>();

//update text
_txtObjects.text = numObjects.ToString();
}
```

In LoadItems(), we make a call to our DataManager instance to retrieve the saved number of collectables in Luna's inventory. The CollectableInventory's numObjects variable is set equal to this value. Subsequently, the onscreen text is updated to match. Thus, LoadItems() ensures that the CollectableInventory's current tally of Luna's inventory matches what is contained in our save data. It is critical to synchronize these values at the start of the game. After all, we wouldn't want the player to save with 50 collectables, then return later to find only five during a future play session. Thus, we call LoadItems() from inside Start(). The remaining portions of the CollectableInventory script remain intact from before:

```
//CollectableInventory script
//Start() function
void Start() {

    //load inventory
    LoadItems();
}
```

In related fashion, we must make sure to synchronize our save data and inventory whenever a new scene is loaded. We can do so by adding this code to the Start() function of our LevelGenerator script:

```
//LevelGenerator script
//excerpt from Start() function
void Start() {

    /*
    Code omitted.
    */

    //update inventory
    CollectableInventory inventory = GameObject.
      FindWithTag("Inventory").GetComponent<CollectableInventory>();
    inventory.LoadItems();

    /*
    Code omitted.
    */
}
```

Since this code is executed every time a level is generated, we ensure that our collectable inventory displays the most up-to-date save data.

Another thing to consider is when data need to be saved. One suggestion is to save our game data every time a new scene is loaded. To do so, we can add a call to

---

our DataManager inside the `SwitchSceneTo()` function of our StateManager script. This automatically saves the latest game data to a file every time a scene changes:

```
//StateManager script
//SwitchSceneTo() function
public void SwitchSceneTo(string theScene) {

    //save
    DataManager.Instance.SaveData();

    //load next scene
    SceneManager.LoadScene(theScene);
}
```

This completes your data management system implementation, although you will surely expand it as you continue to develop your game. On a final note, you may have realized that this implementation creates a single save file named "save.luna." Only that one file is ever saved or loaded. Hence, any time our game data is saved, any previous data are overwritten. Thus, our DataManager only keeps track of the most recent save. However, you could expand this implementation to store a series of saved files. Instead of making the player always continue from the most recent save, you could allow the player to choose from multiple save files. With some UI elements, you would have a save system that looks like many professional games: a list of previous save files from which the player can choose to load when starting the game. Conveniently, you have already implemented the core necessities for saving and loading. The rest can easily be added to your data management system as needs or preferences dictate.

Summary

You have written a data management system that can easily be reused and expanded in the future. Although we only focused on saving a single piece of information in this chapter, the same principles apply to storing other game data. As you expand your game, you can return to your DataSave script and update it to include the necessary data. Conveniently, you can continue to leverage your DataManager script throughout the development process, regardless of how much or what kinds of data you need to save. By now, you should be able to apply all of these game implementation techniques:

- Manage the saving and loading of game data

- Allow the game to be saved and continued across multiple play sessions

- Write custom classes and constructor functions

Truthfully, our game already has more than enough features to produce a compelling gameplay experience. Thus far, we have only tried to implement features in isolation. However, to produce a complete game, we need to consider the design, composition, and application of our features as a whole. Therefore, we will focus on arranging our gameplay features to create a pleasant player experience in the upcoming chapter.

References

Microsoft Corporation. 2015a. Binary Serialization. https://msdn.microsoft.com/library/72hyey7b.aspx (accessed December 28, 2015).

Microsoft Corporation. 2015b. BinaryFormatter.Deserialize Method (Stream). https://msdn.microsoft.com/library/b85344hz.aspx (accessed December 28, 2015).

Microsoft Corporation. 2015c. BinaryFormatter.Serialize Method (Stream, Object). https://msdn.microsoft.com/library/c5sbs8z9.aspx (accessed December 28, 2015).

Microsoft Corporation. 2015d. Constructors (C# Programming Guide). https://msdn.microsoft.com/library/ace5hbzh.aspx (accessed December 28, 2015).

Microsoft Corporation. 2015e. File.Create Method (String). https://msdn.microsoft.com/library/d62kzs03.aspx (accessed December 28, 2015).

Microsoft Corporation. 2015f. File.Exists Method (String) (C# and Visual Basic). https://msdn.microsoft.com/library/system.io.file.exists.aspx (accessed December 28, 2015).

Microsoft Corporation. 2015g. File.Open Method (String, FileMode). https://msdn.microsoft.com/library/b9skfh7s.aspx (accessed December 28, 2015).

Microsoft Corporation. 2015h. FileMode Enumeration. https://msdn.microsoft.com/library/system.io.filemode.aspx (accessed December 28, 2015).

Microsoft Corporation. 2015i. FileStream.Close Method. https://msdn.microsoft.com/library/aa328800.aspx (accessed December 28, 2015).

Microsoft Corporation. 2015j. new (C# Reference). https://msdn.microsoft.com/library/51y09td4.aspx (accessed December 28, 2015).

Microsoft Corporation. 2015k. Serialization (C# and Visual Basic). https://msdn.microsoft.com/library/ms233843.aspx (accessed December 28, 2015).

Microsoft Corporation. 2015l. System.IO Namespace. https://msdn.microsoft.com/library/system.io.aspx (accessed December 28, 2015).

Microsoft Corporation. 2015m. System.Runtime.Serialization.Formatters.Binary Namespace (C# and Visual Basic). https://msdn.microsoft.com/library/system.runtime.serialization.formatters.binary.aspx (accessed December 28, 2015).

Unity Technologies. 2015a. Application.persistentDataPath. http://docs.unity3d.com/ScriptReference/Application-persistentDataPath.html (accessed December 28, 2015).

Unity Technologies. 2015b. MonoBehaviour. http://docs.unity3d.com/ScriptReference/MonoBehaviour.html (accessed December 28, 2015).

Unity Technologies. 2015c. Serializable. http://docs.unity3d.com/ScriptReference/Serializable.html (accessed December 28, 2015).

Unity Technologies. 2015d. SerializeField. http://docs.unity3d.com/ScriptReference/SerializeField.html (accessed December 28, 2015).

7 Design Your World

All of the necessary gameplay mechanics, such as user controls, collisions, and interactions between characters, are implemented. You have everything necessary to create a wonderful game. Yet, your game is currently more of a loose collection of features than something players would enjoy. In this chapter, you get to have some fun designing your game world. By composing the various feature implementations you have already coded, you can create a diverse, engaging game for players to enjoy.

▌ Goals

By the end of this chapter, you will be able to apply these game implementation techniques:

- Design a complete game world

- Determine the overall logic of the game based on characters, scenes, and interactions

- Create multiple scenes to execute the vision of the game

- Add variety to the game while reusing existing code and components

▮ Required Files

In this chapter, you will use the following files from the *Software > Chapter_07* folder (https://www.crcpress.com/Learn-to-Implement-Games-with-Code/Quick/p/book/9781498753388):

- The contents of the Challenge folder to create, code, and test your solution

- The contents of the Solution folder to compare your solution to the example solution

▮ Challenge: Implement Your Design

The core framework for your game already exists. It isn't necessary to do an all-new feature implementation at this point. Hence, much of the work in this challenge entails thinking about the full scope of your game world. From the characters to the scenes to the interactions, there is much designing to do. Once you have a logical design in place, you need to execute it by reusing your existing codebase, as well as making minor changes to your scripts. By the end of this challenge, you will have a fully functional game that can be played from start to finish. The provided challenge project picks up right where you left off at the end of the previous chapter. From there, it's your job to bring the pieces together to form a playable game. The requirements for this challenge are:

1. Design purposeful interactions for all characters

2. Compose multiple scenes into a compelling gameplay experience

3. Determine the win conditions for the game

4. Reuse existing assets to expand the game content and add variety

Take note that many unforeseen issues are likely to arise as you implement your world design. Perhaps you will need to change certain variables or functions in your scripts. You will certainly need to add new information to your DataSave script. You may even end up copying your existing scenes and editing them to create different scenes. Once you solidify the logic behind your design, it is very important to work through your implementation one step at a time. Test extensively along the way. In this manner, you won't get lost or frustrated once things start to get complicated. Indeed, you have everything you need to make a great game. However, it is going to take some effort to tie all of the pieces together in a seamless fashion. Thankfully, the final product is well worth your efforts. Depending on your comfort level, feel free to implement your own unique game world, replicate the provided example solution, or anything in between.

Hint: Think about Characters

To design your game world, we'll review three major considerations: characters, scenes, and win conditions. We'll begin with characters. Return to the

Assets > Prefabs > Characters folder and review its contents (Figure 7.1). As you can see, there are a few different types of characters in our game: dragons, drakes, knights, heroes, and the player. Let's determine a suitable purpose for each character type in our game.

Dragons

There are three dragon prefabs: Dragon_01, Dragon_02, and Dragon_03. These characters are identical, aside from the fact that they come in different colors of red, green, and blue (Figure 7.2). This is an example of reusing the same asset to easily expand our game and add variety. Indeed, we will apply such techniques several times in this chapter. Recall that we previously introduced the Green Dragon as an antagonist who challenges Luna to a game of Star–Sun–Moon (SSM) in the Interaction scene. While we could limit our game world to a single showdown between Luna and the Green Dragon, we could also add more dragons to our world. For instance, incorporating the Red Dragon and the Blue Dragon would give Luna more challenges to overcome and provide the player with an extended experience. Perhaps each dragon could command a different dungeon.

Figure 7.1 Review the contents of the *Assets > Prefabs > Characters* folder to see the different characters from our game world.

Figure 7.2 Dragons of three different colors (red, green, blue) inhabit our game world.

Drakes

Similarly, there are three drake prefabs: Drake_01, Drake_02, and Drake_03. As with our dragons, they are identical, but come in different colors—red, green, and blue (Figure 7.3). The drakes are pesky henchmen that steal Luna's collectables when she collides with them in the Dungeon scene. Previously, our Dungeon scene only included Green Drakes and the Green Dragon. However, we can add more variety to the game by including all of the drakes and dragons. For example, we might even make different types of dungeons for the player to explore, each with its own types of characters.

Knights

Likewise, there are three knight prefabs: Knight_01, Knight_02, and Knight_03. Once again, they are identical aside from their color (Figure 7.4). Early on, we introduced the Red Knight character, who asked Luna whether she wanted to enter the dungeon. In coordination with the concept of introducing more dungeons, how might you incorporate the Green Knight and the Blue Knight characters into your game?

Heroes

The heroes are generically represented by four prefabs: DarkElf, Dryad, Dwarf, and Orc. By name, we know these characters as Luna, Lily, Pink Beard, and Larg (Figure 7.5), respectively. Previously, you created a Group script that allowed Luna to add heroes to her group and lead them around in the game world. You will want to leverage this script again to incorporate the hero characters into your game. Furthermore, you also need to consider how to make the heroes appear in your Interaction scene. That is, once Luna has added some friends to her group, it would be nice to incorporate them into the

Figure 7.3 Drakes of three different colors (red, green, blue) inhabit our game world.

Figure 7.4 Knights of three different colors (red, green, blue) inhabit our game world.

Figure 7.5 Luna, Lily, Pink Beard, and Larg are the heroes of our game world.

Interaction scene. Moreover, rather than placing the characters on the world map for Luna to easily find, you might place them deep within the dungeons. This would challenge the player to find Luna's friends by exploring the dungeons. Any found heroes provide the reward of more assistance during the SSM game against the dragon team.

Player

Quite simply, the Player prefab represents the character that the player controls in our Map and Dungeon scenes. For the most part, this character is already implemented in our game. However, you may need to update certain scripts attached to the Player prefab in order to fulfill your complete design.

Hint: Think about Scenes

Our game is composed of three primary scenes: Map, Dungeon, and Interaction. Consider how each of these scenes can be used.

Map

The Map scene is the gateway to Luna's world. It is a safe place where the player can explore the game's controls and pick up extra collectables. To date, we have only placed the Red Knight on the world map. When Luna interacts with the Red Knight, she chooses whether or not to transit to the Dungeon scene. In a sense, this makes our world map serve as a scene selection screen. For instance, we could add the Green Knight and the Blue Knight to the world map. When Luna interacts with them, they could offer to take her to different dungeon scenes. By using the Red, Green, and Blue Knights in this manner, we can offer Luna a choice of three different places to explore in our game.

Dungeon

Thus far, we have only one Dungeon scene. However, considering that there are nearly three of everything in our game, it makes sense to create three dungeons too. Further, there are three heroes who can accompany Luna on her quest. Thus, if we had three dungeons, we could place a hero for Luna to rescue inside each one. This would give the player plenty to explore, while still maintaining a good degree of variety between the scenes and characters.

Open the Dungeon scene in Unity. Notice the composition of objects in the Hierarchy window (Figure 7.6). Our Dungeon scene is composed of easily editable scripts, objects, and components. These elements could be altered slightly to create entirely new dungeons. For example, changes such as these could be made to create multiple dungeons from the same scene:

- BgMap: swap the tile prefabs to change the color of the dungeon floor

- Stairs: change the tile prefab to change its color

- Drakes: change the tile prefab to change the types of drakes that appear in the dungeon

- Dragons: change the tile prefab to change the dragon that can be encountered in the dungeon

- Heroes: change the tile prefab to change the hero who can be found in the dungeon

Conveniently, you can make a copy of any scene by highlighting it in the Project window and pressing CTRL + D on Windows or CMD + D on Mac (Figure 7.7). Click on the name of the copied scene to rename it (Figure 7.8). Afterward, you can open the scene and edit it as desired. Try copying your Dungeon scene a few times, renaming it, and altering the tile prefabs to create three different styles of dungeons for your game.

Note that any time you create a new scene, you must remember to add it to the project's build settings. Make sure the scene is opened. Then go to File > Build Settings ... (Figure 7.9) and click on the Add Current button (Figure 7.10). This act formally includes the scene in your game and makes it available for testing.

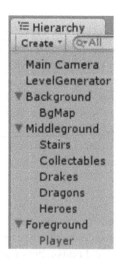

Figure 7.6 The objects that compose our Dungeon scene can be reused to create multiple dungeons for our game world.

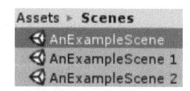

Figure 7.7 You can copy any scene by highlighting it in the Project window and pressing CTRL + D on Windows or CMD + D on Mac.

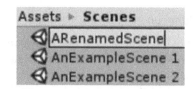

Figure 7.8 After copying a scene, click on its name in the Project window to rename it.

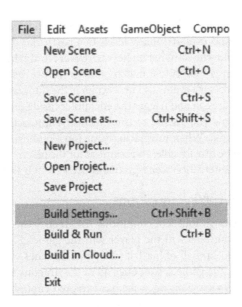

Figure 7.9 After creating a scene, open it and go to File > Build Settings ... to add it to your game.

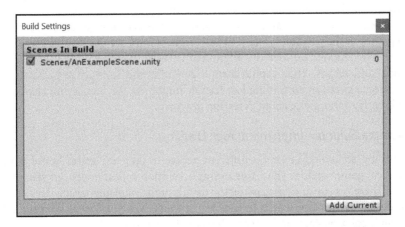

Figure 7.10 In the Build Settings dialogue box, click on the Add Current button to ensure that your newly created scene is added to your game.

Thus far, we have focused mostly on cosmetic changes to our scenes, which can be accomplished with ease. However, don't forget that both the Map and Dungeon scenes rely upon the LevelGenerator script. You may need to make some changes to this script to fulfill the technical side of your game's design.

Interaction

The Interaction scene is the final one we have to work with. Recall that we developed this scene in isolation with plans to integrate it into the broader scope of the game at a later time. That time has come. One idea is to think of the Interaction scene as the final showdown with the dragon of a particular dungeon. Imagine that Luna has dodged the drakes and explored many levels of a particular dungeon. At last, she finds a long-lost friend who joins her on her quest. Next thing they know, the dragon shows up and challenges them to a match of SSM. In this case, we would need to keep track of the necessary events as Luna explores the dungeon. When the time is right, we spawn the dragon and trigger the encounter inside the Interaction scene.

Regardless of how you choose to implement the Interaction scene, put some thought into your logic. When integrating your Interaction scene, you want to do something that will be fun, feasible, and seamless for the player. Once you've decided how to integrate the Interaction scene, gradually implement it and test along the way.

Hint: Think about Win Conditions

No game is complete without win conditions. To identify the win conditions, ask yourself this question: how will the player win the game? For instance, suppose Luna is on a quest to find all of her friends. Once she does, she has won. On the other hand, perhaps the game is won once all of the dragons are defeated. In contrast, maybe Luna is victorious once she has explored enough to collect a certain number of objects. There are many possibilities for win conditions in the context of our game world. The same can be said for losing conditions, if you choose to implement them. Regardless of your choice, you will need to track and save data throughout the game to determine whether the player has won or lost. If ever the player wins or loses, the game should end (or start over). Think about how you will keep track of the win conditions and take the necessary actions in your game.

Furthermore, consider the alignment between your win conditions, characters, and scenes. They should form a coherent and supportive package. For example, a game about finding lost friends might use the scenes and characters differently than a game about defeating dragons.

Example Solution: Implement Your Design

Naturally, we wouldn't expect different people to take our features and design identical game worlds. Thus, this example solution reflects only one designer's view. Therefore, prior to discussing the details of the implementation, let's review the design of the game world. In addition, it would be helpful to play through the example solution game to better understand how it works.

Game Design

The game begins with Luna at the top-left corner of the world map in the Map scene. Three non-player characters (NPCs) are placed on the map: the Red, Green, and Blue Knights. Similar to how our original Red Knight worked, the other knights invite Luna to explore a dungeon. However, each knight is the guardian of a different dungeon. Keeping with the color theme of our characters, there are three dungeon scenes: RedDungeon, GreenDungeon, and BlueDungeon. Each scene is similar in function, but uses different art assets.

Inside each dungeon, Luna can explore to find collectable objects. She moves from room to room infinitely using the stairs that are spawned on each floor. Meanwhile, the drakes chase her and try to steal her collectables. If Luna runs out of collectables at any time, she is booted back to the Map scene and may make another attempt at the dungeon later. While Luna is alive and well inside the dungeon, she can search for her hero friends. One hero is hidden in each dungeon. This character randomly spawns after Luna explores a certain number of rooms. Once Luna finds her friend, that hero joins the group. Subsequently, as Luna enters the next room of the dungeon, she encounters a dragon. One dragon is associated with each dungeon. Upon contact, the dragon and its team of drakes challenge Luna and her team of heroes to a game of SSM in the Interaction scene. If Luna's team wins the interaction, the player is returned to the Map scene victorious. The dungeon is conquered and the associated knight no longer appears on the world map. If Luna's team loses the interaction, the player is returned to the Map scene and may attempt the dungeon again at a later time.

The game is won once Luna has completed each of the three dungeons. That is, she must have explored each dungeon to find all of her missing hero friends and defeated all of the dragons in a game of SSM. After this happens, the game ends.

To review, the example solution design is based on the concept that our world contains three dungeons to explore. The world map is a safe place for the player to rest and learn the controls for the game. The knight characters act as the gatekeepers for each of the three dungeons. Each dungeon is based upon the same core implementation, but is themed to match a different color (red, green, or blue). Luna must find one of her missing hero friends in each dungeon, as well as defeat the dragon that guards each dungeon. Once Luna and her friends have successfully completed all three dungeons, the player wins the game.

Game Implementation

Now that you're familiar with the logic behind the example solution design, let's review how it could be implemented. To begin, the original Dungeon scene was duplicated to produce three different dungeon scenes: DungeonRed, DungeonGreen, and DungeonBlue (Figure 7.11). Inside each scene, different combinations of prefabs are spawned to provide the dungeons with their own unique theme. To accompany the three dungeons, the original Interaction scene was duplicated to make InteractionRed, InteractionGreen, and InteractionBlue (Figure 7.12).

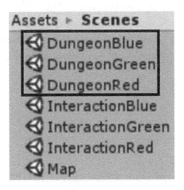

Figure 7.11 The original Dungeon scene was duplicated to produce three different scenes: DungeonRed, DungeonGreen, and DungeonBlue.

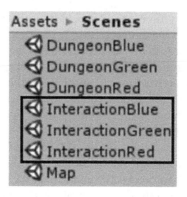

Figure 7.12 The original Interaction scene was duplicated to produce three different scenes: InteractionRed, InteractionGreen, and InteractionBlue.

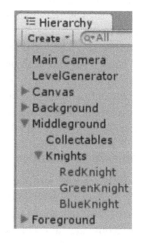

Figure 7.13 The RedKnight, GreenKnight, and BlueKnight characters have been added to the Map scene.

Likewise, each of these scenes uses background tiles that correspond to their associated dungeon. Returning to the Map scene, we find that the RedKnight, GreenKnight, and BlueKnight have been added to the Hierarchy (Figure 7.13). Of course, these characters match their respective dungeons. This covers the extent of modifications that were made in the Unity editor. As you can see, with the reuse of just a few assets, we can create quite a bit of content for our game. Nevertheless, there's more to making our game than swapping assets. We have to create a seamless and integrated experience using our code as well.

Let's review the various snippets of code required to realize the complete game design. As mentioned, three knight characters were placed in the Map scene. These knights allow Luna to enter the three dungeons in our game. Each knight carries the "Knight" tag, but has a unique name assigned in its attached CharacterData script. Thus, to direct Luna to the appropriate dungeon upon collision, we must differentiate between these characters in our UserCollision script. The code that has changed from our previous rendition is in bold:

```
//UserCollision script
//excerpt from OnTriggerEnter2D() function
case "Knight":

//disable input
userMove.SetUserInputEnabled(false);

//update dialogue text
InteractionSystem.Instance.dialogue.CreateDialogueWithText(new
   string[] {
      "Do you dare to enter the dungeon?",
      "Change your choice using the WASD or ARROW keys.",
```

```
        "Press SPACE to confirm your choice."
});

//show
InteractionSystem.Instance.dialogue.Show();

//hide on input
StartCoroutine(InteractionSystem.Instance.dialogue.HideOnInput());

//create selection text
List<string> txtSelection = new List<string>() {
     "Yes",
     "No",
     "Cancel"
};

//create selection
InteractionSystem.Instance.selection.CreateSelection(txtSelection);

//position selection
InteractionSystem.Instance.selection.PositionAt(gameObject);

//show selection
InteractionSystem.Instance.selection.Show();

//make choice
int choice = 2;
yield return StartCoroutine(InteractionSystem.Instance.selection.
StartSelection(txtSelection.Count, value => choice = value));

//check choice
//yes
if (choice == 0) {
     //retrieve character name
     string knightName = theCollider.gameObject.GetComponent
       <CharacterData>().characterName;

     //check name
     if (knightName == "Red Knight") {

          //switch to dungeon scene
          StateManager.Instance.SwitchSceneTo("DungeonRed");
     }
     else if (knightName == "Green Knight") {

          //switch to dungeon scene
          StateManager.Instance.SwitchSceneTo("DungeonGreen");
     }
     else if (knightName == "Blue Knight") {

          //switch to dungeon scene
          StateManager.Instance.SwitchSceneTo("DungeonBlue");
     }
}

//no
else if (choice == 1 || choice == 2) {

     //enable input
     userMove.SetUserInputEnabled(true);
}

break;
```

Notice that our updated collision code retrieves the knight's name from its CharacterData script. Then, based on the name, Luna is directed to the corresponding dungeon scene. Other than that, our knight collision code remains the same as before.

In similar fashion, we need to check the "Dragon" tag in our UserCollision script to direct Luna toward the appropriate interaction scene. Recall that each of the three dungeons has a dragon. As with our knights, the dragons carry the "Dragon" tag and their own CharacterData scripts. Hence, by checking which dragon Luna has collided with, we are able to direct her to the appropriate interaction scene for a given dungeon:

```
//UserCollision script
//excerpt from OnTriggerEnter2D() function
case "Dragon":
    //disable collisions
    gameObject.GetComponent<Collider2D>().enabled = false;

    //disable input
    userMove.SetUserInputEnabled(false);

    //stop movement
    theCollider.gameObject.GetComponent<AIMove>().StopMove();

    //create scene name
    //replace the word "Dungeon" in the scene name with
      "Interaction"
    //e.g. "DungeonRed" becomes "InteractionRed"
    string interactionName = SceneManager.GetActiveScene().name.
      Replace("Dungeon", "Interaction");

    //load interaction scene
    StateManager.Instance.SwitchSceneTo(interactionName);
    break;
```

Previously, there was no check for the "Dragon" tag in our UserCollision script, so let's break this code down. As is customary with our collision checks, we disable collisions and user input immediately. We also stop the dragon's movement. Combined, these actions create a freeze frame effect and set us up to nicely transition to the next scene:

```
//UserCollision script
//excerpt from OnTriggerEnter2D() function
case "Dragon":

    //disable collisions
    gameObject.GetComponent<Collider2D>().enabled = false;

    //disable input
    userMove.SetUserInputEnabled(false);

    //stop movement
    theCollider.gameObject.GetComponent<AIMove>().StopMove();
```

Then, we create a string containing the name of the appropriate scene. To do so, we use SceneManager.GetActiveScene().name (Unity Technologies 2016) in conjunction with Replace() (Microsoft Corporation 2016). Since our scene names follow a consistent format, we can easily swap the word "Interaction" for "Dungeon" to get the appropriate name. For example, if our current scene is DungeonRed, we exchange the words "Dungeon" and "Interaction" to arrive at the InteractionRed scene. Once we determine the name, we place a call to our StateManager to load the scene:

```
//UserCollision script
//excerpt from OnTriggerEnter2D() function
    //create scene name
    //replace the word "Dungeon" in the scene name with
      "Interaction"
    //e.g. "DungeonRed" becomes "InteractionRed"
    string interactionName = SceneManager.GetActiveScene().name.
      Replace("Dungeon", "Interaction");

    //load interaction scene
    StateManager.Instance.SwitchSceneTo(interactionName);
    break;
```

Much of our remaining modifications depend upon save data. Our win conditions entail finding the missing hero and defeating the dragon in each dungeon. Therefore, we can add variables to our DataSave script to track this information. In addition, we initialize the variables to default values in our custom constructor. The entire DataSave script is presented:

```
//DataSave script
//mark class for saving
[Serializable]

public class DataSave {

    //heroes found
    public Dictionary<string, bool> heroData;

    //dungeons completed
    public Dictionary<string, bool> dungeonData;

    //number of collectables
    public int numCollectables;

    //custom constructor
    //create new save data
    public DataSave() {

        //define hero data
        heroData = new Dictionary<string, bool>() {
                {"Lily", false},
                {"Pink Beard", false},
                {"Larg", false}
        };

        //define dungeon data
        dungeonData = new Dictionary<string, bool>() {
                {"Red", false},
                {"Green", false},
                {"Blue", false}
        };
```

```
              //initial number of collectables
              numCollectables = 5;
    }
} //end class
```

With the ability to track which heroes have been found, we can think about our hero group. We'll begin with the Group script, which is attached to our Player prefab. Since we are going to load our heroes based on saved data, we need to make some adjustments to our script. An array is created to store the hero prefabs. In the Unity Inspector window for the Player prefab, the hero prefabs from the *Assets > Prefabs > Characters* folder are assigned to this array. This allows us to load the specified hero prefabs as needed:

```
//Group script
//member prefabs
public GameObject[] prefabs;
```

Meanwhile, the old Start() function is removed from the Group script. In its place, a LoadMembers() function is created:

```
//Group script
//LoadMembers() function
public void LoadMembers() {
    //iterate through existing members
    //start at 1 to skip leader
    for (int i = 1; i < members.Count; i++) {

            //destroy
            Destroy(members[i]);
    }

    //clear group
    members.Clear();

    //add leader from attached object
    members.Add(gameObject);

    //retrieve group data
    Dictionary<string, bool> heroData = DataManager.Instance.
      currentSave.heroData;

    //check each member prefab
    //start at 1 to skip leader
    for (int j = 1; j < prefabs.Length; j++) {

            //retrieve character name
            string charName = prefabs[j].
              GetComponent<CharacterData>().characterName;

            //check whether saved data contains member
            if (heroData[charName] == true) {

                    //clone prefab
                    GameObject newMember = (GameObject)
                      Instantiate(prefabs[j]);

                    //disable collisions
                    newMember.GetComponent<Collider2D>().enabled =
                      false;
```

```
//set position at leader
//set z relative to leader to ensure proper
  layering
Vector3 memberPos = members[0].transform.position;
memberPos.z = gameObject.transform.position.z + j;
newMember.transform.position = memberPos;

//set parent
newMember.transform.parent = gameObject.transform.
  parent;

//add member
members.Add(newMember);
        }
    }
}
```

Every time we load our members from saved data, we want a fresh start. Therefore, we iterate through any existing heroes in the Group script's members List and remove them. Then, we clear the members List. However, we maintain the leader, since there is always at least one character in our group at all times (Luna):

```
//Group script
//excerpt from LoadMembers() function
public void LoadMembers() {

    //iterate through existing members
    //start at 1 to skip leader
    for (int i = 1; i < members.Count; i++) {

        //destroy
        Destroy(members[i]);
    }

    //clear group
    members.Clear();

    //add leader from attached object
    members.Add(gameObject);
```

To determine what other heroes are available, we refer to our saved data:

```
//Group script
//excerpt from LoadMembers() function
    //retrieve group data
    Dictionary<string, bool> heroData = DataManager.Instance.
      currentSave.heroData;
```

We iterate through each hero in the saved data. If the hero has already joined Luna's group, we clone the prefab and add it to Luna's group. The cloning process is similar to that which we applied in previous iterations of our Group script:

```
//Group script
//excerpt from LoadMembers() function
//check each member prefab
```

```
        //start at 1 to skip leader
        for (int j = 1; j < prefabs.Length; j++) {

                //retrieve character name
                string charName = prefabs[j].
                  GetComponent<CharacterData>().characterName;

                //check whether saved data contains member
                if (heroData[charName] == true) {

                        //clone prefab
                        GameObject newMember = (GameObject)
                          Instantiate(prefabs[j]);

                        //disable collisions
                        newMember.GetComponent<Collider2D>().enabled = false;

                        //set position at leader
                        //set z relative to leader to ensure proper
                          layering
                        Vector3 memberPos = members[0].transform.position;
                        memberPos.z = gameObject.transform.position.z + j;
                        newMember.transform.position = memberPos;

                        //set parent
                        newMember.transform.parent = gameObject.transform.
                          parent;

                        //add member
                        members.Add(newMember);
                }
        }
}
```

Thus, by calling LoadMembers(), we ensure that Luna's group of heroes is populated based on the most recent save data. Of course, we must call the function to make this happen. One suggestion is to place the call inside the Start() function of the LevelGenerator script. That way, each time a level is generated, we ensure that Luna's group is updated with the latest information:

```
//LevelGenerator script
//place this code inside the Start() function
//load group
GameObject.FindWithTag("Player").GetComponent<Group>().
LoadMembers();
```

Another aspect of group management is adding heroes to Luna's teams whenever she collides with them. We must update our UserCollision script to account for saved data:

```
//UserCollision script
//excerpt from OnTriggerEnter2D() function
case "Hero":

        //disable collisions
        theCollider.enabled = false;
```

```
//retrieve character name
string heroName = theCollider.gameObject.
  GetComponent<CharacterData>().characterName;

//create dialogue
InteractionSystem.Instance.dialogue.CreateDialogueWithText(
    new string[] {
        heroName + " has joined your party!",
        "Press SPACE to dismiss."
        });

//show
InteractionSystem.Instance.dialogue.Show();

//hide
StartCoroutine(InteractionSystem.Instance.dialogue.
  HideOnInput());

//update game data
DataManager.Instance.currentSave.heroData[heroName] = true;

//update hero group
group.LoadMembers();

//destroy
Destroy(theCollider.gameObject);

break;
```

Notably, when Luna collides with a hero, we make a call to our DataManager to update our save data. Additionally, we call the Group script's LoadMembers() function to display the updated group on screen.

With our hero group implemented, let's consider how it will be integrated into the interaction scenes. Previously, our InteractionGenerator script used a collection of heroes that we assigned in the Unity Inspector. This was just for testing purposes. In reality, we want to leverage our save data to utilize only those heroes who the player has already added to Luna's team. Therefore, we update the Start() function:

```
//InteractionGenerator script
//Start() function
void Start() {

    //create background map
    CreateBgMap();

    //store all characters
    List<GameObject> allChars = new List<GameObject>();

    //add characters to interaction
    //add main character (stored at index 0)
    allChars.Add(heroPrefabs[0]);

    //retrieve hero data
    Dictionary<string, bool> heroData = DataManager.Instance.
      currentSave.heroData;
```

```
        //check each member prefab
        //start at 1 to skip main character
        for (int i = 1; i < heroPrefabs.Length; i++) {

                //retrieve character name
                string charName = heroPrefabs[i].
                  GetComponent<CharacterData>().characterName;

                //if saved data contains member
                if (heroData[charName] == true) {

                        //add character
                        allChars.Add(heroPrefabs[i]);
                }
        }

        //add opponents
        //retrieve number of heroes
        int numHero = allChars.Count;

        //spawn drakes based on number of heroes
        for (int j = 0; j < numHero - 1; j++) {

                //add drake (stored at index 1)
                allChars.Add(opponentPrefabs[1]);
        }

        //add dragon (stored at index 0)
        allChars.Add(opponentPrefabs[0]);

        //create interaction
        InteractionSystem.Instance.CreateInteraction(allChars);

        //start interaction
        StartCoroutine(InteractionSystem.Instance.
          StartInteraction());
}
```

Importantly, we retrieve the hero data from our current save via the DataManager. Then, we iterate through the heroes and only allow those who the player has already found to be included in the interaction. Of course, we ensure that at least one hero, Luna, is a part of the group:

```
//InteractionGenerator script
//excerpt from Start() function
        //add characters to interaction
        //add main character (stored at index 0)
        allChars.Add(heroPrefabs[0]);

        //retrieve hero data
        Dictionary<string, bool> heroData = DataManager.Instance.
          currentSave.heroData;

        //check each member prefab
        //start at 1 to skip main character
        for (int i = 1; i < heroPrefabs.Length; i++) {
```

```
            //retrieve character name
            string charName = heroPrefabs[i].
            GetComponent<CharacterData>().characterName;

            //if saved data contains member
            if (heroData[charName] == true) {

                //add character
                allChars.Add(heroPrefabs[i]);
            }
    }
}
```

On a side note, we can achieve better game balance and fairness for the player by creating an opponent group that is the same size as the hero group. Since the dragon is a must, we ensure it is added to the group automatically. However, a number of generic drakes are spawned based on the number of heroes in Luna's group. This process is demonstrated by the following code snippet:

```
//InteractionGenerator script
//excerpt from Start() function
    //add opponents
    //retrieve number of heroes
    int numHero = allChars.Count;

    //spawn drakes based on number of heroes
    for (int j = 0; j < numHero - 1; j++) {

        //add drake (stored at index 1)
        allChars.Add(opponentPrefabs[1]);
    }

    //add dragon (stored at index 0)
    allChars.Add(opponentPrefabs[0]);
```

Speaking of interactions, let's finish our InteractionSystem script. We already have a way to enter the interaction scenes: through a collision with a dragon in the dungeon. However, we also need a way to exit an interaction scene. Obviously, we should exit the scene once the SSM game is won or lost. Accordingly, the EndInteraction() function serves this purpose:

```
//InteractionSystem script
//EndInteraction() function
public void EndInteraction(bool isHeroWin) {

    //toggle flag
    _isComplete = true;

    //heroes win
    if (isHeroWin == true) {

        //retrieve dungeon data
        string dungeonName = SceneManager.GetActiveScene().
          name.Replace("Interaction","");

        //update save data
        DataManager.Instance.currentSave.
          dungeonData[dungeonName] = true;
```

```
        //update dialogue
        dialogue.UpdateDialogueWithText("Heroes win!");
    }

    //opponents win
    else if (isHeroWin == false) {
        //update dialogue
        dialogue.UpdateDialogueWithText("Dragons win!");
    }

    //switch scene
    StateManager.Instance.SwitchSceneTo("Map");
}
```

The EndInteraction() function receives a Boolean argument that indicates whether Luna's hero team did or did not win the SSM game. Immediately, the InteractionSystem script's _ isComplete variable is toggled to prevent any additional turns from being taken by the characters:

```
//InteractionSystem script
//excerpt from EndInteraction() function
public void EndInteraction(bool isHeroWin) {

    //toggle flag
    _isComplete = true;
```

If Luna's heroes have won the match, the save data is updated to indicate that the dungeon has been completed and an appropriate message is printed to the player:

```
//InteractionSystem script
//excerpt from EndInteraction() function
    //heroes win
    if (isHeroWin == true) {

        //retrieve dungeon data
        string dungeonName = SceneManager.GetActiveScene().
          name.Replace("Interaction","");

        //update save data
        DataManager.Instance.currentSave.
          dungeonData[dungeonName] = true;

        //update dialogue
        dialogue.UpdateDialogueWithText("Heroes win!");
    }
```

On the contrary, if Luna's heroes have lost, no save data is altered, but an appropriate message is printed to the player:

```
//InteractionSystem script
//excerpt from EndInteraction() function
    //opponents win
    else if (isHeroWin == false) {
```

```
        //update dialogue
        dialogue.UpdateDialogueWithText("Dragons win!");
    }
```

Win or lose, once the SSM game is complete, the player is returned to the Map scene to continue playing the game:

```
//InteractionSystem script
//excerpt from EndInteraction() function

        //switch scene
        StateManager.Instance.SwitchSceneTo("Map");
    }
```

Appropriately, `EndInteraction()` is called at the moment we detect the end of the SSM game from inside our existing `CheckInteraction()` function. At last, we have a fully integrated set of interaction scenes:

```
//InteractionSystem script
//CheckInteraction() function
public void CheckInteraction() {

        //check active characters
        List<GameObject> activeOpponents = FindCharacters(true, false);
        List<GameObject> activeHeroes = FindCharacters(true, true);

        //if no opponents remain
        if (activeOpponents.Count <= 0) {

            //heroes win
            EndInteraction(true);
        }

        //if no heroes remain
        else if (activeHeroes.Count <= 0) {

            //heroes lose
            EndInteraction(false);
        }
    }
```

Let's not forget that the LevelGenerator ties together much of our work to create the world map and dungeon scenes. Since we've transitioned from only two scenes (Map and Dungeon) to four (Map, RedDungeon, GreenDungeon, BlueDungeon), it makes sense to reorganize the code in our LevelGenerator script. An enum is used to identify the level. Furthermore, as applicable to the dungeon levels, a hero name can be specified. These variables are public, meaning they can be set in the Unity Inspector. This makes it very easy to create different versions of our dungeon scene by changing just a few parameters:

```
//LevelGenerator script
//level types
public enum LevelType {

        //map
        Map = 0,
```

```
        //dungeon
        Red = 1,
        Green = 2,
        Blue = 3,
}

//current level type
public LevelType levelType;

//name of hero to be found
public string heroName;
```

Since there are some differences between our map and dungeon levels, it makes sense to handle their creation separately. The commonalities, such as spawning the player, remain in Start() as before, whereas level-specific code is broken into different functions. For instance, the Map scene is created by the GenerateMap() function. This function checks the save data to see which dungeons have been completed. The knight characters associated with any completed dungeons are removed from the map. Logically, this is to prevent the player from reentering a dungeon that has already been finished:

```
//LevelGenerator script
//GenerateMap() function
private void GenerateMap() {

        //retrieve game data
        Dictionary<string, bool> dungeonData = DataManager.Instance.
            currentSave.dungeonData;

        //check whether dungeons are completed
        //if so, remove knights
        if (dungeonData["Red"] == true) {

                //destroy
                Destroy(GameObject.Find("RedKnight"));
        }
        if (dungeonData["Green"] == true) {

                //destroy
                Destroy(GameObject.Find("GreenKnight"));
        }
        if (dungeonData["Blue"] == true) {

                //destroy
                Destroy(GameObject.Find("BlueKnight"));
        }

        //collectables
        SpawnObjectsWithTag("Collectable");
}
```

When it comes to the dungeon scenes, the GenerateDungeon() function handles the level-specific code:

```
//LevelGenerator script
//GenerateDungeon() function
private void GenerateDungeon() {
```

```
        //stairs
        SpawnObjectsWithTag("Stairs");

        //retrieve game data
        Dictionary<string, bool> heroData = DataManager.Instance.
          currentSave.heroData;
        Dictionary<string, bool> dungeonData = DataManager.Instance.
          currentSave.dungeonData;

        //check data
        bool isHeroFound = heroData[heroName];
        bool isDungeonComplete = dungeonData[System.Enum.
          GetName(typeof(LevelType), levelType)];

        //hero not yet found
        if (isHeroFound == false) {

                //generate random chance hero will spawn
                float randChance = Random.Range(0, 4);

                //25% chance
                if (randChance == 0) {

                        //spawn hero
                        SpawnObjectsWithTag("Hero");
                }

                //drakes
                SpawnObjectsWithTag("Drake");

                //movement
                MoveObjectsWithTag("Drake");
        }

        //hero found, but dragon not yet defeated
        else if (isHeroFound == true && isDungeonComplete == false) {

                //spawn dragon
                SpawnObjectsWithTag("Dragon");

                //movement
                MoveObjectsWithTag("Dragon");
        }

        //collectables
        SpawnObjectsWithTag("Collectable");
}
```

The GenerateDungeon() function makes sure that the stairs are spawned, so our player doesn't get trapped forever in the dungeon. After this, we retrieve the latest hero and dungeon save data. Local Boolean variables are created to check whether the hero in this dungeon has already been found and whether the dragon in this dungeon has already been defeated:

```
//LevelGenerator script
//excerpt from GenerateDungeon() function
private void GenerateDungeon() {
```

```
//stairs
SpawnObjectsWithTag("Stairs");

//retrieve game data
Dictionary<string, bool> heroData = DataManager.Instance.
    currentSave.heroData;
Dictionary<string, bool> dungeonData = DataManager.Instance.
    currentSave.dungeonData;

//check data
bool isHeroFound = heroData[heroName];
bool isDungeonComplete = dungeonData[System.Enum.
    GetName(typeof(LevelType), levelType)];
```

If the hero has not already been found, we generate a typical dungeon room with drakes. We include a random chance that the missing hero is spawned in this room:

```
//LevelGenerator script
//excerpt from GenerateDungeon() function
    //hero not yet found
    if (isHeroFound == false) {

        //generate random chance hero will spawn
        float randChance = Random.Range(0, 4);

        //25% chance
        if (randChance == 0) {

            //spawn hero
            SpawnObjectsWithTag("Hero");
        }

        //drakes
        SpawnObjectsWithTag("Drake");

        //movement
        MoveObjectsWithTag("Drake");
    }
```

However, if the hero is already found, but the dragon has not been defeated, we spawn the dragon to challenge the heroes to the SSM game:

```
//LevelGenerator script
//excerpt from GenerateDungeon() function
    //hero found, but dragon not yet defeated
    else if (isHeroFound == true && isDungeonComplete == false) {

        //spawn dragon
        SpawnObjectsWithTag("Dragon");

        //movement
        MoveObjectsWithTag("Dragon");
    }
```

Lastly, we spawn the collectables, which appear in all dungeon rooms, to complete the GenerateDungeon() function:

```
//LevelGenerator script
//excerpt from GenerateDungeon() function
    //collectables
    SpawnObjectsWithTag("Collectable");
}
```

Interestingly, the GenerateDungeon() function recreates the appropriate game state, regardless of how many times Luna enters a dungeon. For example, suppose that she finds Lily in a dungeon, but loses the SSM game against the dragon. When Luna reenters the dungeon, our code knows to spawn the dragon immediately, since Lily was already found. This demonstrates the power of our data management system.

Moreover, a simple check in the Start() function differentiates between the level types. Based on the level type, the appropriate generation function is called, either GenerateMap() or GenerateDungeon(). This completes the modifications to our LevelGenerator script:

```
//LevelGenerator script
//excerpt from Start() function
void Start() {

        /*
        Code omitted.
        */

        //check level type
        //map
        if (levelType == LevelType.Map) {

                //generate map
                GenerateMap();
        }

        //dungeon
        else {

                //generate dungeon
                GenerateDungeon();
        }

        /*
        Code omitted.
        */
}
```

Before we wrap up our world design, we have to settle our win conditions. To reiterate, Luna wins the game when she has found all of her missing hero friends and defeated all of the dragons. We already saved the necessary data to our DataSave script. Thus, to determine whether the player has won the game, we need to check our data for the win conditions. This can be done from the StateManager script. Much like we update our save data every time we switch scenes, we can also check to see whether the game has ended every time we switch scenes:

```
//StateManager script
//SwitchSceneTo() function
public void SwitchSceneTo(string theScene) {

    //save
    DataManager.Instance.SaveData();

    //check win conditions
    //retrieve dungeon data
    Dictionary<string, bool> dungeonData = DataManager.Instance.
        currentSave.dungeonData;

    //check if all dungeons completed
    if (dungeonData["Red"] == true &&
            dungeonData["Green"] == true &&
            dungeonData["Blue"] == true) {

        //create dialogue
        InteractionSystem.Instance.dialogue.
            CreateDialogueWithText("The game is won!");

        //show dialogue
        InteractionSystem.Instance.dialogue.Show();
    }

    //otherwise
    else {

        //load next scene
        SceneManager.LoadScene(theScene);
    }
}
```

Before changing scenes, our revised `SwitchSceneTo()` function checks the save data to see if the win conditions are met. If so, we show a congratulatory dialogue box for the time being (we will polish our game to offer the player a more grandiose ending in a future challenge). If not, we simply continue the game by loading the requested scene. With the win conditions in full effect, our designed game world has been realized!

Besides playing through the example solution and reading the provided descriptions of how it was made, you should thoroughly examine the various scenes, prefabs, objects, and scripts involved. Exercise your design skills by changing values. Experiment with how things work and adjust the settings to your liking. You can even take the example solution and rework it into an entirely different game.

Tying all the pieces of a game into a compelling experience is a formidable task. However, it is one that you'll undoubtedly succeed at many times as a game developer. Whether you replicated the example solution, created an entirely different game, or anything inbetween, congratulations on creating a complete game from your various implementations!

Summary

As you can see, once you have coded the core features of your game, it is relatively easy to create an entire game world. By reusing existing implementations, you can add a surprising amount of variety to your game. At this point, you have crafted an entire game world and ensured that it functions properly. You should be able to apply all of these game implementation techniques:

- Design a complete game world

- Determine the overall logic of the game based on characters, scenes, and interactions

- Create multiple scenes to execute the vision of the game

- Add variety to the game while reusing existing code and components

From a gameplay standpoint, everything is in place. However, there are still several things to be done to take our game from functionally complete to release-ready for players. For instance, our game doesn't even have a main menu screen to welcome players. Let's give it one in the next chapter.

References

Microsoft Corporation. 2016. String.Replace Method (String, String). https://msdn. microsoft.com/library/c8f5xwh7.aspx (accessed January 6, 2016).
Unity Technologies. 2016. SceneManager.GetActiveScene. https://docs.unity3d.com/ ScriptReference/SceneManagement.SceneManager.GetActiveScene.html (accessed January 6, 2016).

8 A Proper Introduction

So far, we've always launched our game directly from the Map scene. While this is fine for testing purposes, it wouldn't be very professional to present our final game to players this way. For a better gameplay experience, we should focus on the introduction to our game. Specifically, we will introduce a loading screen and a main menu to better manage resources and create a more professional presentation for players. Nearly all games make use of loading and main menu screens. Once you are proficient at making these, you will be able to rapidly incorporate them into future projects.

▌ Goals

By the end of this chapter, you will be able to apply these game implementation techniques:

- Make a loading screen for the game

- Create a main menu screen for the game

- Preload critical components prior to starting the game

- Allow the game to be started based on user input

▮ Required Files

In this chapter, you will use the following files from the *Software > Chapter_08* folder (https://www.crcpress.com/Learn-to-Implement-Games-with-Code/Quick/p/book/9781498753388):

- The contents of the Challenge folder to create, code, and test your solution

- The contents of the Solution folder to compare your solution to the example solution

▮ Challenge: Create a Loading Screen

Almost all games have one or more loading screens that appear before a main menu. Although they often display credits related to the game, they may also be used to preload necessary components before the game begins. Especially for larger games with hardware-intensive requirements, loading screens may also appear before individual scenes. In that case, they are most certainly used to load resources in advance. The logic behind preloading is that we want to make sure everything is in place before the player enters the game. Should the player enter the game without the minimum necessary resources prepared, a host of undesirable situations can arise, such as crashes and performance hiccups. Thus, our loading screen serves two purposes. First, while the game we're making is not hardware intensive, we can still practice good resource management by preloading our core components. Second, the loading screen provides a branding opportunity where you can credit yourself for creating the game.

In this challenge, you will create a Load scene and an accompanying Load script for your game. You should create both items from scratch inside your Unity project. The requirements for this challenge are:

1. Create a Load script that manages the loading screen.

2. Design a Load scene that the player sees when the game is first started.

Hint: Preload Critical Components

Setting up your initial solution for this challenge should be fairly routine by now. Create a new scene named "Load." Be sure to add it to your project's Build Settings at the 0 position to ensure that it comes before all other scenes. Then, create a Load script. Last, attach the Load script to a `GameObject` in the scene.

Now, think about the logic behind your scene. Recall that you want to preload the critical components that your game relies upon to function. How will you identify these components? Think in terms of the components that exist throughout the duration of your game, such as the singletons you previously implemented. Furthermore, think about what components are relied upon by many other entities throughout your game. These sorts of components are good candidates for preloading. Generally speaking, here is a list of example game components that are likely to be preloaded before a game begins:

- A state manager that manages scene switching

- A data management system that enables saving and loading

- A notification system that presents information to the player

- An audio manager that controls the playback of music and sound effects

On the contrary, here is a list of example game components that are unlikely to be preloaded before the game begins:

- A character that appears only in a specific scene

- A script that generates individual levels

- A subcomponent that represents just one piece of a more complex object

- Any component designed to exist only within a specific scene

Once you've identified your critical components, use your Load script to initialize them. In this manner, you ensure that these components are preloaded before the game begins. Once these components are loaded, feel free to proceed to the next scene in your game via the Load script.

Another thing you may want to include in your Load script is a delay before switching scenes. Not only does this allow your objects to fully load before proceeding, but it also creates a smoother flow for the player. Without any delay, your Load script immediately executes and bypasses the Load scene in an instant. However, with a delay of a few seconds, your loading screen is perceptible to the player before proceeding to the next scene.

Hint: Design the Loading Screen

At this point, you can take a moment to be creative. Your loading screen is functional, thanks to the code in your Load script. However, your Load scene has nothing to show for itself yet. Create whatever kind of loading screen visual you want. For instance, you can add text, such as your name, and images, like a logo, to the scene. You can add a new canvas to your Load scene to display the necessary visuals. This is what will be presented to the player when your game is launched.

Speaking of canvases, think of the existing Canvas object that is placed in our Map scene. It displays things like our dialogue box, selection box, and Luna's inventory of collectables. We want this Canvas object to remain throughout all of our scenes, since we use it regularly. Previously, our game started in the Map scene, so our Canvas started there, too. However, now that we have a proper introduction to our game, we should initialize the Canvas in the Load scene instead. Therefore, you should copy the existing Canvas to your Load scene and delete it from your Map scene.

Note that it is perfectly fine to have multiple canvases in a Unity scene. You can make a separate canvas in your Load scene and use it only to display the specific visuals associated with that scene. Once the next scene loads, it will be gone. At the same time, your persistent Canvas will be preloaded in the Load scene and ready for use in subsequent scenes.

Example Solution: Create a Loading Screen

Take a look at the example solution project to review the design of the loading screen in the Load scene. The sample project uses a separate canvas called LoadCanvas, which contains a background image, text box, and three dragon images (Figure 8.1). In fact, it reuses the same components from our primary Canvas, but with a few minor visual changes. Overall, the LoadCanvas creates what the player sees on the loading screen (Figure 8.2). You may have created an entirely different look for your loading screen, which is perfectly fine.

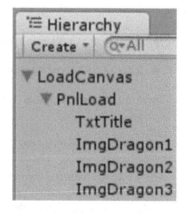

However, let's not forget that our loading screen has an important responsibility beyond its looks. A GameObject

Figure 8.1 The example solution uses a canvas to create the loading screen from a text box and a few images.

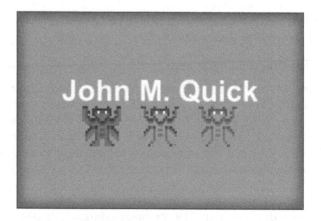

Figure 8.2 The example solution's loading screen.

named Load also exists in the Load scene and has the Load script attached. Our Load script is responsible for initializing the critical components that our game relies upon to function properly. Here is the relatively brief Load script in its entirety:

```
//Load script
public class Load : MonoBehaviour {

    //delay before loading game, in seconds
    public float loadDelay;

    //awake
    void Awake() {

        //load
        StartCoroutine(LoadGame());
    }

    //load
    private IEnumerator LoadGame() {

        //init persistent objects
        InitPersistentObjects();

        //delay
        yield return new WaitForSeconds(loadDelay);

        //load scene
        StateManager.Instance.SwitchSceneTo("Menu");
    }

    //init objects that persist through scenes
    public void InitPersistentObjects() {

        //state manager
        if (StateManager.Instance) {};

        //data manager
        if (DataManager.Instance) {};

        //interaction system
        if (InteractionSystem.Instance) {};

        //canvas
        GameObject canvas = GameObject.FindWithTag("Canvas");
        DontDestroyOnLoad(canvas);
        canvas.GetComponent<CanvasGroup>().alpha = 0.0f;
    }
}
```

A public float named "loadDelay" is declared. This allows us to set a duration at which the loading screen is shown to players before proceeding to the next scene:

```
//Load script
//delay before loading game, in seconds
public float loadDelay;
```

A function named `InitPersistentObjects()` handles the initialization of our critical components:

```
//Load script
//InitPersistentObjects() function
public void InitPersistentObjects() {

        //state manager
        if (StateManager.Instance) {};

        //data manager
        if (DataManager.Instance) {};

        //interaction system
        if (InteractionSystem.Instance) {};

        //canvas
        GameObject canvas = GameObject.FindWithTag("Canvas");
        DontDestroyOnLoad(canvas);
        canvas.GetComponent<CanvasGroup>().alpha = 0.0f;
}
```

Recall that each of our singleton instances (StateManager, DataManager, and InteractionSystem) initialize themselves the first time they are accessed in our code. Thus, empty `if` statements are used to place a call to each singleton in the `InitPersistentObjects()` function. This triggers the singletons to initialize themselves. Furthermore, each singleton already contains an `Awake()` function and `DontDestroyOnLoad()` call, thus ensuring they won't be destroyed. Meanwhile, the Canvas, which was previously in our Map scene, has been transferred to our Load scene instead. Since our Canvas does not have its own script, we must explicitly retrieve it from the scene and call `DontDestroyOnLoad()` to ensure it persists throughout the game. Alternatively, you could write a small script to handle this work and attach it to the Canvas.

Continuing, the overall loading process is handled by the `LoadGame()` coroutine:

```
//Load script
//LoadGame() coroutine
private IEnumerator LoadGame() {

        //init persistent objects
        InitPersistentObjects();

        //delay
        yield return new WaitForSeconds(loadDelay);

        //load scene
        StateManager.Instance.SwitchSceneTo("Menu");
}
```

The `LoadGame()` coroutine places a call to `InitPersistentObjects()` to take care of initializing our critical components. Afterward, it uses `WaitForSeconds()` in conjunction with `loadDelay` to display the loading screen to the player for the desired amount of time. Subsequently, our game progresses to the main menu scene by placing a call to the StateManager's `SwitchSceneTo()` function.

Last, since it is of utmost importance that our Load script executes right away, we place a call to the `LoadGame()` coroutine inside `Awake()`:

```
//Load script
//Awake() function
void Awake() {

    //load
    StartCoroutine(LoadGame());
}
```

Our brief, but vital, Load script is complete. By the way, notice that the example Load script ultimately forwards to the main menu scene (`StateManager.Instance.SwitchSceneTo("Menu");`). Since you have not yet created your main menu, you may go to the Map scene for the time being. However, once your loading screen and main menu scenes are finalized, you will want your Load scene to lead into the Menu scene.

Nevertheless, when you run your Load scene, notice that your critical components appear in the Hierarchy window. The Canvas, StateManager, DataManager, and InteractionSystem are all present. Therefore, by the time the player gets to the game, all of the vital components are already in place. Hence, we have created a nice loading screen to lead the player into our game. Let's proceed to complete our main menu.

▌ Challenge: Create a Main Menu

The main menu is the face of your game. It welcomes the player and entices him or her to enter the world you created. In its simplest form, the main menu acts as a title page. It presents graphics and text that represent the game. The player is allowed to start the game on demand. Your title page should at least accomplish these objectives. In more complex cases, the main menu may include other UI elements. For example, if the game has customizable settings, a tutorial, or loadable files, buttons may be used to link to such pages. These aren't necessary for our current game, but you may want to practice including them anyway. Much like your loading screen, your main menu begins by creating a new scene and script from scratch. The requirements for this challenge are:

1. Create a Menu script that manages the main menu.

2. Design a Menu scene that invites the player into your game world.

3. Allow the player to begin the game based on user input.

Hint: Listen for User Input

The Menu script may be the simplest implementation that you ever code. Your Load script already handles preloading the necessary components to run your game.

Therefore, your Menu script merely acts as a gateway to your game world (or other menu pages, should you choose to include them). As you've done before, you should check for user input, such as a key press. Once the player chooses to enter the game, place a call to the StateManager to transit to the next scene.

Hint: Design the Main Menu

Just like your loading screen, you might create a separate canvas to handle the visuals for your main menu. Be sure to include graphics and text that invite the player into your game world. Once your main menu is complete, remember to test your game several times. At this point, your game should load smoothly and provide a proper introduction to the player, thanks to your Load and Menu scenes.

Example Solution: Create a Main Menu

Have a peek at the example solution project's Menu scene to examine its design. Similar to the Load scene, a separate canvas called "MenuCanvas" was created specifically to handle the visuals for the Menu scene. In the Hierarchy, you can see that MenuCanvas contains text and images (Figure 8.3). The overall look for the Menu scene consists of displaying the game's name, our soon-to-be-famous group of heroes, and an instruction to the player on how to start the game (Figure 8.4).

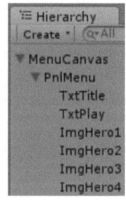

Although you can pick any design you wish for your main menu, remember its key goals. The main menu should welcome your player into the game. That's why main menus usually feature the title of the game and a prominent image—such as a logo,

Figure 8.3 The example solution uses a canvas to create the main menu from a few text boxes and images.

Figure 8.4 The example solution's main menu.

the main character, or an exciting action shot from the game. In addition, your main menu is a gateway to the rest of your game. In the minimalist example solution, this means that the player must provide input in order to start the game. Accordingly, the player is told to "press any key to play" on the main menu. Meanwhile, this functionality is handled by our miniscule Menu script, which has been attached to a Menu GameObject in the scene:

```
//Menu script
public class Menu : MonoBehaviour {

    //whether input is enabled
    private bool _isInputEnabled;

    //init
    void Start() {

        //set flag
        _isInputEnabled = true;
    }

    //update
    void Update() {

        //check user input
        if (_isInputEnabled && Input.anyKeyDown) {

            //toggle flag
            _isInputEnabled = false;

            //start game
            StateManager.Instance.SwitchSceneTo("Map");
        }
    }
}
```

The Menu script establishes a Boolean flag to check for the player's input:

```
//Menu script
public class Menu : MonoBehaviour {

    //whether input is enabled
    private bool _isInputEnabled;
```

In Start(), the flag is set to true, indicating that the player may provide input:

```
//Menu script
//Start() function
void Start() {

    //set flag
    _isInputEnabled = true;
}
```

Then, in `Update()`, we check for any key press using Unity's `Input.any-KeyDown` (Unity Technologies 2016). If the player presses any key, we immediately disable user input. Last, a call is made to the StateManager to load the Map scene:

```
//Menu script
//Update() function
void Update() {

    //check user input
    if (_isInputEnabled && Input.anyKeyDown) {

        //toggle flag
        _isInputEnabled = false;

        //start game
        StateManager.Instance.SwitchSceneTo("Map");
    }
}
```

That's all for your loading screen and main menu. You have rapidly provided players with a proper introduction to your game. Furthermore, your game is steadily improving and making progress toward a release-ready state.

Summary

Your implementations in this chapter served multiple purposes. Not only are the critical resources of your game better managed than before, but you have also created a more professional presentation for players. With the successful creation of a loading screen and main menu, you should be able to apply all of these game implementation techniques:

- Make a loading screen for the game

- Create a main menu screen for the game

- Preload critical components prior to starting the game

- Allow the game to be started based on user input

In the next chapter, we continue our tour of polishing the game and prepping it for release. Our game already has a loading screen, main menu, and several in-game scenes. Transitions are one thing that goes hand in hand with switching between scenes. Thus, our upcoming challenge entails implementing transitions into our game.

Reference

Unity Technologies. 2016. Input.anyKeyDown. http://docs.unity3d.com/ScriptReference/Input-anyKeyDown.html (accessed January 6, 2016).

9 A Proper Transition

Thanks to your efforts in the last chapter, our game is able to switch through a sensible sequence of scenes. The game starts with a loading screen, followed by a main menu, and then the game itself, which is composed of several scenes. While our game can indeed switch scenes, the transition between them is neither smooth nor pleasant. Currently, the player is jolted between scenes in an instant. In line with the concept of polishing our game and creating a better player experience, we are going to improve the transition between scenes. To do so, we will apply the most classic transition used throughout games and cinema: the fade. After completing the challenges in this chapter, you will have a nice fade in and fade out transition that can be applied when switching scenes in this game, as well as many future games to come.

▌▌ Goals

By the end of this chapter, you will be able to apply these game implementation techniques:

- Create fade in and out effects to transition between scenes
- Smooth scene transitions with easing

- Use timing to manage the transition between scenes effectively

- Coordinate game states and scene transitions

▋ Required Files

In this chapter, you will use the following files from the *Software > Chapter_09* folder (https://www.crcpress.com/Learn-to-Implement-Games-with-Code/Quick/p/book/9781498753388):

- The contents of the Challenge folder to create, code, and test your solution

- The contents of the Solution folder to compare your solution to the example solution

▋ Challenge: Fade the Screen In and Out

Your challenge is straightforward. Make the screen fade in and out. To fade in, the screen should start out completely black (or any other color of your choice). Over time, the game world gradually fades in until it is fully revealed to the player. On the other hand, to fade out, the game world begins by being fully visible to the player. Gradually, the screen becomes darker and darker until it is completely black. Figure 9.1 demonstrates the beginning and end states for the fade transitions.

The challenge project still contains everything you've done so far. It is your responsibility to create any objects and scripts necessary to execute the fade transition. Since the fade will occur between all of the scenes in your game, think about how you can manage your transitions efficiently. The requirements for this challenge are:

1. Create a Fade script that implements the fade in and out transitions.

2. Test the fade in and out transitions within a scene to ensure they work.

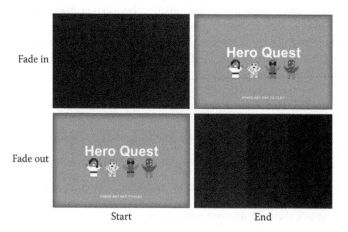

Figure 9.1 The start and end states of the fade in and fade out transitions are displayed.

Hint: Apply the Texture Technique

An age-old game development technique for covering the screen involves the use of a very small, single-color texture. For example, we might create a 1 × 1 pixel (px), 2 × 2 px, or 4 × 4 px opaque black texture that is extremely small and efficient for the computer to process. Subsequently, we can stretch this texture to match the size of the screen. Hence, from a very small texture, we manage to block the player's entire view of the game. Unlike when you try to upsize your family photos on a computer, the texture experiences no pixelation. That's because it is a single, solid color. When it is enlarged, it is still just a solid color. Thus, we can stretch our tiny texture to obscure any screen size.

In Unity, we can use the `Texture2D` class (Unity Technologies 2016k) to create our texture in code. When we create our texture, we can set various parameters, such as its color, size, and transparency. This code snippet demonstrates how to create a 1 × 1 px black texture:

```
//create a new 1 px texture
Texture2D sampleTexture = new Texture2D(1, 1, TextureFormat.ARGB32,
  false);

//color the texture's pixel black
sampleTexture.SetPixel(0, 0, Color.black);

//apply the color change
sampleTexture.Apply();
```

In the preceding sample code, a `Texture2D` named `"sampleTexture"` is initialized using a standard constructor function. The first two arguments in Texture2D(1, 1, TextureFormat.ARGB32, false) indicate that the width and height of the texture are 1 × 1 px. A `TextureFormat` (Unity Technologies 2016n) of ARGB32 is selected to ensure that our texture has an alpha channel, which allows us to modify its transparency. Meanwhile, the remaining argument is set to `false`, as it is irrelevant to our current purpose:

```
//create a new 1 px texture
Texture2D sampleTexture = new Texture2D(1, 1, TextureFormat.ARGB32,
  false);
```

Subsequently, the `SetPixel()` function (Unity Technologies 2016m) is used to set our single pixel to black. Unity provides a convenient shortcut for an opaque black color in the form of `Color.black` (Unity Technologies 2016b), which is used in the sample code. Recall that computers usually start counting from "0," rather than from "1" like us humans, so an index position of (0, 0) is fed into `SetPixel()`. That index position represents the coordinates of our solitary pixel:

```
//color the texture's pixel black
sampleTexture.SetPixel(0, 0, Color.black);
```

Last, to ensure that the changes made in our `SetPixel()` function take effect in our texture, we must call the `Apply()` function (Unity Technologies 2016l):

```
//apply the color change
sampleTexture.Apply();
```

With this code, you can establish an opaque black texture in your Fade script. This is a good place to start for creating your fade transition. However, remember that your texture is only 1 × 1 px at the moment. You need to find a way to stretch it to fill the entire screen.

Hint: Manage the Texture's Alpha Transparency

Furthermore, once we cover the screen with a solid texture, we can proceed to fade it in and out. To do so, we manipulate the alpha transparency of the texture over time. Gradually, we reduce the alpha transparency to make the texture transparent and the screen visible (fade in). Alternatively, we can also make the texture opaque over time to hide the screen (fade out).

Calculating the alpha transparency of the texture is one thing, but applying it is another. In Unity, we can use a special function called `OnGUI()` (Unity Technologies 2016i) to continually update the transparency of our texture. Similar to `Start()` and `Update()`, `OnGUI()` is automatically executed once placed in our script. This function is called rapidly, sometimes even more than once per frame. If we choose to update our texture's transparency in `OnGUI()`, we can be sure that it is always up to date with the latest calculations. The structure of `OnGUI()` is presented in this sample code:

```
//OnGUI() function structure
void OnGUI() {

    /*
    Update the alpha channel of your
    texture's color over time in this
    function.
    */

}
```

In the past, Unity's GUI system was used to handle a game's user interface (UI) and related events (Unity Technologies 2016c). However, the Canvas system (Unity Technologies 2016a) that you've used several times already is currently the more preferred way to create UI. Nevertheless, we can leverage the old GUI system to our benefit when it comes to creating fade transitions. Note that you will need to place some GUI-specific code inside your `OnGUI()` function to make it work. Also, don't forget that you have created a texture that needs to be drawn to the screen. As an added hint, be sure to examine `GUI.color`, `GUI.depth`, and `GUI.DrawTexture()` before coding your `OnGUI()` function (Unity Technologies 2016d, 2016e, 2016f).

Now that you've considered how to create a texture and manipulate its transparency, think about how you want to organize your Fade script. For example, you might write one or more functions in your script to calculate the alpha transparency of your texture. In addition, you can use OnGUI() to ensure that your texture's alpha transparency is continually updated. Moreover, consider what other features you might want to add to your Fade script, such as a time-based mechanism to control how long the transitions take to complete. Implement your Fade script and test it with a scene to make sure you can fade the screen in and out. Then, proceed to the example solution.

Example Solution: Fade the Screen In and Out

The example solution presents one way that you may have implemented your fade transitions. Most of the code takes place in the Fade script. To begin, let's set up a few variables. The minAlpha and maxAlpha variables represent the alpha range that we will use for fading. Most of the time, the maximum possible range, 0–1, will be used. However, these variables allow us to use other ranges as well, such as 0.2–0.8:

```
//Fade script
//alpha limits
public float minAlpha, maxAlpha;
```

A time-based implementation is demonstrated in the example solution. That is, we have the ability to specifically state how many seconds our fade transitions last. To implement our timing mechanism, we must accept the length of the transition (duration) and record when the latest transition started (_startTime):

```
//Fade script
//duration, in seconds
public float duration;

//time when fade cycle started
private float _startTime;
```

Since this is our Fade script after all, we must always keep track of the current alpha value of our texture. Furthermore, isPaused acts as a control variable to ensure that we only bother to update the texture's alpha value when a transition is underway. Moreover, the isFadingIn Boolean flags whether our transition is currently fading in or fading out:

```
//current alpha level
private float _alpha;

//whether fade is paused
private bool isPaused;

//whether currently fading in
private bool isFadingIn;
```

Of course, we need a Texture2D to make this all possible. This texture is going to be sized to match the screen, so we also want to store the screen size in a Rect (Unity Technologies 2016j) as well:

```
//texture used to create effect
private Texture2D _texture;
```

```
//screen rectangle
private Rect _screenRect;
```

With the aforementioned variables, you have everything you need to cover the screen with a texture, fade the texture in or out, and control the timing of the transition. Since our transition takes place as soon as a scene is started, we initialize the variables to relevant variables inside Awake():

```
//Fade script
//Awake() function
void Awake() {

    //set limits
    minAlpha = 0.0f;
    maxAlpha = 1.0f;
    duration = 1.0f;

    //set flags
    isPaused = false;
    isFadingIn = false;

    //set alpha
    _alpha = maxAlpha;

    //create fade texture
    _texture = new Texture2D(1, 1, TextureFormat.ARGB32, false);
    _texture.SetPixel(0, 0, Color.black);
    _texture.Apply();

    //create screen rect
    _screenRect = new Rect(0, 0, Screen.width, Screen.height);
}
```

Briefly, these initialized values give us a 1-second transition with alpha boundaries of 0 (completely transparent) and 1 (completely opaque). We assume that we are not fading in nor paused, while the alpha is set to the maximum value. A 1×1 px texture is made and colored black, then the size of the screen is stored in a rectangle.

The example implementation applies a single UpdateAlpha() function to calculate the current alpha value, regardless of which transition is underway:

```
//Fade script
//UpdateAlpha() function
private void UpdateAlpha() {

    //calculate cumulative duration
    float cumulativeDuration = Time.time - _startTime;

    //calculate percentage of duration complete
    float pct = Mathf.Clamp01(cumulativeDuration / duration);

    //check fade direction
    switch (isFadingIn) {

        //fading in
        case true:
```

```
        //alpha less than max
        if (_alpha < maxAlpha) {

            //update alpha
            _alpha = minAlpha + pct * (maxAlpha - minAlpha);
        }

        //otherwise
        else {

            //set to max
            _alpha = maxAlpha;

            //pause
            isPaused = true;
        }
        break;

    //fading out
    case false:

        //alpha greater than min
        if (_alpha > minAlpha) {

            //update alpha
            _alpha = minAlpha + (1.0f - pct) * (maxAlpha
                - minAlpha);
        }

        //otherwise
        else {

            //set to min
            _alpha = minAlpha;

            //pause
            isPaused = true;
        }
        break;

    //default
    default:
        break;
    }
}
```

Straight away, UpdateAlpha() uses Time.time and our stored _startTime to determine how much time has passed. This time is converted into a percentage value between 0 and 1 using Mathf.Clamp01 (Unity Technologies 2016g). This percentage is later used to adjust the alpha value, thereby ensuring that the transition lasts precisely for the specified duration:

```
//Fade script
//excerpt from UpdateAlpha() function
    //calculate cumulative duration
    float cumulativeDuration = Time.time - _startTime;
```

```
//calculate percentage of duration complete
float pct = Mathf.Clamp01(cumulativeDuration / duration);
```

The remainder of the function exists within a `switch` statement. The `switch` statement checks the `isFadingIn` flag to determine whether the screen is fading in or out:

```
//Fade script
//excerpt from UpdateAlpha() function
    //check fade direction
    switch (isFadingIn) {

        //fading in
        case true:

            /*
            Code omitted.
            */

        //fading out
        case false:

            /*
            Code omitted.
            */

        //default
        default:
            break;
    }
```

When fading in, we check that the current alpha is less than the maximum limit. If so, our `_alpha` variable is calculated based on the percentage of time complete thus far. If not, the transition has ended. Thus, we fix our alpha at the maximum and toggle the pause flag:

```
//Fade script
//excerpt from UpdateAlpha() function
//fading in

        case true:

            //alpha less than max
            if (_alpha < maxAlpha) {

                //update alpha
                _alpha = minAlpha + pct * (maxAlpha - minAlpha);
            }

            //otherwise
            else {

                //set to max
                _alpha = maxAlpha;

                //pause
                isPaused = true;
            }
            break;
```

Similarly, if fading out, we check that the current alpha is greater than the minimum. If so, we again calculate the _alpha value based on the time passed thus far. Otherwise, the transition has ended, so we fix the alpha at the minimum and pause the script:

```
//Fade script
//excerpt from UpdateAlpha() function
//fading out
        case false:

                //alpha greater than min
                if (_alpha > minAlpha) {

                    //update alpha
                    _alpha = minAlpha + (1.0f - pct) * (maxAlpha
                      - minAlpha);

                }

                //otherwise
                else {

                    //set to min
                    _alpha = minAlpha;

                    //pause
                    isPaused = true;

                }
                break;
```

That's all there is to our UpdateAlpha() function. It simply checks the status of the transition and calculates the appropriate alpha value. Since the alpha needs to be calculated repeatedly over the duration of the transition (except when the script is paused), UpdateAlpha() is called from Update():

```
//Fade script
//Update() function
void Update() {

    //if not paused
    if (isPaused == false) {

        //update alpha
        UpdateAlpha();

    }
}
```

Naturally, we must remember to update our texture with our newly calculated alpha values. This is where OnGUI() comes into play:

```
//Fade script
//OnGUI() function
```

```
void OnGUI() {

    //update color
    Color color = Color.black;
    color.a = _alpha;
    GUI.color = color;

    //place texture in front of all objects
    GUI.depth = -100;

    //draw texture over screen
    GUI.DrawTexture(_screenRect, _texture);

}
```

Inside OnGUI(), we create a local color variable and set its alpha channel equal to our calculated _alpha value. Subsequently, we set the overall GUI color to match:

```
//Fade script
//excerpt from OnGUI() function
    //update color
    Color color = Color.black;
    color.a = _alpha;
    GUI.color = color;
```

Remember that our goal is to cover the entire screen with a texture. If that texture is not in front of everything else, it won't have any impact on the visuals presented to the player. Therefore, we set our GUI depth to a lucrative value that ensures it is in front of all other layers in our game:

```
//Fade script
//excerpt from OnGUI() function
    //place texture in front of all objects
    GUI.depth = -100;
```

To complete OnGUI(), we physically draw our texture over the screen:

```
//Fade script
//excerpt from OnGUI() function
    //draw texture over screen
    GUI.DrawTexture(_screenRect, _texture);
}
```

At this point, the nuts and bolts of our Fade script are in place. However, we need a way to trigger the events of the Fade script to take place from elsewhere in our game. Enter the ToggleFade() function:

```
//Fade script
//ToggleFade() function
public void ToggleFade() {

    //reverse flag
    isFadingIn = !isFadingIn;
```

```
//unpause
isPaused = false;

//reset start time
_startTime = Time.time;
}
```

Any time ToggleFade() is called, our isFadingIn flag is reversed. Hence, if we previously faded the screen in, we will fade the screen out. Or, if we last faded out, we will now fade in. Also, the isPause flag is set to false, and the _startTime is reset to the current time. Effectively, these actions begin a new transition immediately. Since our scenes always fade in when loaded and then out before exited, ToggleFade() gives us a convenient way to trigger these events. For reference, the complete Fade script is provided:

```
//Fade script
public class Fade : MonoBehaviour {

    //alpha limits
    public float minAlpha, maxAlpha;

    //duration, in seconds
    public float duration;

    //time when fade cycle started
    private float _startTime;

    //current alpha level
    private float _alpha;

    //whether currently fading in
    private bool isFadingIn;

    //whether fade is paused
    private bool isPaused;

    //texture used to create effect
    private Texture2D _texture;

    //screen rectangle
    private Rect _screenRect;

    //awake
    void Awake() {

        //set limits
        minAlpha = 0.0f;
        maxAlpha = 1.0f;
        duration = 1.0f;

        //set flags
        isPaused = false;
        isFadingIn = false;

        //set alpha
        _alpha = maxAlpha;
```

```
        //create fade texture
        _texture = new Texture2D(1, 1, TextureFormat.ARGB32,
          false);
        _texture.SetPixel(0, 0, Color.black);
        _texture.Apply();

        //create screen rect
        _screenRect = new Rect(0, 0, Screen.width, Screen.height);
    }

    //update
    void Update() {

        //if not paused
        if (isPaused == false) {

            //update alpha
            UpdateAlpha();
        }
    }

    //toggle fade
    public void ToggleFade() {

        //reverse flag
        isFadingIn = !isFadingIn;

        //unpause
        isPaused = false;

        //reset start time
        _startTime = Time.time;

    }

    //update alpha
    private void UpdateAlpha() {

        //calculate cumulative duration
        float cumulativeDuration = Time.time - _startTime;

        //calculate percentage of duration complete
        float pct = Mathf.Clamp01(cumulativeDuration / duration);

        //check fade direction
        switch (isFadingIn) {

            //fading in
            case true:

                //alpha less than max
                if (_alpha < maxAlpha) {

                    //update alpha
                    _alpha = minAlpha + pct * (maxAlpha
                      - minAlpha);
                }

                //otherwise
                else {
```

```
            //set to max
            _alpha = maxAlpha;

            //pause
            isPaused = true;

        }
        break;

    //fading out
    case false:

        //alpha greater than min
        if (_alpha > minAlpha) {

            //update alpha
            _alpha = minAlpha + (1.0f - pct) * (maxAlpha
                - minAlpha);
        }

        //otherwise
        else {

            //set to min
            _alpha = minAlpha;

            //pause
            isPaused = true;

        }

        break;

    //default
    default:
        break;

    }

}

//update texture
void OnGUI() {

    //update color
    Color color = Color.black;
    color.a = _alpha;
    GUI.color = color;

    //place texture in front of all objects
    GUI.depth = -100;

    //draw texture over screen
    GUI.DrawTexture(_screenRect, _texture);

}

}
```

Later on, we will manage all of our fade transitions from a centralized source. At the moment, find a sensible way to test your fade in and out transitions. For instance, you could open your Load scene and add a temporary object with a Fade script attached. Call to its `ToggleFade()` function to execute both the fade in and fade out transitions. Running a test such as this will allow you to see that your Fade script is functioning properly. Make adjustments as needed until you have it working.

■ Challenge: Ease the Fade Transition

Currently, your fade transitions operate in a *linear* fashion. That is, per each unit of time, your texture's alpha transparency increases or decreases by the same amount. In fact, you could calculate the exact change in transparency per unit of time by using this formula:

(end alpha – start alpha) / duration

For instance, if we fade in from 0 to 1 alpha over a period of 1,000 milliseconds (1 second), we know that our alpha increases by 1/1,000 per millisecond: (1 – 0) / 1,000. Since the transition is linear, the alpha will always change by 1/1,000 every millisecond.

In contrast, we can apply *easing* to change the way our transition works. Easing involves the use of mathematical formulas to alter the rate at which events occur. Figure 9.2 provides a comparison between linear and eased fade in transitions.

It may be helpful to think of easing as a gradual acceleration or deceleration, rather than as a linear change. Imagine a race car speeding around a track at top speed. When the driver applies the brakes, the car rapidly decelerates at first. As the car slows in speed, its deceleration also slows. Therefore, it takes quite some time until the car gently rolls to a complete stop. This pattern of deceleration can be represented by a mathematical equation. Indeed, a wide variety of movement patterns can be represented through easing.

Easing is a common game development technique that helps make things feel more natural and appealing. Often, easing is applied to movement, physics, animations, and UI. Actually, you already practiced a similar effect when you smoothed the movement of your camera way back in Chapter 1. However, this time around, you will more formally explore the use of easing equations

Start   End

Figure 9.2 Examples of linear and eased fade in transitions are demonstrated across several frames. Both begin completely black and end fully visible. However, the linear transition reveals the screen consistently, while the eased transition accelerates to reveal the screen slowly at first, then rapidly toward the end.

to produce a smooth transition between your scenes. The requirements for this challenge are:

1. Apply an easing equation to adjust the fade in and out transitions.

2. Test the fade in and out transitions within a scene to ensure they work.

Hint: Select an Easing Equation

There are very many easing equations to choose from. You could also create your own, if you are so inclined. The most common easing equations apply exponential functions, such as quadratic (x^2), cubic (x^3), or quartic (x^4), to gradually increase or decrease a value toward a desired target. For example, consider a linear transition from 0 to 1, where we add 0.2 at each step. Our sequence would go like this: 0, 0.2, 0.4, 0.6, 0.8, 1.0. On the other hand, consider an eased transition where we square each step. We would arrive at this sequence: 0, 0.04, 0.16, 0.36, 0.64, 1.0. As you can see, the first few steps are very close together, whereas the last few make huge leaps. In terms of a fade in transition, this would appear as a black screen that slowly changes at first, but ends by rapidly revealing the game screen. Hence, easing gives the impression that the transition is affected by inertia and momentum, which gives it a more lifelike quality. This is but one of many ways that you can use easing to subtly change your transitions. For more information and examples, see Robert Penner's easing functions (Penner, n.d.). Take some time to review this reference and experiment with different easing equations. Once you find a look that is suitable for your fade transitions, proceed to the next section.

Hint: Apply an Easing Equation

So, you've selected an easing equation. Regardless of your choice, it's time to implement it inside your Fade script. The key thing to consider is that the easing equation alters your existing linear calculations. Thus, you can work with what you already have. For instance, the previous example solution calculated the alpha for fading in like this:

```
//Fade script
//excerpt from UpdateAlpha() function
//fade in alpha calculation
_alpha = minAlpha + pct * (maxAlpha - minAlpha);
```

In words, this code starts with minimum possible alpha (0 in our case). The percentage of time completed thus far is multiplied by the maximum alpha minus the minimum alpha (1 − 0 in our case). The final alpha value is calculated by adding these two values together. You know that this is a linear equation, because each percentage of time that passes is treated the same. For example, every 1% of the total duration that passes is guaranteed to add 0.01 to the alpha value, calculated as 0 + 0.01 * (1 − 0). Thus, if you want to ease this transition, you need to find a way to manipulate the alpha values calculated over time. Instead of adding the same amount of alpha for every timeframe, you want to apply an easing equation to determine the alpha calculation at each step. You could accomplish this in a variety of ways in your Fade script, such as writing functions to apply the easing adjustment or directly modifying your alpha calculation equations. Note that your calculations may differ based on whether you are fading in or out. See if you can apply easing in your code and test the resulting fade transitions in your game.

Example Solution: Ease the Fade Transition

The example solution builds from the previous linear Fade script and incorporates certain changes to implement easing. The updates to the Fade script are highlighted. To begin, we add two Boolean flags to our Fade script. These flags make it easy for us optionally apply easing to our transitions:

```
//Fade script
//easing flags
public bool isEaseIn, isEaseOut;
```

These flags are defaulted to `true` in `Awake()`:

```
//Fade script
//excerpt from Awake() function
isEaseIn = true;
isEaseOut = true;
```

Two new functions manage the application of our easing equations. For fading in, we have `EaseIn()`:

```
//Fade script
//EaseIn() function
private float EaseIn(float thePctTime, int thePower) {

    //percent complete
    float pct;

    //calculate percent complete
    pct = Mathf.Pow(thePctTime, thePower);

    //return
    return pct;
}
```

The `EaseIn()` function accepts arguments that represent the percentage of time completed thus far and the power of our easing equation. Conveniently, this function can accept any power, so it is easy for us to apply a quadratic (x^2), cubic (x^3), quartic (x^4), or any similar easing equation. With `Mathf.Pow()` (Unity Technologies 2016h), the percentage of time complete is raised to the indicated power and returned. For fading out, the `EaseOut()` function is nearly identical, with the exception that the percentage of time complete is gradually decreased:

```
//Fade script
//EaseOut() function
private float EaseOut(float thePctTime, int thePower) {

    //percent complete
    float pct;
```

```
//calculate percent complete
pct = 1.0f - Mathf.Pow(1.0f - thePctTime, thePower);

//return
return pct;
}
```

The logic behind the EaseIn() and EaseOut() functions is to manipulate the percentage of time complete when calculating the _alpha value inside UpdateAlpha(). Interestingly, our overall transition still lasts for the same amount of time. That's because we only adjust the percentage when calculating our eased alpha value. See the bolded code in our revised UpdateAlpha() function:

```
//Fade script
//UpdateAlpha() function
private void UpdateAlpha() {

    //calculate cumulative duration
    float cumulativeDuration = Time.time - _startTime;

    //calculate percentage of duration complete
    float pct = Mathf.Clamp01(cumulativeDuration / duration);

    //check fade direction
    switch (isFadingIn) {

        //fading in
        case true:

            //if easing in
            if (isEaseIn == true) {

                //update pct for easing
                pct = EaseIn(pct, 2);

            }

            //alpha less than max
            if (_alpha < maxAlpha) {

                //update alpha
                _alpha = minAlpha + pct * (maxAlpha - minAlpha);

            }

            //otherwise
            else {

                //set to max
                _alpha = maxAlpha;

                //pause
                isPaused = true;

            }

            break;
```

```
        //fading out
        case false:

            //if easing out
            if (isEaseOut == true) {

                //update pct for easing
                pct = EaseIn(pct, 2);

            }

            //alpha greater than min
            if (_alpha > minAlpha) {

                //update alpha
                _alpha = minAlpha + (1.0f - pct) * (maxAlpha
                    - minAlpha);

            }

            //otherwise
            else {

                //set to min
                _alpha = minAlpha;

                //pause
                isPaused = true;

            }

            break;

        //default
        default:

            break;

    }
}
```

The two Boolean flags we previously created are used to determine whether or not to apply easing. This allows us to use any combination of easing, such as none, ease in only, ease out only, or both ease in and ease out. If easing is applied, the associated function is called either `EaseIn()` or `EaseOut()`. Again, these functions adjust the `pct` variable prior to calculating the current `_alpha` value. Effectively, this applies easing by adjusting the alpha value to match our choice easing equation, rather than using a linear gradient. In the example code, a power of 2 is used, which indicates a quadratic easing equation. That's all you need to update to apply easing to your Fade script. Test different easing combinations and powers to witness the impact on your fade transitions. For the record, the entire example Fade script is presented:

```
//Fade script
public class Fade : MonoBehaviour {
```

```
//alpha limits
public float minAlpha, maxAlpha;

//duration, in seconds
public float duration;

//easing flags
public bool isEaseIn, isEaseOut;

//time when fade cycle started
private float _startTime;

//current alpha level
private float _alpha;

//whether currently fading in
private bool isFadingIn;

//whether fade is paused
private bool isPaused;

//texture used to create effect
private Texture2D _texture;

//screen rectangle
private Rect _screenRect;

//awake
void Awake() {

    //set limits
    minAlpha = 0.0f;
    maxAlpha = 1.0f;
    duration = 1.0f;

    //set easing
    isEaseIn = true;
    isEaseOut = true;

    //set flags
    isPaused = false;
    isFadingIn = false;

    //set alpha
    _alpha = maxAlpha;

    //create fade texture
    _texture = new Texture2D(1, 1, TextureFormat.ARGB32,
    false);
    _texture.SetPixel(0, 0, Color.black);
    _texture.Apply();

    //create screen rect
    _screenRect = new Rect(0, 0, Screen.width, Screen.height);
}

//update
void Update() {
```

```
        //if not paused
        if (isPaused == false) {

            //update alpha
            UpdateAlpha();
        }
    }

    //toggle fade
    public void ToggleFade() {

        //reverse flag
        isFadingIn = !isFadingIn;

        //unpause
        isPaused = false;

        //reset start time
        _startTime = Time.time;
    }

    //ease in
    private float EaseIn(float thePctTime, int thePower) {

        //percent complete
        float pct;

        //calculate percent complete
        pct = Mathf.Pow(thePctTime, thePower);

        //return
        return pct;
    }

    //ease out
    private float EaseOut(float thePctTime, int thePower) {

        //percent complete
        float pct;

        //calculate percent complete
        pct = 1.0f - Mathf.Pow(1.0f - thePctTime, thePower);

        //return
        return pct;
    }

    //update alpha
    private void UpdateAlpha() {

        //calculate cumulative duration
        float cumulativeDuration = Time.time - _startTime;

        //calculate percentage of duration complete
        float pct = Mathf.Clamp01(cumulativeDuration / duration);

        //check fade direction
        switch (isFadingIn) {
```

```
//fading in
case true:

    //if easing in
    if (isEaseIn == true) {

        //update pct for easing
        pct = EaseIn(pct, 2);

    }

    //alpha less than max
    if (_alpha < maxAlpha) {

        //update alpha
        _alpha = minAlpha + pct * (maxAlpha
        - minAlpha);

    }

    //otherwise
    else {

        //set to max
        _alpha = maxAlpha;

        //pause
        isPaused = true;

    }

    break;

//fading out
case false:

    //if easing out
    if (isEaseOut == true) {

        //update pct for easing
        pct = EaseIn(pct, 2);

    }

    //alpha greater than min
    if (_alpha > minAlpha) {

        //update alpha
        _alpha = minAlpha + (1.0f - pct) * (maxAlpha
          - minAlpha);

    }

    //otherwise
    else {

        //set to min
        _alpha = minAlpha;
```

```
                    //pause
                    isPaused = true;

                }

                break;

            //default
            default:
                break;
        }
    }

    //update texture
    void OnGUI() {

        //update color
        Color color = Color.black;
        color.a = _alpha;
        GUI.color = color;

        //place texture in front of all objects
        GUI.depth = -100;

        //draw texture over screen
        GUI.DrawTexture(_screenRect, _texture);
    }

} //end class
```

▌ Challenge: Coordinate the Timing

You've completed your Fade script. It's time to get serious about implementing it throughout your game. Up to this point, you may just have been testing your script to make sure it works in a single scene. Now you need to step up your implementation and apply it to all scenes. Think about how you will manage your transitions throughout the entire game. You may want to do so from a centralized source in your code. For this challenge, you should apply your fade in and fade out transitions to every scene in the game. Hence, every scene will fade in from black when loaded and fade out to black when exited. After implementing your transitions, you need to test your entire game to ensure that no unexpected factors interfere with the player experience. This requires some coordination between the timing of your transitions and gameplay elements. The requirements for this challenge are:

1. Apply the fade in and fade out transitions to all scenes in the game.

2. Coordinate the timing of scene transitions and gameplay elements to ensure a smooth player experience.

Hint: Use Time-Based Scene Transitions

As is often true with our implementations, the Fade script doesn't run itself. It needs to be triggered by an outside entity to work. The StateManager is an excellent choice to be the arbiter of transitions. It already handles all of the scene switching in our game. Since all scenes have transitions, it makes sense that the StateManager handles them too.

However, we have introduced an added element of time into our game. Previously, our StateManager's `SwitchSceneTo()` function immediately transitioned from one scene to another. Thus, you need to update your `SwitchSceneTo()` function to accommodate time-based transitions. Basically, you don't want the scene to be switched until after the entire fade out transition is complete. For example, when moving from your Load scene to your Menu scene, you want the loading screen to completely finish fading out before progressing to the main menu. Otherwise, your transition would get cut off as Unity deletes everything in the scene and loads the subsequent one. This would be jarring and unpleasant to the player. Find a way to adjust your StateManager script to handle our time-based transitions appropriately.

After adding the necessary bits to your StateManager script, you may need to update any existing calls to the `SwitchSceneTo()` function throughout your game. Once finished, you should be able to begin your game as normal. With your Fade script and StateManager coordinated, notice that every scene fades in and out pleasantly and professionally.

Hint: Be Aware of Unexpected Gameplay Events

The timing of our transitions impacts more than just scene switching. Most importantly, we never want to allow a visual effect to interfere with our gameplay. If you played through your game with a careful eye, you might notice some problems that have cropped up. We want to make adjustments to subdue these problems, so they aren't a nuisance to the player.

For example, one problem occurs in the dungeon scenes. If a drake is spawned in the vicinity of Luna when the scene loads, it will immediately start chasing after her. However, the screen is fading in from black when the level is loaded. This creates an unfair situation for the player. To fix this problem, we could delay the movement of the drakes, ensure that they always spawn far enough away from Luna, or choose from a host of alternative solutions. Pick one and implement it.

A related problem occurs when exiting our dungeon scenes. Once Luna takes the stairs, the scene takes time to fade out, but the drakes keep moving! This puts Luna in a completely defenseless position for the duration of the transition. Again, we must eliminate this possibility. To fix this problem, we could do something like stop the movement of the drakes or disable collision detection once Luna safely reaches the stairs.

You definitely want to correct these gameplay faults in the dungeon scene. Play through your game and look for any other instances where your gameplay can be adjusted to accommodate transitions. Also, in the future, be wary of how polishing refinements such as this may interfere with your existing gameplay. Always be sure to make revisions where necessary to ensure a fair player experience.

Example Solution: Coordinate the Timing

Let's review the final modifications required to fully implement transitions into our game. The Fade script does not require any adjustments beyond the previous challenges. However, the StateManager should take control of all transitions in the game. Therefore, in our StateManager script, we add a Fade script as a variable:

```
//StateManager script
public Fade fade;
```

Next, inside our accessor, we initialize the Fade script as part of our singleton instance. Hence, our Fade script becomes attached to our StateManager. This allows the StateManager to control our game's transitions:

```
//StateManager script
//excerpt from singleton accessor
_Instance.fade = StateManagerObj.AddComponent<Fade>();
```

Then, we update the SwitchSceneTo() function. Here, the function is transformed into a coroutine. This allows us to easily use WaitForSeconds() to introduce delays that accommodate our fade transitions. The modifications are in bold:

```
//StateManager script
//SwitchSceneTo() function
public IEnumerator SwitchSceneTo(string theScene) {

    //save
    DataManager.Instance.SaveData();

    //fade
    fade.ToggleFade();

    //delay
    yield return new WaitForSeconds(fade.duration);

    //check win conditions
    //retrieve dungeon data
    Dictionary<string, bool> dungeonData = DataManager.Instance.
      currentSave.dungeonData;

        //check if all dungeons completed
        if (dungeonData["Red"] == true &&
        dungeonData["Green"] == true &&
        dungeonData["Blue"] == true) {

        //create dialogue
        InteractionSystem.Instance.dialogue.
        CreateDialogueWithText("The game is won!");

        //show dialogue
        InteractionSystem.Instance.dialogue.Show();
    }
```

```
    //otherwise
    else {

        //load next scene
        SceneManager.LoadScene(theScene);
    }

    //fade
    fade.ToggleFade();
}
```

Any time the StateManager's SwitchSceneTo() function is called, we use the Fade script's ToggleFade() function to start the fade out transition. Meanwhile, we use WaitForSeconds() to delay the scene switch until after the transition is complete. Last, just after the next scene is loaded, we call ToggleFade() again to fade it in. With these few lines of code, we have ensured that all of our scenes fade in and out.

Notice that we turned our SwitchSceneTo() function into a coroutine. This means we need to update all of the calls throughout our game to use StartCoroutine(). Thus far, our InteractionSystem, Load, Menu, and UserCollision scripts all make calls to SwitchSceneTo(). Make sure to update the calls to SwitchSceneTo() in these scripts. See the example solution code to verify your changes.

With the transitions taken care of, we must remember to fix the aforementioned gameplay problems that were introduced in our dungeon scenes. One strategy is to stop the movement of any drakes and dragons once the transition begins to prevent them from pursuing Luna. This requires some changes to our LevelGenerator's MoveObjectsWithTag() function:

```
//LevelGenerator script
//MoveObjectsWithTag function
public IEnumerator MoveObjectsWithTag(string theTag, bool
theIsEnabled, float theDelay = 0.0f) {

    //delay
    yield return new WaitForSeconds(theDelay);

    //retrieve objects associated with tag
    GameObject[] objects = GameObject.
      FindGameObjectsWithTag(theTag);

    //iterate through objects
    for (int i = 0; i < objects.Length; i++) {

        //retrieve movement script
        AIMove move = objects[i].GetComponent<AIMove>();

        //update movement
        //enabled
        if (move == true && theIsEnabled == true) {

            //start move
            move.StartMove();
        }
```

```
        //disabled
        else if (move == true && theIsEnabled == false) {

            //stop move
            move.StopMove();
        }
    }
}
```

Our expanded MoveObjectsWithTag() function has been converted into a coroutine. It receives an additional Boolean argument (theIsEnabled) to signify whether the characters' movements are being started or stopped, as well as an optional float to specify a delay. If a delay is specified, WaitForSeconds() is applied to suspend the function's execution. Just as before, all characters with the specified tag and their AIMove scripts are retrieved. Then, the Boolean argument is used to either call the characters' StartMove() or StopMove() functions, as appropriate. Thus, our revised MoveObjectsWithTag() function allows us to either start or stop the movement of all characters with a given tag. We can optionally introduce a delay beforehand as well.

One negative impact of the transitions on our gameplay occurs when a drake or dragon pursues Luna before the screen has fully faded in. This is an unfair disadvantage for the player. Therefore, inside LevelGenerator, we apply our revised MoveObjectsWithTag() coroutine to ensure that the drakes and dragons only begin moving after the screen has fully faded in. We do so by incorporating a delayed start to the characters' movement in the GenerateDungeon() function:

```
//LevelGenerator script
//excerpt from GenerateDungeon() function
private void GenerateDungeon() {

    /*
    Code omitted.
    */

    //hero not yet found
    if (isHeroFound == false) {

        /*
        Code omitted.
        */

        //movement
        StartCoroutine(MoveObjectsWithTag("Drake", true, 1.0f));
    }

    //hero found, but dragon not yet defeated
    else if (isHeroFound == true && isDungeonComplete == false) {

        /*
        Code omitted.
        */

        //movement
```

```
        StartCoroutine(MoveObjectsWithTag("Dragon", true, 1.0f));
    }

    /*
    Code omitted.
    */
}
```

On the flip side, when exiting our dungeon scene, we also want to stop all drake and dragon movement. This prevents the player from being unfairly pursued while the screen is fading out. Returning to our UserCollision script, our OnTriggerEnter2D() function stores a local copy of the LevelGenerator script for convenience:

```
//UserCollision script
//excerpt from OnTriggerEnter2D() function
//place code just before switch statement
//retrieve level generator
LevelGenerator levelGen = GameObject.FindWithTag("LevelGenerator").
  GetComponent<LevelGenerator>();
```

With our LevelGenerator, we put a stop to all drakes and dragons when Luna reaches the stairs. There is no need to define the MoveObjectWithTag() function's optional delay argument in this case, since we want to stop the movement immediately:

```
//UserCollision script
//excerpt from OnTriggerEnter2D() function
//stairs collision
case "Stairs":

    //disable collisions
    gameObject.GetComponent<Collider2D>().enabled = false;

    //disable input
    userMove.SetUserInputEnabled(false);

    //disable drakes and dragons
    StartCoroutine(levelGen.MoveObjectsWithTag("Drake", false));
    StartCoroutine(levelGen.MoveObjectsWithTag("Dragon", false));

    //continue to next dungeon level
    StartCoroutine(StateManager.Instance.
      SwitchSceneTo(SceneManager.GetActiveScene().name));

    break;
```

Similarly, we put a halt to the drakes when Luna runs out of collectables and is transported back to the Map scene. This is the other time in our game when we transition out of the dungeon scene and need to stop all non-player characters (NPCs) from moving:

```
//UserCollision script
//excerpt from OnTriggerEnter2D() function
//drake collision
```

```
case "Drake":

    /*
    Code omitted.
    */

    //if inventory is empty
    if (inventory.numObjects <= inventory.minObjects) {

        //disable collisions
        gameObject.GetComponent<Collider2D>().enabled = false;

        //disable input
        userMove.SetUserInputEnabled(false);

        //disable drakes
        StartCoroutine(levelGen.MoveObjectsWithTag("Drake",
          false));

        //switch scene
        StartCoroutine(StateManager.SwitchSceneTo("Map"));
    }
    break;
```

Congratulations on fully implementing your fade in and fade out transitions! Not only did you put your transitions to work, but you also accommodated them nicely within the scope of your game to ensure a pleasant player experience. Play through your game and enjoy the pageantry of majestic fade sequences.

Summary

In this chapter, you created the most widespread and effective transition known to games. All of your scenes pleasantly fade in and out as they switch between one another. In addition, you experimented with easing effects to fine-tune your fade transitions. Furthermore, you practiced adjusting your game's timing to accommodate scene transitions. Having succeeded in these challenges, you should be able to apply all of these game implementation techniques:

- Create fade in and out effects to transition between scenes

- Smooth scene transitions with easing

- Use timing to manage the transition between scenes effectively

- Coordinate game states and scene transitions

Your game is looking better by the hour and progressing towards release. However, there are still a couple of major elements that we have yet to explore. Without them, no game can be considered complete. In the next chapter, we'll tackle animation, which is a topic of tremendous importance. Excitingly, the time has come to transform our static sprites into living, breathing characters.

References

Penner, R. n.d. Robert Penner's Easing Functions. http://robertpenner.com/easing/ (accessed January 7, 2016).

Unity Technologies. 2016a. Canvas. http://docs.unity3d.com/Manual/class-Canvas.html (accessed January 7, 2016).

Unity Technologies. 2016b. Color.black. http://docs.unity3d.com/ScriptReference/Color-black.html (accessed January 7, 2016).

Unity Technologies. 2016c. GUI. http://docs.unity3d.com/ScriptReference/GUI.html (accessed January 7, 2016).

Unity Technologies. 2016d. GUI.color. http://docs.unity3d.com/ScriptReference/GUI-color.html (accessed January 7, 2016).

Unity Technologies. 2016e. GUI.depth. http://docs.unity3d.com/ScriptReference/GUI-depth.html (accessed January 7, 2016).

Unity Technologies. 2016f. GUI.DrawTexture. http://docs.unity3d.com/ScriptReference/GUI.DrawTexture.html (accessed January 7, 2016).

Unity Technologies. 2016g. Mathf.Clamp01. http://docs.unity3d.com/ScriptReference/Mathf.Clamp01.html (accessed January 7, 2016).

Unity Technologies. 2016h. Mathf.Pow. http://docs.unity3d.com/ScriptReference/Mathf.Pow.html (accessed January 7, 2016).

Unity Technologies. 2016i. MonoBehaviour.OnGUI(). http://docs.unity3d.com/ScriptReference/MonoBehaviour.OnGUI.html (accessed January 7, 2016).

Unity Technologies. 2016j. Rect. http://docs.unity3d.com/ScriptReference/Rect.html (accessed January 7, 2016).

Unity Technologies. 2016k. Texture2D. http://docs.unity3d.com/ScriptReference/Texture2D.html (accessed January 7, 2016).

Unity Technologies. 2016l. Texture2D.Apply. http://docs.unity3d.com/ScriptReference/Texture2D.Apply.html (accessed January 7, 2016).

Unity Technologies. 2016m. Texture2D.SetPixel. http://docs.unity3d.com/ScriptReference/Texture2D.SetPixel.html (accessed January 7, 2016).

Unity Technologies. 2016n. TextureFormat. http://docs.unity3d.com/ScriptReference/TextureFormat.html (accessed January 7, 2016).

10 The World Is in Motion

One of the best things you can do to make your game world come to life is to introduce animations. No matter how good your core implementations are, they can't compensate for the fact that your world feels static and lifeless. However, by animating your game, you can greatly improve its appeal. In the challenges ahead, you will use code to transform simple sprites into living, breathing characters. Further, you will create a system that allows you to manage several animations for each character in your game world.

Goals

By the end of this chapter, you will be able to apply these game implementation techniques:

- Animate the characters of the game world.

- Slice a sprite sheet into individual animation frames using code.

- Create timed, looping animations composed of frames.

- Manage multiple animations for a variety of different characters.

■ Required Files

In this chapter, you will use the following files from the *Software > Chapter_10* folder (https://www.crcpress.com/Learn-to-Implement-Games-with-Code/Quick/p/book/9781498753388).

- The contents of the Challenge folder to create, code, and test your solution

- The contents of the Solution folder to compare your solution to the example solution

■ Challenge: Slice the Sprite Sheet

Open the provided challenge project. Navigate to the *Assets > Sprites* folder and find the SpriteSheet image (Figure 10.1). Recall that all of the visuals in our game have been condensed into a single sprite sheet image (Figure 10.2). Focus on the first few rows of the sprite sheet. As you can see, each character in our game has several different frames. We will use these different images to make our characters do things like walk in different directions, call for help, and celebrate victory. Conveniently, we can use code to slice a single sprite sheet into many individual animation frames. This is the first step towards building our animation system. Once we isolate the individual frames, we can proceed to animate them. The requirements for this challenge are:

1. Create a SpriteSlicer script that slices a sprite sheet into individual animation frames.

2. Ensure that the animation frames are stored and accessible throughout the game.

Hint: Slice the Sprite Sheet into Frames

As you know, we have a single sprite sheet that is composed of many individual 64×64 pixel (px) images (Figure 10.2). We want to code our SpriteSlicer script to take our sprite sheet, break it down, and store each individual image. From there, we will be able to use the individual images as animation frames.

When crafting your SpriteSlicer script, think about how you will store the original sprite sheet, as well as the collection of individual animation frames. You used the `Texture2D` class to create your fade transition in Chapter 9. Conveniently, your sprite sheet can be stored as a `Texture2D` in your SpriteSlicer script. You can think of your sprite sheet as a tile map, similar to the backgrounds used throughout your scenes. For instance, your Map scene's background is made up of different grass tiles, which are placed at row and column positions to form a grid. Likewise, you can treat your sprite sheet as a grid composed of individual images. Therefore, you can iterate over the rows and columns of your sprite sheet. As you do so, you can extract

Figure 10.1 Find the SpriteSheet image in the *Assets > Sprites* folder.

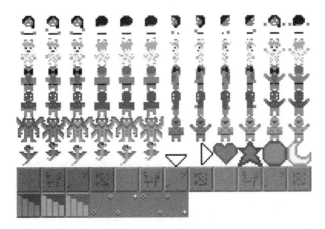

Figure 10.2 All of our game's graphics have been condensed into a single sprite sheet image.

the individual animation frames using the `Sprite` class (Unity Technologies 2016a) and the `Sprite.Create()` function (Unity Technologies 2016b). Once you have iterated through your entire sprite sheet, you should have a collection of individual animation frames stored for future reference.

Hint: Integrate the Sprite Slicer

At this point, your SpriteSlicer script should traverse your sprite sheet and break it into a collection of individual animation frames. Now, it is ready to be integrated into your game. You may choose to treat your SpriteSlicer as a persistent object that exists throughout the duration of the game. This allows you to chop up the sprite sheet when the game is initially loaded. From that point forward, any time you need to animate something, you can refer to the SpriteSlicer's collection of sprites. For this method, you should return to your Load scene, create a `GameObject`, and add the SpriteSlicer script to it. Importantly, remember to prevent your SpriteSlicer from being destroyed when your game switches scenes. You want it to stick around throughout the game, since you will be animating characters throughout every scene.

Example Solution: Slice the Sprite Sheet

Your SpriteSlicer script can be composed of as little as a few variables and one primary function. In accord with the responsibilities of the script, we store variables to hold the original sprite sheet, the collection of sliced frames, and the size of our sprites:

```
//SpriteSlicer script
public class SpriteSlicer : MonoBehaviour {

    //sprite sheet
    public Texture2D spriteSheet;

    //sprite size, in pixels
    public int spriteSize;

    //individual frames
    public Sprite[,] frames;
```

Since we want our SpriteSlicer to endure throughout the game, we apply DontDestroyOnLoad() in its Awake() function:

```
//SpriteSlicer script
//Awake() function
void Awake() {

    //prevent destruction
    DontDestroyOnLoad(this);
}
```

The heart of our SpriteSlicer script lies in the SliceSprites() function, which we will break down, piece by piece:

```
//SpriteSlicer script
public Sprite[,] SliceSprites(Texture2D theSheet, int
  theSpriteSize) {

    //retrieve dimensions
    int numRow = theSheet.height / theSpriteSize;
    int numCol = theSheet.width / theSpriteSize;

    //store frames
    Sprite[,] allFrames = new Sprite[numRow, numCol];

    //iterate through rows
    for (int row = 0; row < numRow; row++) {

        //iterate through columns
        for (int col = 0; col < numCol; col++) {

            //create rectangle at position in sheet
            Rect sliceRect = new Rect(
                col * theSpriteSize,
                row * theSpriteSize,
                theSpriteSize,
                theSpriteSize
                );

            //create pivot point
            Vector2 slicePivot = new Vector2(0.5f, 0.5f);

            //create slice
            Sprite slice = Sprite.Create(theSheet, sliceRect,
              slicePivot);

            /*
            Modify the row calculation to switch the sprite sheet
            origin from bottom-left (default) to top-left. This
            allows the sprite sheet locations to be read from top
            to bottom, left to right.
            */
            //add to collection
            allFrames[numRow - 1 - row, col] = slice;
        }
    }

    //return
    return allFrames;
}
```

The `SliceSprites()` function returns a 2D array of the `Sprite` type. Remember that our sprite sheet can be seen as a grid of rows and columns with each individual image occupying one coordinate position. The 2D array is a mathematical representation of that grid. Hence, this function returns what is ultimately our collection of animation frames. In addition, `SliceSprites()` accepts the original sprite sheet and the size of our frames, in pixels:

```
//SpriteSlicer script
//excerpt from SliceSprites() function
public Sprite[,] SliceSprites(Texture2D theSheet, int
    theSpriteSize) {
```

To calculate the number of rows and columns for our 2D array, we divide the dimensions of the sprite sheet by the dimensions of our frames. Next, we initialize a local version of the 2D array to store the animation frames:

```
//SpriteSlicer script
//excerpt from SliceSprites() function
//retrieve dimensions
int numRow = theSheet.height / theSpriteSize;
int numCol = theSheet.width / theSpriteSize;

//store frames
Sprite[,] allFrames = new Sprite[numRow, numCol];
```

Then, we iterate over every spot in our 2D array using nested `for` loops. This ensures we traverse every row and column position in our sprite sheet:

```
//SpriteSlicer script
//excerpt from SliceSprites() function
//iterate through rows
for (int row = 0; row < numRow; row++) {

    //iterate through columns
    for (int col = 0; col < numCol; col++) {

        /*
        Code omitted.
        */
}
```

For each position, we execute the same actions. First, we create a rectangle that is located at the row–column position in our sprite sheet and has dimensions equal to the size of our animation frames:

```
//SpriteSlicer script
//excerpt from SliceSprites() function
//create rectangle at position in sheet
Rect sliceRect = new Rect(
    col * theSpriteSize,
    row * theSpriteSize,
    theSpriteSize,
    theSpriteSize
    );
```

Second, we establish a pivot point for the frame in `Vector2` format (Unity Technologies 2016d), which Unity uses as the origin of the image (Unity Technologies 2016c). We could technically set any pivot point we want, but since almost everything in Unity uses a center origin, we maintain that tradition by using x–y values of 0.5:

```
//SpriteSlicer script
//excerpt from SliceSprites() function
//create pivot point
Vector2 slicePivot = new Vector2(0.5f, 0.5f);
```

Third, we're ready to place a call to the Sprite.Create() function, which creates a brand new Sprite by copying the data located at the selected position in our sprite sheet. We pass into the Sprite.Create() function our sprite sheet, the rectangle defining the frame to extract, and the pivot point we previously made:

```
//SpriteSlicer script
//excerpt from SliceSprites() function
//create slice
Sprite slice = Sprite.Create(theSheet, sliceRect, slicePivot);
```

At this point, we have extracted an animation frame from our sprite sheet and saved it as a Sprite. Our fourth and final step is to add it to our collection for safe keeping:

```
//SpriteSlicer script
//excerpt from SliceSprites() function
/*
Modify the row calculation to switch the sprite sheet
origin from bottom-left (default) to top-left. This
allows the sprite sheet locations to be read from top
to bottom, left to right.
*/
//add to collection
allFrames[numRow - 1 - row, col] = slice;
```

As noted, the index value was manipulated to yield a 2D array of frames that matches our original sprite sheet as read from top-to-bottom, left-to-right. This makes the top-left image in our 2D array to have a (0, 0) index. Hence, it is easy to refer to the original sprite sheet and count rows and columns to find the exact animation frames that you want (Figure 10.3). If you simply add the frames without making this adjustment, the bottom-left image of our original sprite sheet would be stored in the (0, 0) position in our 2D array instead. Either way, we will need to refer to these frames by their exact index positions later on. Therefore, make sure you have a good understanding of how your 2D array is organized.

Last, we want to slice our sprite sheet while our game is being loaded. Therefore, in Start(), we go ahead and set our collection of frames equal to the result of our SliceSprites() function:

```
//SpriteSlicer script
//Start() function
void Start() {

    //slice sprite sheet into frames
    frames = SliceSprites(spriteSheet, spriteSize);
}
```

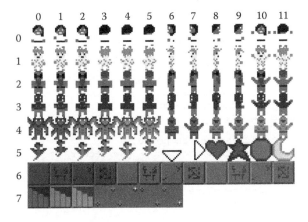

Figure 10.3 The rows (horizontal) and columns (vertical) have been numbered for easy reference to our 2D array.

For convenience, the entire SpriteSlicer script is presented:

```
//SpriteSlicer script
public class SpriteSlicer : MonoBehaviour {

    //sprite sheet
    public Texture2D spriteSheet;

    //sprite size, in pixels
    public int spriteSize;

    //individual frames
    public Sprite[,] frames;

    //awake
    void Awake() {

        //prevent destruction
        DontDestroyOnLoad(this);
    }

    //init
    void Start() {

        //slice sprite sheet into frames
        frames = SliceSprites(spriteSheet, spriteSize);
    }

    //get frames from sprite sheet
    public Sprite[,] SliceSprites(Texture2D theSheet, int
      theSpriteSize) {

        //retrieve dimensions
        int numRow = theSheet.height / theSpriteSize;
        int numCol = theSheet.width / theSpriteSize;

        //store frames
        Sprite[,] allFrames = new Sprite[numRow, numCol];

        //iterate through rows
        for (int row = 0; row < numRow; row++) {
```

```
            //iterate through columns
            for (int col = 0; col < numCol; col++) {
                //create rectangle at position in sheet
                Rect sliceRect = new Rect(
                    col * theSpriteSize,
                    row * theSpriteSize,
                    theSpriteSize,
                    theSpriteSize
                    );

                //create pivot point
                Vector2 slicePivot = new Vector2(0.5f, 0.5f);

                //create slice
                Sprite slice = Sprite.Create(theSheet, sliceRect,
                    slicePivot);

                /*
                Modify the row calculation to switch the sprite
                    sheet
                origin from bottom-left (default) to top-left. This
                allows the sprite sheet locations to be read from
                    top to bottom, left to right.
                */
                //add to collection
                allFrames[numRow - 1 - row, col] = slice;
            }
        }

        //return
        return allFrames;
    }

} //end class
```

This completes the SpriteSlicer script. Remember to create a GameObject in the Load scene and add your script to it. Further, assign the sprite sheet stored in the *Assets > Sprites* folder to the script and set the sprite size to 64 px (Figure 10.4). Subsequently, when the game is started, the sprite sheet will automatically be sliced into frames and stored in the SpriteSlicer script. Thereafter, we can reference our individual frames as needed to create animations.

Figure 10.4 Attach your SpriteSlicer script to a GameObject in the Load scene and set its properties in the Unity editor.

▌ Challenge: Create a Frame Animation

While your SpriteSlicer retrieves individual images from your sprite sheet, your FrameAnimation script places sequences of images together into frame-based animations. The goal for this challenge is to code a generic FrameAnimation script that can be used to create any animation sequence out of frames. For example, your script can use a few images of Luna to create a walking animation or a couple of images to make the Red Knight call for attention. Conveniently, your FrameAnimation script will be reused many times over to create animation sequences for every character in the game. Later, you will efficiently manage multiple animations for specific characters. Before that happens, you need to focus on the FrameAnimation script, which represents one complete animation sequence. To accomplish this challenge, follow these requirements:

1. Create a FrameAnimation script that represents an individual, time-based animation composed of frames.

2. Add relevant controls to your FrameAnimation script.

3. Manage the overall state of an animation, including looping, within your FrameAnimation script.

Hint: Use Frame Animation

All of the animations you will create for your game are based on the same concept. Essentially, multiple static images, called frames, are presented in sequence for a specified period of time. The result is the impression of animated motion. For instance, consider the two frames depicted in Figure 10.5. The first frame shows Luna standing still and facing to the right. The second frame shows Luna taking a step to the right. If we frequently swap the display of these two images while the player moves Luna across the screen, it gives the impression that Luna is walking. We will create many such animations for our game using the various frames that are stored in our sprite sheet.

When designing your FrameAnimation script, remember to think in terms of a single frame–based animation. Of course, storing the necessary frames is essential for making these animations work. However, timing is also an important factor to consider. Make sure to build timing into your script. Ideally, you can specify how fast the frames are swapped on screen or how long the entire animation sequence lasts. This will allow you to experiment with different timings and find the best duration for each animation you wish to create.

Finally, any time a particular frame is selected, you actually need to display it on screen. Assume that your FrameAnimation script will be attached to each character. All of our characters have `SpriteRenderer` components, which display

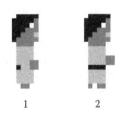

1   2

Figure 10.5 Two frames composing a right-facing walk animation for Luna are depicted. Swapping these frames quickly while moving Luna across the screen would give the impression that she is walking.

an image of the `Sprite` type. Since our SpriteSlicer already stores our animation frames in a `Sprite` collection, you can assign a `Sprite` to a character's `SpriteRenderer` component to make it appear on screen. In fact, every time you want to swap the frame displayed for a character, you can assign a different `Sprite` to its `SpriteRenderer` component.

Hint: Provide Controls

Again, focus on the idea of scripting a single frame–based animation. You want to play different animations at different times throughout your game. Sometimes you may need to stop an animation in place. At other times, you may rapidly switch between two animations, such as when Luna turns to move in a different direction. Similar to using a remote control to facilitate the playback of a movie, your animations can be controlled through actions like play, pause, and stop. Here are some ideas for control functions that you may want to include in your FrameAnimation script:

- Create a new animation sequence, given a series of frames

- Play an animation sequence with optional looping

- Stop an animation sequence, perhaps at a specified frame

- Reset an animation sequence, so it can be played again

Hint: Execute the Animation

Besides controlling the playback of our animations, we must also control the overall state of a given animation. Often, frame-based animations will loop continuously until they are changed. Within each loop of an animation, each frame should be displayed on the screen. Further, you want to implement a time-based mechanism to control how long each frame is displayed. You've successfully implemented time-based systems in the past, such as the fade transition in Chapter 9. Feel free to leverage what you've already done to gain insights into the current challenge.

Generally speaking, you want to keep track of when an animation is started, how long it lasts, and which frames are displayed at which times. Once an animation is complete, loop back to the beginning and start the process all over again. Work to implement a state management system in your FrameAnimation script. For a concrete example, think back to the animation depicted in Figure 10.5. If you had just those frames provided to your script, how would you ensure they are displayed in order, for a specified amount of time, in a repeating loop?

Example Solution: Create a Frame Animation

In this challenge, you needed to create a FrameAnimation script that represents a single frame–based animation sequence. Our FrameAnimation script has these core features: establishing a frame-based animation, controlling playback, and managing the overall animation state. These variables support the stated features:

```
//FrameAnimation script
public class FrameAnimation : MonoBehaviour {
```

```
//animation name
public string animName;

//animation frames
private Sprite[] _frames;

//frames to display per second
private float _fps;

//whether the animation loops
private bool _isLoop;

//time at which current frame started
private float _startTime;

//current frame index
private int _currentFrame;

//whether animation is playing
private bool _isPlaying;
```

The animName gives our animation a name, while the _frames array stores the specific frames associated with the animation. The _fps indicates how many frames per second (fps) are displayed. This is how our time-based mechanism is implemented. It is common to think of animations in terms of the number of frames displayed per second. Continuing, _isLoop is a Boolean flag that determines whether our animation will loop endlessly or stop after a single iteration. Meanwhile, _startTime tracks how long the current frame has been displayed, while _currentFrame is the current frame's index value from the _frames array. Another Boolean variable, _isPlaying, flags whether our animation is currently in progress.

Remember that we need to update the Sprite associated with a character's SpriteRenderer to display a frame on the screen. This is accomplished by the UpdateSprite() function:

```
//FrameAnimation script
//UpdateSprite() function
private void UpdateSprite(Sprite theSprite) {

    //update sprite
    gameObject.GetComponent<SpriteRenderer>().sprite = theSprite;

    //update start time
    _startTime = Time.time;
}
```

Simply, the UpdateSprite() function receives the desired frame as a Sprite argument, updates the attached SpriteRenderer, and resets the _startTime to accurately portray how long the frame has been displayed.

Now we are prepared to create a new animation with our custom initialization function, named InitFrameAnimation():

```
//FrameAnimation script
//InitFrameAnimation() function
public void InitFrameAnimation(string theName, Sprite[] theFrames =
  null, float theFPS = 1.0f, bool theIsLoop = true) {
```

```
//init
animName = theName;
_frames = theFrames;
_fps = theFPS;
_isLoop = theIsLoop;
_currentFrame = 0;
_isPlaying = false;

//update sprite
if (_frames != null) {
    UpdateSprite(_frames[_currentFrame]);
}
}
```

The `InitFrameAnimation()` sets up the basic necessities for any frame-based animation we create. It requires only a name as an argument. Optional arguments include the frames associated with the animation, fps, and whether the animation loops. These are set to default values if they aren't provided. Moreover, we assume the initial frame is 0 (logically, the first index position of the `_frames` array) and that the animation is not yet playing. Last, if frames were provided, we call `UpdateSprite()` to display the initial frame on screen.

Note that the use of optional arguments, as well as default values, gives us some flexibility in how we create frame-based animations. One way is to create them somewhat generically, without specified frames, timing, and other details. The other way is to specify exactly the animation we want and provide all the details. Depending on how we are animating our game, we may want to use both methods at different times. This is why the initialization function allows for both. Of course, you could also create multiple overloaded functions if you prefer to separate these usages into different functions.

Let's focus on our control functions. The example solution uses four different control functions, including `Play()`, `Stop()`, `GoToFrameAndPlay()`, and `GoToFrameAndStop()`. The `Play()` function checks the `_isPlaying` flag. If not already playing, the flag is flipped and the `_startTime` is reset:

```
//FrameAnimation script
//Play() function
public void Play() {

    //if not already playing
    if (_isPlaying == false) {

        //toggle flag
        _isPlaying = true;

        //reset start time
        _startTime = Time.time;
    }
}
```

The `Stop()` function stops all playback of our animation by flipping the `_isPlaying` flag. Effectively, you can think of this function as accomplishing a pause effect as well:

```
//FrameAnimation script
//Stop() function
public void Stop() {
```

```
//toggle flag
_isPlaying = false;
}
```

Furthermore, the GoToFrameAndPlay() function allows us to specify a frame index at which to begin the animation. This is useful if we want to start the animation somewhere other than the first frame or if we want to restart our animation from a specific place after stopping it. The GoToFrameAndPlay() function accepts the frame index as an argument, updates the _currentFrame variable, updates the displayed sprite, and plays the animation:

```
//FrameAnimation script
//GoToFrameAndPlay() function
public void GoToFrameAndPlay(int theFrameIndex) {

    //update frame index
    _currentFrame = theFrameIndex;

    //update sprite
    UpdateSprite(_frames[_currentFrame]);

    //play
    Play();
}
```

Similarly, GoToFrameAndStop() stops all playback at a specific frame. It also accepts a frame index argument, and then updates the _currentFrame variable and the displayed sprite:

```
//FrameAnimation script
//GoToFrameAndStop() function
public void GoToFrameAndStop(int theFrameIndex) {

    //stop
    Stop();

    //update frame index
    _currentFrame = theFrameIndex;

    //update sprite
    UpdateSprite(_frames[_currentFrame]);
}
```

With these functions, we have solid command over the playback of our animations. The final portion of our FrameAnimation script that needs to be implemented is state management. When it is time to switch frames, our UpdateFrame() function handles the job:

```
//FrameAnimation script
//UpdateFrame() function
private void UpdateFrame() {

    //update frame index
    _currentFrame = ++_currentFrame % _frames.Length;

    //if index exceeds bounds and looping
    if (_currentFrame >= _frames.Length && _isLoop == true) {
```

```
    //return to start
    GoToFrameAndPlay(0);
}

//if index exceeds bounds and not looping
else if (_currentFrame >= _frames.Length && _isLoop == false) {

    //stop
    Stop();
}

//otherwise, use valid frame
else {

    //update sprite
    UpdateSprite(_frames[_currentFrame]);
}
}
```

Importantly, we want to make sure to never select a frame index that extends beyond the number of frames in our animation. Therefore, we make a clever calculation to start off the UpdateFrame() function. In words, we use the modulus operator (%) to calculate the new _currentFrame as the remainder of the total number of frames (_frames.Length) divided by 1 plus the old frame index (++_currentFrame). This ensures that we will cycle through our frames one by one and never exceed the highest index value in our _frames array. To verify, try plugging some values into the equation and testing it out:

```
//FrameAnimation script
//excerpt from UpdateFrame() function
//update frame index
_currentFrame = ++_currentFrame % _frames.Length;
```

Next, we use an if statement to sort out the possible animation states. If we happen to reach the final frame and the animation is set to loop, we return to the initial frame and play the animation anew:

```
//FrameAnimation script
//excerpt from UpdateFrame() function
//if index exceeds bounds and looping
if (_currentFrame >= _frames.Length && _isLoop == true) {

    //return to start
    GoToFrameAndPlay(0);
}
```

However, if we reach the final frame in an animation that does not loop, we stop it all together:

```
//FrameAnimation script
//excerpt from UpdateFrame() function
//if index exceeds bounds and not looping
else if (_currentFrame >= _frames.Length && _isLoop == false) {

    //stop
    Stop();
}
```

Yet, if we have not yet reached the end frame in our animation, we continue to update our on-screen display with the current frame:

```
//FrameAnimation script
//excerpt from UpdateFrame() function
//otherwise, use valid frame
else {

    //update sprite
    UpdateSprite(_frames[_currentFrame]);
}
```

Thus, the UpdateFrame() function covers all conditions related to switching from one frame to another in our animation sequence. Still, there is another state-based matter to attend. The CheckFrame() function controls the timing of our frame changes:

```
//FrameAnimation script
//CheckFrame() function
private void CheckFrame() {

    //duration of current frame
    float duration = Time.time - _startTime;

    //duration limit for a single frame
    float limit = 1.0f / _fps;

    //if limit exceeded
    if (duration >= limit) {

        //update frame
        UpdateFrame();
    }
}
```

In CheckFrame(), we calculate the duration that the current frame has been displayed. Since the duration is in seconds form, we divide 1 by the fps to arrive at the amount of time each individual frame should be displayed. Should the duration of the current frame exceed the limit for the current frame, we call UpdateFrame() to switch to the next frame in the sequence.

As is often the case, our trusty Update() function is the final arbiter of state management in our FrameAnimation script. It checks whether the animation is currently playing. If so, it allows our CheckFrame() function to be called, thereby initiating the entire chain of events:

```
//FrameAnimation script
//Update() function
void Update() {

    //if playing
    if (_isPlaying == true) {

        //check frame
        CheckFrame();
    }
}
```

To summarize, the entire FrameAnimation script is provided:

```
//FrameAnimation script
public class FrameAnimation : MonoBehaviour {

    //animation name
    public string animName;

    //animation frames
    private Sprite[] _frames;

    //frames to display per second
    private float _fps;

    //whether the animation loops
    private bool _isLoop;

    //time at which current frame started
    private float _startTime;

    //current frame index
    private int _currentFrame;

    //whether animation is playing
    private bool _isPlaying;

    //custom init
    public void InitFrameAnimation(string theName, Sprite[] theFrames
       = null, float theFPS = 1.0f, bool theIsLoop = true) {

        //init
        animName = theName;
        _frames = theFrames;
        _fps = theFPS;
        _isLoop = theIsLoop;
        _currentFrame = 0;
        _isPlaying = false;

        //update sprite
        if (_frames != null) {
        UpdateSprite(_frames[_currentFrame]);
        }
    }

    //update
    void Update() {

        //if playing
        if (_isPlaying == true) {

            //check frame
            CheckFrame();
        }
    }

    //check whether frame needs to change
    private void CheckFrame() {

        //duration of current frame
        float duration = Time.time - _startTime;
```

```
        //duration limit for a single frame
        float limit = 1.0f / _fps;

        //if limit exceeded
        if (duration >= limit) {

            //update frame
            UpdateFrame();
        }
    }

    //update the current frame
    private void UpdateFrame() {

        //update frame index
        _currentFrame = ++_currentFrame % _frames.Length;

        //if index exceeds bounds and looping
        if (_currentFrame >= _frames.Length && _isLoop == true) {

            //return to start
            GoToFrameAndPlay(0);
        }

        //if index exceeds bounds and not looping
        else if (_currentFrame >= _frames.Length && _isLoop ==
          false) {

            //stop
            Stop();
        }

        //otherwise, use valid frame
        else {

            //update sprite
            UpdateSprite(_frames[_currentFrame]);
        }
    }

    //update the current sprite
    private void UpdateSprite(Sprite theSprite) {

        //update sprite
        gameObject.GetComponent<SpriteRenderer>().sprite =
          theSprite;

        //update start time
        _startTime = Time.time;
    }

    //play
    public void Play() {

        //if not already playing
        if (_isPlaying == false) {

            //toggle flag
            _isPlaying = true;
```

```
        //reset start time
        _startTime = Time.time;
    }
}

//pause
public void Stop() {
    //toggle flag
    _isPlaying = false;
}

//go to a specific animation frame and play
public void GoToFrameAndPlay(int theFrameIndex) {

    //update frame index
    _currentFrame = theFrameIndex;

    //update sprite
    UpdateSprite(_frames[_currentFrame]);

    //play
        Play();
}

//go to a specific animation frame and stop
public void GoToFrameAndStop(int theFrameIndex) {

    //stop
    Stop();

    //update frame index
    _currentFrame = theFrameIndex;

    //update sprite
    UpdateSprite(_frames[_currentFrame]);
}

} //end class
```

You have succeeded in slicing a sprite sheet into individual frames and defining a frame-based animation in your game world. Excitingly, the next phase of this implementation entails managing entire groups of animations. This is where you get to define the various animations that will make your characters come to life!

▌▌ Challenge: Manage Multiple Animations

Your FrameAnimation script allows you to define individual animations. However, if you look at your sprite sheet (Figure 10.2), you'll find that several different frames exist for each character. Since most of our animations only require two frames, we have the resources to create several animations for each character. However, to keep things organized, we need to implement a system for managing all of the animations a character has.

In this challenge, you will create a CharacterAnimator script that can be attached to every character in your game. This script will allow you to define the specific frame animations that are associated with each character. So, by the time you're done, you will have animations established for all of your characters. That puts you one step closer to animating your game world. Specifically, the requirements for this challenge are:

1. Create a CharacterAnimator script that manages multiple frame animations for a given character.

2. Use a CharacterAnimator script to define the animations for each character.

Hint: Manage Characters' Animations

Conceptually, we know that each character can have multiple animations. Since our FrameAnimation script defines any animation we want, we are able to give our different characters different animations. Furthermore, our CharacterAnimator script acts as the centralized source for each character. It will store all of the animations available for a particular character and allow them to be executed as needed throughout the game.

Critically, our CharacterAnimator must store data about a character's animations in a way that is complete and easy to reference. Recall that our FrameAnimation has an `animName` variable, which defines the name of an animation. In addition, the individual frames available to us are stored in the SpriteSlicer script's `frames` array. Hence, referencing the correct animation data requires associating the name of an animation with its frames. Thus, the CharacterAnimator should provide a method for retrieving this information.

Dictionary

One way to associate animation names and frame locations is through a *dictionary*. A dictionary is a type of collection that stores data in key-value pairs (Microsoft Corporation 2016b). A value represents data stored in the collection, while a key allows the data to be accessed. For instance, we could have a key of "MyHero" that allows us to retrieve the value of "Luna." Conveniently, the keys and values in a dictionary do not need to be of the same data type. For example, we could have a `string` key called "NumCollectables" that returns an `int` value of 5.

Things get even more interesting with the dictionary collection. We aren't limited to primitive data types. We can put composite objects, multidimensional arrays, entire collections, and a host of other data into dictionaries. This makes dictionaries quite handy when we need to associate keys and values in complex ways that the array or `List` cannot. However, note that dictionaries are not indexed or ordered like other collections. That means we must always retrieve values from a dictionary using the associated keys. Since the keys are linked to specific values, all of the keys in a dictionary should be unique. However, values may be duplicated. Never assume any particular order for the values stored in a dictionary, because there isn't one. We cannot iterate over dictionaries with an index value and `for` loop like we are accustomed to with other collections. Instead, dictionary iteration should be done with a `foreach` loop.

The following code demonstrates the fundamental usage of dictionaries in C#. After reviewing this information, see if you can implement a dictionary to associate character's animation names and frame locations inside your CharacterAnimator script:

```
//C# dictionary examples
//NOTE: replace KEY and VALUE with data types

//declare a dictionary
Dictionary<KEY, VALUE> exampleDictionary;

//initialize a dictionary
exampleDictionary = new Dictionary<KEY, VALUE>();

//add a key-value pair
exampleDictionary.Add(exampleKey, exampleValue);

//remove a key-value pair
exampleDictionary.Remove(exampleKey);

//remove all key-value pairs from the dictionary
exampleDictionary.Clear();

//retrieve a value using its key
exampleDictionary[exampleKey];

//set the value for a specific key
exampleDictionary[exampleKey] = exampleValue;

//manipulate a value, only if the key exists
//useful for checking if a key exists first to avoid errors
VALUE exampleValue;
if (exampleDictionary.TryGetValue(exampleKey, out exampleValue)) {
    /*
    It's safe to utilize the exampleValue here.
    */
}

//iterate over all key-value pairs
foreach (KeyValuePair aPair in exampleDictionary) {
    /*
    Refer to each key-value pair by the pseudonym, aPair.
    */
}
```

Hint: Implement the Character Animator

It's time to code your CharacterAnimator script. Primarily, this script represents a sort of animation database for an individual character. In contrast, your SpriteSlicer holds the raw frame data for the entire game, while the FrameAnimation represents a single animation composed of any selection of frames. Hence, your CharacterAnimator pulls everything together to create a unique collection of animations that can be associated with a specific character. As mentioned, you need to represent a character's collection of animations in some way, such as a dictionary. Furthermore, you need to be able to access the appropriate frames from the SpriteSlicer and employ a FrameAnimation on demand to execute a character's animations whenever necessary.

Since you only want to create a single CharacterAnimator script and reuse it for every character, your code should be written to facilitate this process. However, every character may have a different set of animations and definitely make use of different frames from the sprite sheet. Thus, you need to think about how you will define the exact animations for each character. This may be a good opportunity to use the Unity editor. You can set up a generic backend system in your CharacterAnimator script, and then define the exact frames and animations for individual characters in the Unity editor.

Hint: Integrate the Character Animator

The final step in this challenge entails deploying the CharacterAnimator script in your game. You should attach your CharacterAnimator script to every character in the *Assets > Prefabs > Characters* folder. Furthermore, define the animation names and frames for each character. Based on the contents of our original sprite sheet (Figure 10.2), here are some suggested animations for the different characters:

- Heroes (Luna, Lily, Pink Beard, Larg)

  - Walk down (facing player)

  - Walk up (facing away from player)

  - Walk left (facing left)

  - Walk right (facing right)

  - Raise arms (facing player)

  - Raise arms (facing away from player)

- Drakes (Red, Green, Blue)

  - Fly/move

- Dragons (Red, Green, Blue)

  - Raise arms (facing player)

- Knights (Red, Green, Blue)

  - Raise arms (facing player)

Example Solution: Manage Multiple Animations

With the help of your CharacterAnimator script and the Unity editor, you can arrange all of your characters' animations. In the example solution, all of a character's animations are stored in a dictionary:

```
//CharacterAnimator script
//animation collection
private Dictionary<string, int[,]> _animations;
```

The _animations dictionary uses a string key, which represents the name of each animation. Meanwhile, the values are stored as a 2D integer array to represent the row and column positions of the frames that compose the animation. Unfortunately, without some custom trickery beyond the scope of this book, the Unity editor doesn't allow us to define values for a dictionary. Therefore, we add two additional public variables, which will show up in the Unity editor and can be defined when attaching a CharacterAnimator script to a character prefab:

```
//CharacterAnimator script
//animation names
public string[] animNames;

//frame locations (name index, row, col)
//set in Unity Inspector
public Vector3[] animLocs;
```

The string array, animNames, will hold the names of a character's animations. Interestingly, a Vector3 array, animLocs, is declared to store the frame positions. The logic behind this system is that we must associate the animNames and animLocs to populate our _animations dictionary. The animNames array will have a number of index values based on the number of animations a character has. The animLocs array will store the individual row and column positions for every frame used by our character. These positions require only two values. Yet, a Vector3 provides us with room for three values. To align the animation names to the appropriate frame locations, we can use the extra slot from our animLocs Vector3 to identify an index value from animNames. For example, suppose Luna's "raise arms" animation is the first one listed in her animNames array and has an index of 0. We identify two frames located at (0, 0) and (0, 10) from our sprite sheet to make this animation. In animLocs, we'll use the first value (x) of our Vector3 to refer to the index of "raise arms" in the animNames array: 0. Then, we'll use the second (y) and third (z) values in our Vector3 to refer to the frames' row and column positions: (0, 0) and (0, 10). Thus, in the end, our animNames contains "raise arms" at index 0. Meanwhile, our animLocs contains (0, 0, 0) at index 0 and (0, 0, 10) at index 1. Later, we can easily match up the values stored in animNames and animLocs to populate our _animations dictionary.

In addition, we establish a FrameAnimation variable. This single FrameAnimation will be reused by our CharacterAnimator script any time an animation is played. Not only is that efficient, but a character can only display one animation at a time, so we really only need one script. Since this FrameAnimation represents the current animation at a moment in time, it is named currentAnim:

```
//CharacterAnimator script
//current frame animation
public FrameAnimation currentAnim;
```

As stated, the animNames and animLocs arrays are defined in the Unity editor for each character prefab. As an example, Figure 10.6 depicts a potential setup for Luna. Of course, you can review the entire example solution project to see how the other characters are arranged. Next, inside Awake(), we use

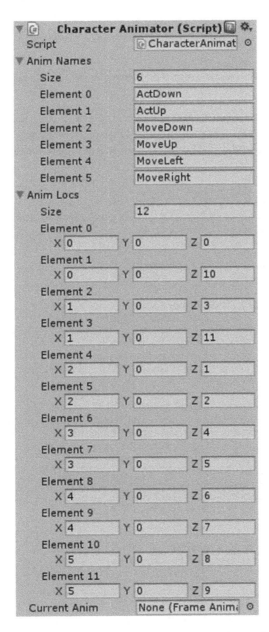

Figure 10.6 A potential CharacterAnimator setup for Luna is depicted.

the `animNames` and `animLocs` arrays to populate our `_animations` dictionary. We also attach a FrameAnimation script to fulfill our `currentAnim` variable:

```
//CharacterAnimator script
//Awake() function
void Awake() {
```

```
//populate animation dictionary
_animations = CreateAnimDict(animNames, animLocs);

//init animation
currentAnim = gameObject.AddComponent<FrameAnimation>();
}
```

Notice the use of a custom CreateAnimDict() function to populate our _animations array. This function takes care of the work necessary to combine our animNames and animLocs arrays into a complete collection of a character's animations:

```
//CharacterAnimator script
//CreateAnimDict() function
private Dictionary<string, int[,]> CreateAnimDict(string[]
    theNames, Vector3[] theLocs) {

    //store result
    Dictionary<string, int[,]> anim = new Dictionary<string,
      int[,]>();

    //loop through animation names
    for (int i = 0; i < theNames.Length; i++) {

        //find locations for animation
        //x = index matching animation name
        Vector3[] vLocs = Array.FindAll(theLocs, loc =>
          loc.x == i);

        //convert locations to int
        //each animation has N rows with 2 frame columns
        int[,] iLocs = new int[vLocs.Length, 2];
        for (int j = 0; j < vLocs.Length; j++) {

            //j = frame index
            //y = row value; z = col value
            iLocs[j, 0] = (int)vLocs[j].y;
            iLocs[j, 1] = (int)vLocs[j].z;
        }

        //add to dictionary
        anim.Add(theNames[i], iLocs);
    }

    //return
    return anim;
}
```

Without surprise, CreateAnimDict() returns a dictionary that matches the profile of our _animations variable. Likewise, it accepts array arguments that match our animNames and animLocs variables. To start, the function initializes a local version of the dictionary:

```
//CharacterAnimator script
//excerpt from CreateAnimDict() function
private Dictionary<string, int[,]> CreateAnimDict(string[]
    theNames, Vector3[] theLocs) {
```

```
//store result
Dictionary<string, int[,]> anim = new Dictionary<string,
    int[,]>();
```

A `for` loop iterates through every animation name provided in the `theNames` argument:

```
//CharacterAnimator script
//excerpt from CreateAnimDict() function
//loop through animation names
for (int i = 0; i < theNames.Length; i++) {
    /*
    Code omitted.
    */
}
```

Inside the loop, a process is repeated for every animation the character has. Recall that we used a `Vector3` to store not only the row and column positions for frames but also their associated animation names. Using the `Array.FindAll()` function (Microsoft Corporation 2016a) in conjunction with a clever lambda expression, we search through the first value (x) of each `Vector3` in our locations array and store the matches in a local array. In other words, we take our animation's index value, search through first `Vector3` value (x) in the frame locations, and take out only those frames that match the animation we are currently working with:

```
//CharacterAnimator script
//excerpt from CreateAnimDict() function
//find locations for animation
//x = index matching animation name
Vector3[] vLocs = Array.FindAll(theLocs, loc => loc.x == i);
```

Truthfully, we only wanted `Vector3` variables so that we could enter values into the Unity editor and accomplish the preceding step. Our actual `_animations` dictionary stores frame coordinates as a 2D integer array. Therefore, we need to convert our `Vector3` coordinates into the appropriate format. To do so, we create a local version of the 2D integer array, iterate over all of the `Vector3` locations, and extract only their row (y) and column (z) values. This leaves us with a 2D integer array that represents the coordinates of our animation frames. Inside the 2D array, each row represents a single frame, while two columns represent the location of the frame in our sprite sheet:

```
//CharacterAnimator script
//excerpt from CreateAnimDict() function
//convert locations to int
//each animation has N rows with 2 frame columns
int[,] iLocs = new int[vLocs.Length, 2];
for (int j = 0; j < vLocs.Length; j++) {

    //j = frame index
    //y = row value; z = col value
    iLocs[j, 0] = (int)vLocs[j].y;
    iLocs[j, 1] = (int)vLocs[j].z;
}
```

Once the animation's name and frame locations are fully prepared, we add them to our local dictionary. We continue this loop until all of the character's animations have been added:

```
//CharacterAnimator script
//excerpt from CreateAnimDict() function
//add to dictionary
anim.Add(theNames[i], iLocs);
```

The last step in our CreateAnimDict() function is to return the local dictionary. Since we previously called CreateAnimDict() back in Awake(), the returned dictionary becomes our fully populated _ animations dictionary:

```
//CharacterAnimator script
//excerpt from CreateAnimDict() function
//return
return anim;
```

At this point, our CharacterAnimator has just a couple of important responsibilities to executed.

The CharacterAnimator acts as an intermediary between the SpriteSlicer, FrameAnimator, our characters, and the rest of the game world. Whenever we want to display a specific animation, we need to access our SpriteSlicer to retrieve a subset of the frames from our sprite sheet. This is accomplished by the FindFramesFor() function:

```
//CharacterAnimator script
//FindFramesFor() function
private Sprite[] FindFramesFor(string theName) {

    //check animation
    int[,] frameLoc;
    if (_animations.TryGetValue(theName, out frameLoc)) {

        //retrieve number of frame locations
        int numFrames = frameLoc.GetLength(0);

        //store frames
        Sprite[] frames = new Sprite[numFrames];

        //retrieve master set of frames
        Sprite[,] allFrames = GameObject.FindWithTag("SpriteSlicer").
          GetComponent<SpriteSlicer>().frames;

        //loop through locations
        for (int i = 0; i < numFrames; i++) {

            //retrieve frame from master set
            frames[i] = allFrames[frameLoc[i, 0], frameLoc[i, 1]];
        }

        //return
        return frames;
    }

    //return
    return null;
}
```

This function accepts an animation name as an argument and returns a Sprite array that contains its frames:

```
//CharacterAnimator script
//excerpt from FindFramesFor() function
private Sprite[] FindFramesFor(string theName) {
```

To prevent an error, we check whether the requested animation can be found in our _animations dictionary using TryGetValue() (Microsoft Corporation 2016c):

```
//CharacterAnimator script
//excerpt from FindFramesFor() function
//check animation
int[,] frameLoc;
if (_animations.TryGetValue(theName, out frameLoc)) {
```

Should the animation not exist, we return null immediately. If indeed the animation exists, we retrieve its quantity of frames. The number of frames is equivalent to the number of rows in the animation's 2D array, hence the use of GetLength(0). We use this value to initialize a local Sprite array. In addition, we retrieve the master set of all frames from our SpriteSlicer. Note that, in this example, the SpriteSlicer has been tagged as "SpriteSlicer" to facilitate use of the GameObject.FindWithTag() function to retrieve it:

```
//CharacterAnimator script
//excerpt from FindFramesFor() function
//retrieve number of frame locations
int numFrames = frameLoc.GetLength(0);

//store frames
Sprite[] frames = new Sprite[numFrames];

//retrieve master set of frames
Sprite[,] allFrames = GameObject.FindWithTag("SpriteSlicer").
  GetComponent<SpriteSlicer>().frames;
```

Next, we iterate through all of the animation's frames and extract the matching ones from our SpriteSlicer script's master set. This yields a subset of frames that matches the requested animation:

```
//CharacterAnimator script
//excerpt from FindFramesFor() function
//loop through locations
for (int i = 0; i < numFrames; i++) {

    //retrieve frame from master set
    frames[i] = allFrames[frameLoc[i, 0], frameLoc[i, 1]];
}
```

Last, we return the frames that were found, so that they can be further utilized to create the animation sequence:

```
//CharacterAnimator script
//excerpt from FindFramesFor() function
//return
return frames;
```

As the glue that holds our animation system together, the CharacterAnimator also needs to pass the retrieved frames to our FrameAnimation variable, currentAnim. Thus, we create a SetUpAnimationWithName() function that can be called any time to prepare a new animation for a character:

```
//CharacterAnimator script
//SetUpAnimationWithName() function
public void SetUpAnimationWithName(string theName, float
  theFPS = 1.0f, bool theIsLoop = true) {

    //find frames
    Sprite[] frames = FindFramesFor(theName);

    //init animation
    currentAnim.InitFrameAnimation(theName, frames, theFPS,
      theIsLoop);
}
```

The SetUpAnimationWithName() function accepts a name and, optionally, other details about the animation. It makes a call to FindFramesFor() to retrieve the necessary frames to execute the animation. Then, it references the currentAnim variable's InitFrameAnimation() function to initialize the animation. This is the go-to function that will be called any time we need to animate a character in our game. For clarity, the entire CharacterAnimator script is presented:

```
//CharacterAnimator script
public class CharacterAnimator : MonoBehaviour {

    //animation collection
    private Dictionary<string, int[,]> _animations;

    //animation names
    public string[] animNames;

    //frame locations (name index, row, col)
    //set in Unity Inspector
    public Vector3[] animLocs;

    //current frame animation
    public FrameAnimation currentAnim;

    //awake
    void Awake() {

        //populate animation dictionary
        _animations = CreateAnimDict(animNames, animLocs);

        //init animation
        currentAnim = gameObject.AddComponent<FrameAnimation>();
    }

    //create animation dictionary from names and locations
    private Dictionary<string, int[,]> CreateAnimDict(string[]
      theNames, Vector3[] theLocs) {

        //store result
        Dictionary<string, int[,]> anim = new Dictionary<string,
          int[,]>();
```

```
        //loop through animation names
        for (int i = 0; i < theNames.Length; i++) {

            //find locations for animation
            //x = index matching animation name
            Vector3[] vLocs = Array.FindAll(theLocs, loc =>
              loc.x == i);

            //convert locations to int
            //each animation has N rows with 2 frame columns
            int[,] iLocs = new int[vLocs.Length, 2];
            for (int j = 0; j < vLocs.Length; j++) {

                //j = frame index
                //y = row value; z = col value
                iLocs[j, 0] = (int)vLocs[j].y;
                iLocs[j, 1] = (int)vLocs[j].z;
            }

            //add to dictionary
            anim.Add(theNames[i], iLocs);
        }

        //return
        return anim;
    }

    //find frames for specific animation
    private Sprite[] FindFramesFor(string theName) {

        //check animation
        int[,] frameLoc;
        if (_animations.TryGetValue(theName, out frameLoc)) {

            //retrieve number of frame locations
            int numFrames = frameLoc.GetLength(0);

            //store frames
            Sprite[] frames = new Sprite[numFrames];

            //retrieve master set of frames
            Sprite[,] allFrames = GameObject.FindWithTag
              ("SpriteSlicer").GetComponent<SpriteSlicer>().
                  frames;

            //loop through locations
            for (int i = 0; i < numFrames; i++) {

                //retrieve frame from master set
                frames[i] = allFrames[frameLoc[i, 0],
                  frameLoc[i, 1]];
            }

                //return
                return frames;
        }

        //return
        return null;
    }
```

```
//set up animation
public void SetUpAnimationWithName(string theName, float
  theFPS = 1.0f, bool theIsLoop = true) {

  //find frames
  Sprite[] frames = FindFramesFor(theName);

  //init animation
  currentAnim.InitFrameAnimation(theName, frames, theFPS,
    theIsLoop);
}

} //end class
```

As you can see, the CharacterAnimator script facilitates communication between various parts of our game. Other parts of our game will refer to a character's CharacterAnimator script any time an animation needs to be displayed. With your SpriteSlicer, FrameAnimation, and CharacterAnimator scripts in place, your core animation system is complete. Now, it's time to apply the animations throughout your game.

Challenge: Apply the Animations

You have created an animation system, but not yet used it to animate anything in your game. In this final challenge, you will implement animations throughout your game. To do so, think about the various places in your game where animations can support the player experience. Then, use your animation system to make it happen. There is but one requirement for this challenge:

1. Implement animations throughout your game.

Hint: Think about Characters

Characters are the primary aspect of your game that will be animated. To animate a character, retrieve its CharacterAnimator script, set up the desired animation, and then control it via the FrameAnimation. For instance, suppose we want to display Luna's "walk left" animation. You can retrieve the CharacterAnimator script attached to Luna. Then, call its SetUpAnimationWithName() function with an argument of "walk left." Thereafter, the "walk left" animation is stored in the currentAnim variable of your CharacterAnimator script. Since currentAnim is of the FrameAnimation type, you can use your control functions (Play(), Stop(), and so forth) to display the animation on screen.

Now that you know how to execute animations, think about when and where you want them to occur throughout your game. Basically, any time a character is doing something in your game, it should be animated. Here are a few ideas for where you might implement character animations:

- The player moves Luna around the screen.

- The heroes follow Luna as members of the group.

- The drakes or dragons chase Luna in the dungeon.

Hint: Think about Interactions

Another way to think about animations is in terms of the interactions that occur in your game. Potentially, an animation could occur any time a player provides user input into your game world. You can also apply animations whenever your characters encounter one another. Furthermore, any time a collision occurs is a time that is likely to be animated in some way. As you are reviewing the status of your game, look for opportunities to incorporate animations wherever interactions occur. Here are some examples:

- A character selects an action during the Star–Sun–Moon (SSM) game.

- A team of characters wins the SSM game.

- A knight or hero wants to get the player's attention.

- A drake or dragon collides with the player.

Example Solution: Apply the Animations

The way you apply animations throughout your game is ultimately up to you. Thus, this example solution provides an overview of the areas in your game where animations could be applied. Let's handle our heroes first. A primary animation need appears when the player moves Luna about the screen. We want Luna's movement (up, down, left, or right) to be accompanied by animations. Therefore, we update the CheckUserInput() function in our UserMove script, which is attached to the Player GameObject in our scene. We begin by retrieving the CharacterAnimator attached to the same object. Then, based on the type of movement, we create and control animations as necessary through the CharacterAnimator script:

```
//UserMove script
//excerpt from CheckUserInput() function
//check user input
private void CheckUserInput() {

    //animation
    //retrieve animator
    CharacterAnimator animator = gameObject.GetComponent<Character
      Animator>();

    //key released
    if (/* Code omitted */) {

        /*
        Code omitted.
        */

        //animation
        //stop and reset
        animator.currentAnim.GoToFrameAndStop(0);
}
```

```
//no key held
else if (/* Code omitted */) {

    /*
    Code omitted.
    */

    //animation
    //if not already set
    if (animator.currentAnim.animName != "ActDown") {

        //update animation
        animator.SetUpAnimationWithName("ActDown", 2.0f);
    }

    //play
    animator.currentAnim.Play();
}

/*
Code omitted.
*/

//move up
if (/* Code omitted */) {

    /*
    Code omitted.
    */

    //animation
    //if not already set
    if (animator.currentAnim.animName != "MoveUp") {

        //update animation
        animator.SetUpAnimationWithName("MoveUp", 6.0f);
    }

    //play
    animator.currentAnim.Play();

}

//move down
else if (/* Code omitted */) {

    /*
    Code omitted.
    */

    //animation
    //if not already set
    if (animator.currentAnim.animName != "MoveDown") {

        //update animation
        animator.SetUpAnimationWithName("MoveDown", 6.0f);
    }

    //play
    animator.currentAnim.Play();
}
```

```
//move left
else if (/* Code omitted */) {

    /*
    Code omitted.
    */

    //animation
    //if not already set
    if (animator.currentAnim.animName != "MoveLeft") {

        //update animation
        animator.SetUpAnimationWithName("MoveLeft", 6.0f);
    }

    //play
    animator.currentAnim.Play();
}

//move right
else if (/* Code omitted */) {

    /*
    Code omitted.
    */

    //animation
    //if not already set
    if (animator.currentAnim.animName != "MoveRight") {

        //update animation
        animator.SetUpAnimationWithName("MoveRight", 6.0f);

    }

    //play
    animator.currentAnim.Play();
}

/*
Code omitted.
*/
}
```

While the UserMove script takes care of our lead hero, Luna, we mustn't forget to update the heroes who follow her. So, we'll add animations to the Group script as well. In this example, special functions are written to keep the animation component distinct from other operations. The UpdateAnimations() function calculates a hero's movement distance on the x and y axes. Whichever distance is greatest will trigger the matching animation:

```
//Group script
//UpdateAnimations() function
public void UpdateAnimations(CharacterAnimator theAnimator, float
theXDistMoved, float theYDistMoved) {

    //x axis dist greater than y axis
    if (Mathf.Abs(theXDistMoved) > Mathf.Abs(theYDistMoved)) {
```

```
//positive
if (theXDistMoved > 0) {

    //animation
    if (theAnimator.currentAnim.animName != "MoveRight") {

        //set up animation
        theAnimator.SetUpAnimationWithName("MoveRight",
            6.0f);
    }

    //play
    theAnimator.currentAnim.Play();
}

//negative
else if (theXDistMoved <= 0) {

    //animation
    if (theAnimator.currentAnim.animName != "MoveLeft") {

        //set up animation
        theAnimator.SetUpAnimationWithName("MoveLeft",
            6.0f);
    }

    //play
    theAnimator.currentAnim.Play();
}
}

//y axis dist greater than x axis
else if (Mathf.Abs(theXDistMoved) < Mathf.Abs(theYDistMoved)) {

    //positive
    if (theYDistMoved > 0) {

        //animation
        if (theAnimator.currentAnim.animName != "MoveUp") {

            //set up animation
            theAnimator.SetUpAnimationWithName("MoveUp",
                6.0f);
        }

        //play
        theAnimator.currentAnim.Play();
    }

    //negative
    else if (theYDistMoved < 0) {

        //animation
        if (theAnimator.currentAnim.animName != "MoveDown") {

            //set up animation
            theAnimator.SetUpAnimationWithName("MoveDown",
                6.0f);
        }
```

```
            //play
            theAnimator.currentAnim.Play();
        }
    }

    //otherwise
    else {

        //animation
        if (theAnimator.currentAnim.animName != "ActDown") {

            //set up animation
            theAnimator.SetUpAnimationWithName("ActDown", 2.0f);
        }

        //reset
        theAnimator.currentAnim.GoToFrameAndStop(0);
    }
}
```

We want to update the heroes' animations whenever movement occurs. Therefore, we add a call to UpdateAnimations() at the very end of our existing UpdatePos() function's for loop:

```
//Group script
//excerpt from UpdatePos() function
public void UpdatePos(float theSpeed, Vector2 theDir) {

    /*
    Code omitted.
    */

        //animation
        UpdateAnimations(animator, xDistMoved, yDistMoved);
    }
}
```

For convenience, we also introduce a StopAnimations() function, which provides us with an easy way to stop all of the heroes' animations on demand:

```
//Group script
//StopAnimations() function
public void StopAnimations() {

    //iterate through members
    foreach (GameObject aMember in members) {

        //retrieve animator
        CharacterAnimator animator = aMember.GetComponent
          <CharacterAnimator>();

        //animation
        if (animator.currentAnim.animName != "ActDown") {

            //set up animation
            animator.SetUpAnimationWithName("ActDown", 2.0f);
        }

        //reset
        animator.currentAnim.GoToFrameAndStop(0);
    }
}
```

Our heroes are taken care of, so let's move on to animate the drakes, dragons, and knights. We'll add a function to our LevelGenerator script named AnimateObjectsWithTag(). It is similar to the existing functions in our script, except that it focuses on handling animations for a specific type of character:

```
//LevelGenerator script
//AnimateObjectsWithTag() function
private void AnimateObjectsWithTag(string theTag) {

    //retrieve objects associated with tag
    GameObject[] objects = GameObject.
      FindGameObjectsWithTag(theTag);

    //iterate through objects
    for (int i = 0; i < objects.Length; i++) {

        //retrieve animator
        CharacterAnimator animator = objects[i].GetComponent
          <CharacterAnimator>();

        //if valid
        if (animator) {

            //check tag
            switch (theTag) {

                //knights
                case "Knight":

                    //set up animation
                    animator.SetUpAnimationWithName("ActDown",
                      3.0f);

                    break;

                //hero
                case "Hero":

                    //set up animation
                    animator.SetUpAnimationWithName("ActDown",
                      6.0f);
                    break;

                //drake
                case "Drake":

                    //set up animation
                    animator.SetUpAnimationWithName("Fly", 3.0f);

                    break;

                //boss
                case "Dragon":

                    //set up animation
                    animator.SetUpAnimationWithName("ActDown",
                      3.0f);

                    break;
```

```
            //default
            default:
                Debug.Log("[LevelGenerator] Animation tag not
                    recognized");

                break;
        }

        //play animation
        animator.currentAnim.Play();

    }
  }
}
```

Depending on the type of character, we call the `AnimatObjectsWithTag()` function from different places in our LevelGenerator script:

```
//LevelGenerator script
//assorted calls to AnimateObjectsWithTag() function

//knights
//add this line to the end of the GenerateMap() function
AnimateObjectsWithTag("Knight");

//drakes
//add this line after the drakes are spawned in GenerateDungeon()
AnimateObjectsWithTag("Drake");

//dragons
//add this line after the dragons are spawned in GenerateDungeon()
AnimateObjectsWithTag("Dragon");
```

Another place that requires animations is our collision system. We want to change our animations based on the collisions that occur between characters. Therefore, we update our UserCollision script's `OnTriggerEnter2D()` function. Mostly, we want to stop our characters' animations when a collision occurs. Incorporate the following lines of code into your UserCollision script to make it happen:

```
//UserCollision script
//excerpt from OnTriggerEnter2D() function

//store collided character's CharacterAnimator for convenience
//place code before switch statement
CharacterAnimator collideAnim = theCollider.gameObject.GetComponent
  <CharacterAnimator>();

/*
The following code is associated with
the respective tag inside the switch
statement.
*/

//stairs collision
//stop all hero animations
group.StopAnimations();
```

```
//knight collision
//stop all hero animations
group.StopAnimations();

//stop animation at default frame
collideAnim.currentAnim.GoToFrameAndStop(0);

//hero collision
//stop all hero animations
group.StopAnimations();

//stop animation at default frame
collideAnim.currentAnim.GoToFrameAndStop(0);

//drake collision
if (inventory.numObjects <= inventory.minObjects) {

    /*
    Code omitted.
    */

    //stop all hero animations
    group.StopAnimations();

    //stop drake animation
    collideAnim.currentAnim.GoToFrameAndStop(0);

    /*
    Code omitted.
    */
}

//dragon collision
//stop all hero animations
group.StopAnimations();

//stop dragon animation
collideAnim.currentAnim.GoToFrameAndStop(0);
```

With that, all of our characters are animated throughout the world map and dungeon scenes. Take the game for a test run to see how much better it looks with animations.

Perhaps you've noticed the basic animation system formula through this example solution. Basically, we retrieve a character's CharacterAnimator script and call SetUpAnimationWithName() to prepare an animation. Later, we use the control functions placed in the currentAnim FrameAnimator variable to execute the animation. This is how the animations in the example solution are implemented. You can follow the same process to introduce more animations into your game. If you're in the mood for a bonus challenge, try animating your interaction scenes as well. When we left off working on our interaction system, we had no animations. Only text provided an indication of what is happening with the characters during the SSM game. However, some animation would add a much-needed special touch to the interaction scenes. Imagine your characters holding up their arms when selecting an action. Just above, you could show an icon of the star, sun, or moon that the character played on that turn (these graphics are included in the sprite sheet). Also, when a character is eliminated, you could let the player know by fading out the sprite, playing a different animation, or a similar method. Further, you may want to experiment with different timing, such as with `WaitForSeconds()`, to find a better flow for your SSM game. You're encouraged to add some lively animations to your interaction scenes and are fully capable of doing so. See the example solution project's InteractionSystem and InteractionGenerator scripts for one approach to animating the interaction scenes. Moreover, feel free to add any other animations to your game that would spruce things up but weren't demonstrated in the example solution.

Summary

From breaking down a sprite sheet with code, to timing frame-based sequences, to managing all of your characters' visuals, you have brought your game world to life through animation. Your game is really starting to look great and is one giant leap closer to completion. You should be able to apply all of these game implementation techniques:

- Animate the characters of the game world

- Slice a sprite sheet into individual animation frames using code

- Create timed, looping animations composed of frames

- Manage multiple animations for a variety of different characters

With animations in place, there is one remaining major implementation that we would be remiss to leave out in any game. In Chapter 11, you will implement audio in the form of music and sound effects. Combined with animations, audio will make your game truly come to life.

References

Microsoft Corporation. 2016a. Array.FindAll<T> Method (T[], Predicate<T>). https://msdn.microsoft.com/library/1kkxfxdd.aspx (accessed January 8, 2016).

Microsoft Corporation. 2016b. Dictionary<TKey, TValue> Class. https://msdn.microsoft.com/library/xfhwa508.aspx (accessed January 8, 2016).

Microsoft Corporation. 2016c. Dictionary<TKey, TValue>.TryGetValue Method (TKey, TValue). https://msdn.microsoft.com/library/bb347013.aspx (accessed January 8, 2016).

Unity Technologies. 2016a. Sprite. http://docs.unity3d.com/ScriptReference/Sprite.html (accessed January 8, 2016).

Unity Technologies. 2016b. Sprite.Create. http://docs.unity3d.com/ScriptReference/Sprite.Create.html (accessed January 8, 2016).

Unity Technologies. 2016c. Sprite Editor. http://docs.unity3d.com/Manual/SpriteEditor.html (accessed January 8, 2016).

Unity Technologies. 2016d. Vector2. http://docs.unity3d.com/ScriptReference/Vector2.html (accessed January 8, 2016).

11 The World Can Be Heard

It's almost unbelievable that we've made it this far without adding music and sound effects to our game. Without doubt, audio is a must-have feature. In this chapter, we'll focus on incorporating music and sound effects into our game world. Not only will you work with Unity's audio features, but you'll also code an audio management system that will serve you well now and in the future. Audio fills the last major gap in the development of our game, thus bringing us very close to release.

▮ Goals

By the end of this chapter, you will be able to apply these game implementation techniques:

- Incorporate audio into the game world

- Manage music and sound effects from multiple audio sources and clips

- Control the playback, volume, and fading for in-game audio

- Use audio to enhance scenes and interactions throughout the game

▐ Required Files

In this chapter, you will use the following files from the *Software > Chapter_11* folder (https://www.crcpress.com/Learn-to-Implement-Games-with-Code/Quick/p/book/9781498753388):

- The contents of the Challenge folder to create, code, and test your solution

- The contents of the Solution folder to compare your solution to the example solution

▐ Challenge: Manage Music and Sound Effects

Open the challenge project in Unity. In addition to what you've already created to date, a number of audio files have been included in the project. You can see all of the available audio files in the *Assets > Audio* folder (Figure 11.1). The music tracks are prefixed with the letters *bgm* (background music), while the sound effects are prefixed with *sfx* (sound effect). Before we proceed, let's credit the sources of the audio files used in this chapter. The background music tracks were originally composed by an artist named HalcyonicFalconX and entered the public domain as part of the Open Game Art Bundle (Commonly.cc, n.d.). Meanwhile, the sound effects were generated by John M. Quick using Tomas Pettersson's *sfxr* software (Pettersson 2007), which is governed by the MIT license (Open Source Initiative, n.d.).

This challenge encompasses the entirety of creating your audio management system. You'll need to learn about Unity's built-in options for utilizing audio sources and clips. Additionally, you'll want to code a script from scratch to manage all of your game's audio. The requirements for this challenge are:

1. Create an AudioManager script that manages the audio for your entire game.

2. The AudioManager should control the playback, volume, and fade transitions for your game's music and sound effects.

3. Ensure that your AudioManager script is accessible throughout the game.

Hint: Use Sources and Clips

When working with audio in Unity, you want to become familiar with the AudioSource and AudioClip classes. An AudioSource can be attached to a GameObject to control the volume and playback of sounds (Unity Technologies 2016b). Meanwhile, an AudioClip represents an individual sound that can be utilized by an AudioSource (Unity Technologies 2016a). These two audio classes are essential to the implementation of your audio management system.

Let's look at some usage examples for the AudioSource and AudioClip classes. You could use code to create these classes. However, there are many different properties and settings available to each. There are also several different audio files in your project. This means that your code can get long, repetitive, and unwieldy at times. Therefore, this is a case where it makes sense to leverage the Unity editor to set up the basics.

For instance, you can create a `GameObject` in your scene and add an `AudioSource` to it. As you can see in Figure 11.2, there are several settings available to an `AudioSource`, such as looping, volume, and which `AudioClip` it is associated with. Think of each `AudioSource` as a separate channel. One channel can only play one clip at a time, but different channels can play their clips simultaneously. Hence, you may want to use more than one `AudioSource` in your game, depending on how many simultaneous sounds you need to play. However, you do not need an `AudioSource` for each individual `AudioClip`, since the clip associated with a source can be changed.

On the other hand, every `AudioClip` is like an individual sound that can be played by an `AudioSource`. Since all your files are nicely arranged in the *Assets > Audio* folder (Figure 11.1) already, the easiest thing to do is to add `public AudioClip` variables to a script to represent each audio file. Then, in the Unity editor, associate each file with its designated `AudioClip` variable. This concept is demonstrated in Figure 11.3.

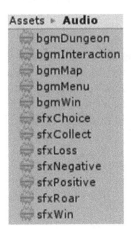

Figure 11.1 Several audio files have been placed in your project's *Assets > Audio* folder.

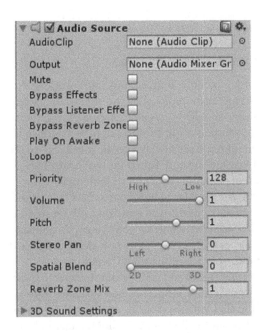

Figure 11.2 There are several settings available to configure the AudioSource component.

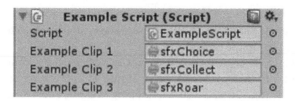

Figure 11.3 The Unity editor can be used to conveniently associate audio files with AudioClip variables in a script.

That said, we will use code to craft an overarching audio management system for our game. To get started, create an AudioManager script and add it to a GameObject in your Load scene. Then, think about how you can use sources and clips to manage the audio files in your game. Here are a few examples of how you can use code to manipulate the AudioSource and AudioClip variables inside your AudioManager script:

```
//example AudioSource and AudioClip manipulations
//associate a clip with a source
exampleSource.clip = exampleClip;

//play a source's clip
exampleSource.Play();

//stop a source's playback
exampleSource.Stop();

//change a source's volume
//float value between 0.0f (min) and 1.0f (max)
exampleSource.volume = 0.5f;
```

Hint: Implement the Audio Manager

You know the basics of how sources and clips work. It's time to use your AudioManager script and audio files to make the magic happen. Your AudioManager script should be capable of controlling the playback of audio files. For example, you may want to start, stop, or pause sounds during gameplay. Since you should reuse the few sources in your script to play many different sounds, you might include custom functions that control playback and associate clips with sources on demand. Also, you should implement a fade transition for your background music. Similar to how your scenes fade in and out visually, you want your music to fade in and out as well. This will create an even more professional transition between the scenes in your game. You already have experience fading things in and out. This time, your task is only slightly different, because you are working with volume, rather than transparency.

Once coded, remember to add your AudioManager to a GameObject in the Load scene. Set any necessary properties and variables in the Unity editor, such as associating audio files with your script's AudioClip variables (Figure 11.3). Moreover, remember not to allow your AudioManager to be destroyed. It needs to stick around for the entire game and manage audio across all scenes.

Example Solution: Manage Music and Sound Effects

We'll review an example implementation of the audio management system. This solution leverages the capabilities of the Unity editor to establish AudioSource and AudioClip variables and the AudioManager script to manage the overall audio system. It begins with the creation of a GameObject in the Load scene named AudioManager. This GameObject is tagged as "AudioManager," and our AudioManager script is attached to it. Next, we add two children objects named BgmSource and SfxSource (Figure 11.4). Each of these child objects has an AudioSource component attached to it. The configurations of these components are shown in Figures 11.5 and 11.6, respectively. Essentially, we are using two audio sources in our game. The BgmSource handles all background music for our scenes, while switching to the appropriate track as necessary. Likewise, the SfxSource plays all sound effects in our game and swaps between them as needed. Hence, despite the number of audio clips in our game, we only need two sources. We simply swap the AudioClip associated with each source whenever we need to.

Figure 11.4 The AudioManager GameObject has two children objects that represent our audio sources, BgmSource and SfxSource.

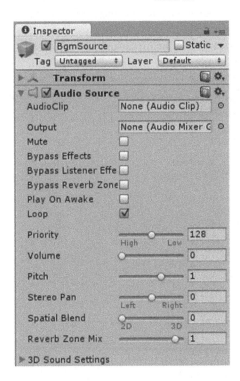

Figure 11.5 The AudioSource component configuration for BgmSource is shown.

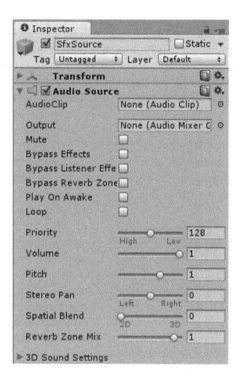

Figure 11.6 The AudioSource component configuration for SfxSource is shown.

Speaking of clips, one AudioClip variable is established in the AudioManager script for each audio file in our project. Similarly, our two sources are also declared as variables. After being declared, these variables are initialized using the Unity editor (Figure 11.7). This allows us to refer to each audio file in our code according to its variable name:

```
//AudioManager script
//audio sources
public AudioSource bgmSource;
public AudioSource sfxSource;

//audio clips
//music
public AudioClip bgmMenu;
public AudioClip bgmMap;
public AudioClip bgmDungeon;
public AudioClip bgmInteraction;
public AudioClip bgmWin;

//sound effects
public AudioClip sfxChoice;
public AudioClip sfxCollect;
public AudioClip sfxLoss;
public AudioClip sfxNegative;
public AudioClip sfxPositive;
public AudioClip sfxRoar;
public AudioClip sfxWin;
```

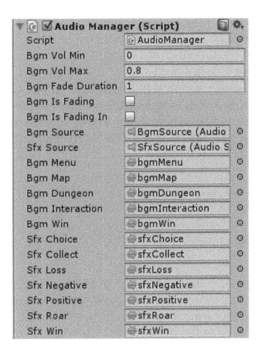

Figure 11.7 All of the AudioManager script's AudioClip variables are defined in the Unity editor.

Recall that we want our AudioManager to stick around throughout the game and not be destroyed during scenes. Therefore, we establish it as a singleton. However, unlike our previous singletons, which created themselves on demand, this one already exists in our scene. Therefore, we can implement a much simpler version of our familiar singleton design pattern:

```
//AudioManager script
//singleton implementation

//singleton instance variable
private static AudioManager _Instance;

//public getter to access instance variable
public static AudioManager Instance {
     get { return _Instance; }
}

//Awake() function
void Awake() {

     //check for existing instance
     //if no instance
     if (_Instance == null) {

          //find object in scene
          _Instance = GameObject.FindWithTag("AudioManager").
            GetComponent<AudioManager>();
```

```
        //prevent destruction
        DontDestroyOnLoad(_Instance);
    }
}
```

To facilitate playback, we create three custom functions. Each of these functions generically refers to AudioClip and AudioSource variables, which allows us
to use them across all of our clips and sources with ease. The simplest function,
StopSource(), receives an AudioSource as an argument and simply stops
its playback:

```
//AudioManager script
//StopSource() function
public void StopSource(AudioSource theSource) {

    //stop
    theSource.Stop();
}
```

Meanwhile, we create two overloaded versions of the
PlayClipFromSource() function. The first version accepts an AudioClip
and AudioSource as arguments. Then, it makes sure the source stops any
existing playback, updates the clip associated with the source, and begins playback again:

```
//AudioManager script
//PlayScriptFromSource() function
public void PlayClipFromSource(AudioClip theClip, AudioSource
    theSource) {

    //stop
    theSource.Stop();

    //set the clip
    theSource.clip = theClip;

    //play
    theSource.Play();
}
```

Basically, the first version instantly plays the desired clip. Therefore, it is great
for sound effects, which usually need to be played right away. The second version
of PlayClipFromSource() is almost identical. Yet, in contrast, it applies a
coroutine to introduce a delay before the audio is switched:

```
//AudioManager script
//PlayScriptFromSource() coroutine
public IEnumerator PlayClipFromSource(AudioClip theClip,
AudioSource theSource, float theDelay) {

    //delay
    yield return new WaitForSeconds(theDelay);

    //stop
    theSource.Stop();
```

```
//set the clip
theSource.clip = theClip;

//play
theSource.Play();
}
```

Hence, our coroutine version of `PlayClipFromSource()` is excellent for our background music. That's because we usually want to transition nicely between music tracks, such as through a fade transition, and not swap them in a way that will be jarring to players.

On that note, let's consider how the fade transition can be executed. Logically, whenever a scene is loaded, we want to fade in our music. Whenever a scene is exited, we want to fade out our music. We establish some control variables in our AudioManager script:

```
//AudioManager script
//volume limits
public float bgmVolMin;
public float bgmVolMax;

//whether currently fading
public bool bgmIsFading;

//whether fading in or out
public bool bgmIsFadingIn;

//duration of fade, in seconds
public float bgmFadeDuration;

//time at which latest fade started
private float _bgmFadeStartTime;
```

The `bgmVolMin` and `bgmVolMax` variables establish the limits of our background music volume. While 0 is an obvious choice for the minimum (silent), we might choose to play the background music at a lower maximum volume than sound effects, such as 0.8. This helps the music blend into the background, keeping the action-packed sound effects front and center. Continuing, the `bgmIsFading` and `bgmIsFadingIn` Boolean variables tell us whether we are currently in transition and what direction the fade is moving at a given time. Meanwhile, `_bgmFadeStartTime` records the time at which the latest fade cycle began and `bgmFadeDuration` determines how long the transition lasts. As you review this implementation, it should look pretty familiar to the time-based systems that you have implemented in prior chapters. Inside `Start()`, we establish that the music is neither fading nor fading in:

```
//AudioManager script
//Start() function
void Start() {

    //set defaults
    bgmIsFading = false;
    bgmIsFadingIn = false;
}
```

The CheckFade() function handles the actual fade process:

```
//AudioManager script
//CheckFade() function
private void CheckFade() {

    //calculate fade duration thus far
    float fadeDuration = Time.time - _bgmFadeStartTime;

    //convert to percentage
    float fadePct = Mathf.Clamp01(fadeDuration /
      bgmFadeDuration);

    //retrieve current volume
    float vol = bgmSource.volume;

    //check fade direction
    switch (bgmIsFadingIn) {

        //fade in
        case true:

            //current vol is less than max
            if (vol < bgmVolMax) {

                //update vol
                vol = fadePct;
            }

            //vol has reached max
            else {

                //update vol
                vol = bgmVolMax;

                //stop fade
                bgmIsFading = false;
            }

            break;

        //fade out
        case false:

            //current vol is greater than min
            if (vol > bgmVolMin) {

                //update vol
                vol = 1.0f - fadePct;
            }

            //vol has reached max
            else {

                //update vol
                vol = bgmVolMin;

                //stop fade
                bgmIsFading = false;
            }
```

```
                    break;

                //default
                default:
                        break;
        }

        //update vol
        bgmSource.volume = vol;
}
```

Here, we will break down the details of `CheckFade()`. It begins by calculating how long the current fade cycle has run, and storing the volume of our music source in a local variable:

```
//AudioManager script
//excerpt from CheckFade() function
//calculate fade duration thus far
float fadeDuration = Time.time - _bgmFadeStartTime;

//convert to percentage
float fadePct = Mathf.Clamp01(fadeDuration / bgmFadeDuration);

//retrieve current volume
float vol = bgmSource.volume;
```

Next, a `switch` statement is called on `bgmIsFadingIn` to determine whether the music is currently fading in or out:

```
//AudioManager script
//excerpt from CheckFade() function
switch (bgmIsFadingIn) {

        //fade in
        case true:

                /*
                Code omitted.
                */

        //fade out
        case false:

                /*
                Code omitted.
                */
}
```

When fading in, we check whether the current volume is less than the maximum. If so, we update our local volume variable based on the percentage of the duration completed thus far. Otherwise, if the maximum is exceeded, we set the volume to the maximum and end the transition by toggling the `bgmIsFading` flag:

```
//AudioManager script
//excerpt from CheckFade() function
//current vol is less than max
if (vol < bgmVolMax) {
```

```
        //update vol
        vol = fadePct;
}

//vol has reached max
else {

        //update vol
        vol = bgmVolMax;

        //stop fade
        bgmIsFading = false;
}

break;
```

The other case in our switch statement handles fading out quite similarly. If the minimum volume has not been reached, we update the volume based on how much of the duration has been completed. Otherwise, we set the volume to the minimum and end the transition by flipping our bgmIsFading flag:

```
//AudioManager script
//excerpt from CheckFade() function
//current vol is greater than min
if (vol > bgmVolMin) {

        //update vol
        vol = 1.0f - fadePct;
}

//vol has reached min
else {

        //update vol
        vol = bgmVolMin;

        //stop fade
        bgmIsFading = false;
}

break;
```

Last, our CheckFade() script updates the actual volume of our background music source based on the preceding calculations:

```
//AudioManager script
//excerpt from CheckFade() function
//update vol
bgmSource.volume = vol;
```

To control the fade transition, we use our bgmIsFading flag to call CheckFade() from Update() only when our music is in transition:

```
//AudioManager script
//Update() function
void Update() {
```

```
        //if fading
        if (bgmIsFading == true) {

            //check fade
            CheckFade();
        }
}
```

Last, we need a way to trigger the fade transition. Thus, our `ToggleFade()` function completes the job by reversing the fade direction, resetting the start time, and restarting the transition:

```
//AudioManager script
//ToggleFade() function
public void ToggleFade() {

        //reverse fade direction
        bgmIsFadingIn = !bgmIsFadingIn;

        //update start time
        _bgmFadeStartTime = Time.time;

        //toggle flag
        bgmIsFading = true;
}
```

This completes the AudioManager script, which is presented in its entirety:

```
//AudioManager script
public class AudioManager : MonoBehaviour {

    //volume limits
    public float bgmVolMin, bgmVolMax;

    //whether currently fading
    public bool bgmIsFading;

    //whether fading in or out
    public bool bgmIsFadingIn;

    //duration of fade, in seconds
    public float bgmFadeDuration;

    //time at which latest fade started
    private float _bgmFadeStartTime;

    //audio sources
    //defined in Unity Inspector
    public AudioSource bgmSource, sfxSource;

    //audio clips
    //defined in Unity Inspector
    //music
    public AudioClip bgmMenu;
    public AudioClip bgmMap;
    public AudioClip bgmDungeon;
    public AudioClip bgmInteraction;
    public AudioClip bgmWin;
```

```
//sound effects
public AudioClip sfxChoice;
public AudioClip sfxCollect;
public AudioClip sfxLoss;
public AudioClip sfxNegative;
public AudioClip sfxPositive;
public AudioClip sfxRoar;
public AudioClip sfxWin;

//singleton instance
private static AudioManager _Instance;

//public getter
public static AudioManager Instance {
    get { return _Instance; }
}

//awake
void Awake() {

    //check for existing instance
    //if no instance
    if (_Instance == null) {

        //find object in scene
        _Instance = GameObject.FindWithTag("AudioManager").
            GetComponent<AudioManager>();

                //prevent destruction
                DontDestroyOnLoad(_Instance);
    }
}

//init
void Start() {

    //set defaults
    bgmIsFading = false;
    bgmIsFadingIn = false;
}

//update
void Update() {

    //if fading
    if (bgmIsFading == true) {

        //check fade
        CheckFade();
    }
}

//play an audio clip using a given source
public void PlayClipFromSource(AudioClip theClip, AudioSource
  theSource) {

    //stop
    theSource.Stop();

    //set the clip
    theSource.clip = theClip;
```

```
    //play
    theSource.Play();
}

//play an audio clip using a given source
//delay for transitions, animations, etc.
public IEnumerator PlayClipFromSource(AudioClip theClip,
  AudioSource theSource, float theDelay) {

    //delay
    yield return new WaitForSeconds(theDelay);

    //stop
    theSource.Stop();

    //set the clip
    theSource.clip = theClip;

    //play
    theSource.Play();
}

//stop a given source
public void StopSource(AudioSource theSource) {

    //stop
    theSource.Stop();
}

//toggle fade for music
public void ToggleFade() {

    //reverse fade direction
    bgmIsFadingIn = !bgmIsFadingIn;

    //update start time
    _bgmFadeStartTime = Time.time;

    //toggle flag
    bgmIsFading = true;
}

//check fade for music
private void CheckFade() {

    //calculate fade duration thus far
    float fadeDuration = Time.time - _bgmFadeStartTime;

    //convert to percentage
    float fadePct = Mathf.Clamp01(fadeDuration /
      bgmFadeDuration);

    //retrieve current volume
    float vol = bgmSource.volume;

    //check fade direction
    switch (bgmIsFadingIn) {

        //fade in
        case true:

            //current vol is less than max
            if (vol < bgmVolMax) {
```

```
                        //update vol
                        vol = fadePct;
                }

                //vol has reached max
                else {

                        //update vol
                        vol = bgmVolMax;

                        //stop fade
                        bgmIsFading = false;
                }
                break;

        //fade out
        case false:

                //current vol is greater than min
                if (vol > bgmVolMin) {

                        //update vol
                        vol = 1.0f - fadePct;
                }

                //vol has reached min
                else {

                        //update vol
                        vol = bgmVolMin;

                        //stop fade
                        bgmIsFading = false;
                }
                break;

        //default
        default:
                break;
        }

        //update vol
        bgmSource.volume = vol;
   }

} //end class
```

Conveniently, your AudioManager script can be called from anywhere in your game to manage music and sound effects on demand. Thus, you need to use your audio management system to execute the myriad of music and sound effects throughout your game. Proceed to do so in the next challenge.

▌ Challenge: Apply Music and Sound Effects

Your audio management system is in place. However, you still need to incorporate all of the music and sound effects into your game. To do so, you can make calls to the AudioManager instance from the appropriate points in your code. For example, you might start a background music track when the Map scene is loaded or play a sound effect any time Luna collides with a collectable object. For this challenge, you will need to think about everywhere in your game that audio can be used. The requirements are straightforward:

1. Add background music to every scene in your game.

2. Ensure that background music volume transitions align with your scene's alpha transparency transitions.

3. Add sound effects for all relevant events in your game.

Hint: Think about Scenes

Every one of your scenes should have background music associated with it. To play the music, you can make a call to your AudioManager script's PlayClipFromSource() coroutine, while providing the appropriate source and clip as arguments. Do not forget to provide a delay as well. Ideally, the delay should match the duration of the alpha fade transition in your scenes. In that case, the audio and visual of your scene will be perfectly synced, which makes for a nice transition. The key factor to playing a music track is to know when and where to call it within your game's code. Work through each scene in your game and find the best place to trigger their background tracks.

Besides playing individual music tracks, you want to make sure that your audio source is faded in and out for every scene. A good place to look for pointers is your alpha transparency fade transition from Chapter 9. There, you used the StateManager to ensure that the fade transition was triggered every time a new scene was loaded. You could execute a similar strategy to fade your background music in and out as the scenes are switched.

Listen to the background music files in your project. Think about which is suitable for each scene. Here are some suggestions for implementing background music into your game:

- Apply the designated audio files to their corresponding scenes:

  - Play bgmDungeon during the DungeonRed, DungeonGreen, and DungeonBlue scenes

  - Play bgmInteraction during the InteractionRed, InteractionGreen, and InteractionBlue scenes

  - Play bgmMap during the Map scene

  - Play bgmMenu during the Menu scene

  - No audio is necessary for the Load scene

- Make sure the music fades in and out whenever a new scene is loaded

- Match the timing of the music's volume transition to the scene's alpha transparency transition

Hint: Think about Interactions

Whereas your scenes utilize background music, the various interactions in your game use your sound effects. Several sound effect audio files were provided in your project. Furthermore, unlike music, which is often associated with a single scene, sound effects can sometimes be applied to multiple interactions. For example, games typically use the same button click sound throughout all menus and choices in the game. Likewise, the same positive jingle could be used when a player finds a hidden object, gains a level, or wins the entire game. That said, you do not want to overuse any one sound too much, as it will lose its effectiveness.

Once again, the key is to know when and where to apply sound effects. Once you have decided, a simple call to your AudioManager script's `PlayClipFromSource()` function will do the trick. Therefore, you should listen to the sound effects provided and play through your game. Look for any time two things interact during the course of play. For instance, any collision between objects or decision made by a character is an excellent opportunity to include a sound effect. Although you may think of many other places to add sound effects, here are a few suggestions:

- Play sfxChoice when the player makes a choice

- Play sfxCollect whenever Luna picks up a collectable object

- Play sfxRoar whenever Luna collides with a drake

- Play sfxWin if the hero team wins a game of Star–Sun–Moon (SSM)

Example Solution: Apply Music and Sound Effects

As with the animations you implemented in Chapter 10, you had the liberty to implement audio in a wide variety of ways during this challenge. Therefore, the example solution will highlight some of the key areas where music and sound effects can improve the player experience. You may want to implement even more audio in your game.

Playing audio in our game involves a simple call to the AudioManager instance. You will see this code appear throughout the example solution. This sample code demonstrates the basic process for playing audio in our game:

```
//basic usage of AudioManager to play audio
/*
Replace CLIPNAME with the variable name
that represents the desired clip and
SOURCENAME with the corresponding source.
*/
AudioManager.Instance.PlayClipFromSource(
     AudioManager.Instance.CLIPNAME,
     AudioManager.Instance.SOURCENAME
);
```

Certainly, we want to add background music to all of our scenes. However, we have to find a sensible place to execute the background track for each scene.

The following code describes how you could add background music to your world map, dungeon, interaction, and menu scenes:

```
//where to add background music

//world map scene
//LevelGenerator script
//excerpt from GenerateMap() function
//place code at very end of function

//play music
AudioManager.Instance.PlayClipFromSource(
      AudioManager.Instance.bgmMap,
      AudioManager.Instance.bgmSource
);

//fade music
AudioManager.Instance.ToggleFade();

//dungeon scenes
//LevelGenerator script
//excerpt from GenerateDungeon() function
//place code at very end of function

//if dungeon music is not already playing
if (AudioManager.Instance.bgmSource.clip !=
    AudioManager.Instance.bgmDungeon) {

      //play music
      AudioManager.Instance.PlayClipFromSource(
            AudioManager.Instance.bgmDungeon,
            AudioManager.Instance.bgmSource
            );

      //fade music
      AudioManager.Instance.ToggleFade();
}

//interaction scenes
//InteractionGenerator script
//excerpt from Start() function
//place code at top of function

//play music
AudioManager.Instance.PlayClipFromSource(
      AudioManager.Instance.bgmInteraction,
      AudioManager.Instance.bgmSource
      );

//fade music
AudioManager.Instance.ToggleFade();

//menu scene
//Menu script
//excerpt from Start() function
//place code at top of function

//play music
AudioManager.Instance.PlayClipFromSource(
```

```
AudioManager.Instance.bgmMenu,
AudioManager.Instance.bgmSource
);

//fade music
AudioManager.Instance.ToggleFade();
```

Each scene calls the AudioManager instance's `PlayClipFromSource()` function somewhere in its initialization code. Since these are background music tracks, they all use `bgmSource` along with a matching audio file. After that, we call `ToggleFade()` to apply our fade in transition.

Notice that there is extra code for the dungeon scenes. Recall that, when Luna is in a dungeon, she can explore countless levels. We accomplish this by reloading our dungeon scene each time Luna reaches the stairs. So long as Luna is inside the dungeon, we should not fade the music in and out. For a more seamless experience, we keep the background music running throughout the entire time Luna is in the dungeon, even as she moves from room to room. Therefore, before starting the dungeon music, we check whether it is already playing. If so, we know Luna is already in the dungeon, and we just let the music continue playing. However, if she were to enter the dungeon for the first time or change to a different scene, our code would handle the necessary music adjustments.

We also need to make sure that the background music for our scenes makes use of the volume fade when transiting out of the scene. This can be accomplished by modifying our StateManager script's `SwitchSceneTo()` function. The key changes are in bold:

```
//StateManager script
//SwitchSceneTo() function
public IEnumerator SwitchSceneTo(string theScene, float theDelay =
  0.0f) {

    //save
    DataManager.Instance.SaveData();

    //delay
    yield return new WaitForSeconds(theDelay);

    //fade
    fade.ToggleFade();

    //audio
    /*
    Note: Only fade audio if a source clip is defined
    and a different scene is loaded (i.e. continue music
    across repeated scenes).
    */
    if (AudioManager.Instance.bgmSource.clip != null &&
        SceneManager.GetActiveScene().name != theScene) {
        AudioManager.Instance.ToggleFade();
    }
    /*
    Code omitted.
    */
}
```

A couple of additions were made to `SwitchSceneTo()`. First, an optional delay was added to the function. This is useful in case you want to play an audio clip right before changing a scene. This allows time for the audio clip to finish playing before moving to the next scene. Second, we add code to fade out the music in the current scene, prior to switching to the next scene. However, some conditions are applied. If there is no clip defined (`AudioManager.Instance.bgmSource. clip != null`), we do not want to attempt to play one, as that would cause an error. This is the case in our Load scene, which has no background music. Furthermore, if the scene we are switching to is the same as our current scene (`SceneManager. GetActiveScene().name != theScene`), we just want the audio to keep playing rather than fading. This was previously described in the case of our dungeon scenes, which repeat indefinitely until the proper conditions are met.

With that, all of the background music in our game is implemented and includes our pleasant fade transitions. Now, let us focus on the sound effects. Again, these could be implemented in myriad ways, so only some key examples will be presented. Let us begin with collisions. Go to your UserCollision script's `OnTriggerEnter2D()` function. Nearly every collision can have sound effects associated with it, including collectables, heroes, drakes, and dragons:

```
//UserCollision script
//excerpts from OnTriggerEnter2D() function

//collectables
case "Collectable":

        //inventory has space remaining
        if (inventory.numObjects < inventory.maxObjects) {

                /*
                Code omitted.
                */

                //play sound effect
                AudioManager.Instance.PlayClipFromSource(
                        AudioManager.Instance.sfxCollect,
                        AudioManager.Instance.sfxSource
                        );
        }
        break;

//heroes
case "Hero":

        /*
        Code omitted.
        */

        //play sound effect
        AudioManager.Instance.PlayClipFromSource(
                AudioManager.Instance.sfxCollect,
                AudioManager.Instance.sfxSource
                );
        break;

//drakes
case "Drake":
```

```
/*
Code omitted.
*/

//inventory has items remaining
if (inventory.numObjects > inventory.minObjects) {

        /*
        Code omitted.
        */

        //play sound effect
        AudioManager.Instance.PlayClipFromSource(
                AudioManager.Instance.sfxRoar,
                AudioManager.Instance.sfxSource
                );
}

//if inventory is empty
if (inventory.numObjects <= inventory.minObjects) {

        //disable collisions
        /*
        Code omitted.
        */

        //stop music
        AudioManager.Instance.StopSource(
                AudioManager.Instance.bgmSource);

        //play sound effect
        AudioManager.Instance.PlayClipFromSource(
                AudioManager.Instance.sfxLoss,
                AudioManager.Instance.sfxSource
                );

        //delay
        yield return new WaitForSeconds(8.0f);

        /*
        Code omitted.
        */
}
break;

//dragons
case "Dragon":

        /*
        Code omitted.
        */

        //play sound effect
        AudioManager.Instance.PlayClipFromSource(
                AudioManager.Instance.sfxRoar,
                AudioManager.Instance.sfxSource
                );

        /*
        Code omitted.
        */
        break;
```

Each of these collisions calls to the AudioManager instance's `PlayClipFromSource()` function at the point of collision to produce a sound effect. Notably, the drake collision also applies a delay after the sound effect is called. Recall that, in our game, when Luna collides with a drake, but has no collectables left, she is booted back to the world map. This is a good opportunity to play an unfortunate-sounding tune to let the player know what has happened. With the delay, our tune plays in its entirety before switching scenes.

Besides collisions, the interaction scene is another place where a lot of action is occurring between characters. It is also a good place to include some sound effects. One way is to provide positive or negative feedback that indicates the outcome of a showdown between two characters. For example, suppose that Luna chooses a Star in a faceoff against the Green Dragon. If the Green Dragon chooses Sun, we play a positive sound effect to indicate the player's victory. On the other hand, if the Green Dragon chooses Moon, we play a negative sound effect to indicate the player's loss. These conditions can be implemented in the InteractionSystem script's `ApplyActionToTarget()` function:

```
//InteractionSystem script
//excerpt from ApplyActionToTarget() function
public void ApplyActionToTarget(GameObject theActor, GameObject
theTarget) {

    /*
    Code omitted.
    */

    //check result
    switch (actorOutcome) {

        //win
        case (int)Outcomes.Win:

            /*
            Code omitted.
            */

            //audio
            //if player wins
            if (actorData.isHero == true) {

                //play sound effect
                AudioManager.Instance.PlayClipFromSource(
                    AudioManager.Instance.sfxPositive,
                    AudioManager.Instance.sfxSource
                    );
            }

            //if player loses
            else if (actorData.isHero == false) {

                //play sound effect
                AudioManager.Instance.PlayClipFromSource(
                    AudioManager.Instance.sfxNegative,
                    AudioManager.Instance.sfxSource
                    );
            }
            break;
```

```
            //lose
            case (int)Outcomes.Lose:

                    /*
                    Code omitted.
                    */

                    //audio
                    //if player loses
                    if (actorData.isHero == true) {

                            //play sound effect
                            AudioManager.Instance.PlayClipFromSource(
                                    AudioManager.Instance.sfxNegative,
                                    AudioManager.Instance.sfxSource
                                    );
                    }

                    //if player wins
                    else if (actorData.isHero == false) {

                            //play sound effect
                            AudioManager.Instance.PlayClipFromSource(
                                    AudioManager.Instance.sfxPositive,
                                    AudioManager.Instance.sfxSource
                                    );
                    }

                    break;

            /*
            Code omitted.
            */
        }
}
```

Similarly, when we determine the overall outcome of the SSM game, we can support it with audio. We can play a positive tune for the heroes' win or a negative one if they lose. As with the aforementioned drake collision, the scene changes after the SSM game ends. Therefore, we need to add a delay to allow our audio to finish before switching scenes. These features can be implemented in the InteractionSystem script's EndInteraction() function:

```
//InteractionSystem script
//excerpt from EndInteraction() function
public void EndInteraction(bool isHeroWin) {

        /*
        Code omitted.
        */

        //heroes win
        if (isHeroWin == true) {

                /*
                Code omitted.
                */
```

```
            //stop music
            AudioManager.Instance.StopSource(
                AudioManager.Instance.bgmSource
                );

            //play sound effect
            AudioManager.Instance.PlayClipFromSource(
                AudioManager.Instance.sfxWin,
                AudioManager.Instance.sfxSource
                );
    }

    //opponents win
    else if (isHeroWin == false) {

            /*
            Code omitted.
            */

            //stop music
            AudioManager.Instance.StopSource(
                AudioManager.Instance.bgmSource
                );

            //play sound effect
            AudioManager.Instance.PlayClipFromSource(
                AudioManager.Instance.sfxLoss,
                AudioManager.Instance.sfxSource
                );
    }

    //switch scene
    StartCoroutine(StateManager.Instance.
      SwitchSceneTo("Map", 8.0f));
}
```

Another key area to include sound effects is when a decision is made by the player. That is, any time our user interface (UI) presents choices and the player makes a selection, we should play a small sound effect. This provides feedback to the player and lets him or her know that the choice has been received. Conveniently, we can implement a sound effect for every choice made by editing only the Selection and Targeting scripts. These two scripts handle all of the player's choices and can incorporate sound effects, like so:

```
//add sound effects to player-made choices

//Selection script
//excerpt from WaitForChoice() function
public IEnumerator WaitForChoice(int theNumChoices, SelectedChoice
theChoice) {

    /*
    Code omitted.
    */

    //while input has not been received
    bool isChoiceSelected = false;
    while (isChoiceSelected == false) {
```

```
//check input
//select current option
if (Input.GetKeyUp(KeyCode.Space)) {

    //play sound effect
    AudioManager.Instance.PlayClipFromSource(
        AudioManager.Instance.sfxChoice,
        AudioManager.Instance.sfxSource
        );

    /*
    Code omitted.
    */
}

/*
Code omitted.
*/
    }
}

//Targeting script
//excerpt from WaitForChoice() function
public IEnumerator WaitForChoice(int theNumChoices, SelectedChoice
theChoice, List<GameObject> theTargets) {

    /*
    Code omitted.
    */

    //while input has not been received
    bool isChoiceSelected = false;
    while (isChoiceSelected == false) {

        //check input
        //select current option
        if (Input.GetKeyUp(KeyCode.Space)) {

            //play sound effect
            AudioManager.Instance.PlayClipFromSource(
                AudioManager.Instance.sfxChoice,
                AudioManager.Instance.sfxSource
                );

            /*
            Code omitted.
            */
        }

        /*
        Code omitted.
        */
    }
}
```

Just those few changes give you pretty good coverage for sound effects. However, these were but a few examples of the many potential sound effects that could be included in your game. With both music and sound effects in your game and your audio management system running the show, give your game a test run. Hear how much more alive your world is, now that audio is included. Also look for opportunities to incorporate even more audio into your game.

Summary

Much like animations, the implementation of audio has added a whole new dimension to your game and vastly improved the player experience. You effectively managed all of the music and sound effects throughout your game. You also applied audio in a professional manner to accompany your scenes and interactions. With your audio system complete, you should be able to apply all of these game implementation techniques:

- Incorporate audio into the game world

- Manage music and sound effects from multiple audio sources and clips

- Control the playback, volume, and fading for in-game audio

- Use audio to enhance scenes and interactions throughout the game

Your game is quite complete at this point. Therefore, the final chapter will focus on some last-minute touch-ups, as well as on how to export your game for players to enjoy.

References

Commonly.cc. n.d. The Open Game Art Bundle. http://open.commonly.cc (accessed January 10, 2016).
Open Source Initiative. n.d. The MIT License (MIT). https://opensource.org/licenses/MIT (accessed January 10, 2016).
Pettersson, T. 2007. sfxr. http://www.drpetter.se/project_sfxr.html (accessed January 10, 2016).
Unity Technologies. 2016a. AudioClip. http://docs.unity3d.com/ScriptReference/AudioClip.html (accessed January 10, 2016).
Unity Technologies. 2016b. AudioSource. http://docs.unity3d.com/ScriptReference/AudioSource.html (accessed January 10, 2016).

12 Celebrate Victory

The funny thing about game development is that no game is ever truly complete. You could work to refine and polish a game for all eternity and still discover more things to implement that could make it better. However, practical limitations require that we eventually decide our games are good enough to be shared with a public audience. You've come a long way to prepare your game for release. In this chapter, we'll put a few finishing touches on the game to make it extra special. After that, it's time to move on. Therefore, we'll export the game in a format that players can enjoy.

▮ Goals

By the end of this chapter, you will be able to apply these game implementation techniques:

- Create a celebration scene for players who have won the game

- Reset the game, so that it can be played again

- Add additional polish to the game to improve player experience

- Export the final version of the game for players to enjoy

▎ Required Files

In this chapter, you will use the following files from the *Software > Chapter_12* folder (https://www.crcpress.com/Learn-to-Implement-Games-with-Code/Quick/p/book/9781498753388).

- The contents of the Challenge folder to create, code, and test your solution

- The contents of the Solution folder to compare your solution to the example solution

▎ Challenge: Create a Win Scene

It's always nice to give players the chance to relish the moment of victory after working so hard to complete an entire game. In this challenge, you'll create a Win scene that allows players to celebrate. Your StateManager already detects when the game is won. So, you can easily insert your Win scene into the flow of the game. In addition, from a functional standpoint, we need a way to reset the game. Since our game continually saves after each scene switch, if we don't reset our data after the game is won, the player will be forever stuck at our Win scene. Hence, we must build in a way to give the player a fresh start, so the game can be enjoyed all over again. With that in mind, the requirements for this challenge are:

1. Create a Win scene that allows players to celebrate after completing the game.

2. Allow the game to be reset after it is won, so that it can be played over again.

Hint: Create the Win Scene

Your Win scene has two components: the physical creation of the scene in the Unity editor and the underlying code that runs it. Create a new scene in your project and have at it. Of course, you can reuse the things that are already in your game to make this scene. For example, you might add some characters to the scene to congratulate the player. Whatever you do, create something that will make the player feel special about completing your game. That's what the Win scene is all about.

Besides the design, you also want to have a Win script that controls your scene. Similar to other scripts, such as the Menu script for the Menu scene, this will take care of certain necessities. For instance, you need to set up the scene and provide a way for the player to exit the scene. You could do something like display a celebratory message to the player using your dialogue box, and then let a certain key press exit the scene and return to the main menu.

Hint: Reset the Game

Importantly, you need a way to reset the game once the player has finished. Thus far, our game automatically saves when the scene is switched. It also automatically loads the latest save data. This becomes problematic once the player has won the game. If we didn't do anything, the player would continually load into the Win scene for all eternity. However, it's likely that the player would enjoy progressing through our game a second or third time. Therefore, you need to think of a way to allow the player to have a fresh start. This entails resetting the save data and ensuring the game starts over without a hitch. Honestly, this is easier said than done. Often, little bugs and discrepancies can arise when trying to restart a game fresh. You have to make sure that you can completely clean the slate before returning the player to the start of the game. Make sure to test your solution several times over to see that it is working properly. To make things easier, you might zip yourself right to the Win scene for testing purposes. That lets you rapidly test the process of moving from a completed game to the fresh reset.

Example Solution: Create a Win Scene

Have a look at the example solution project to see how your Win scene could be structured. In the example Win scene, characters from all over have come to congratulate our heroes. Therefore, a number of objects are added as children in the Middleground (Figure 12.1). Each of these has a MapSpawn script to spread the

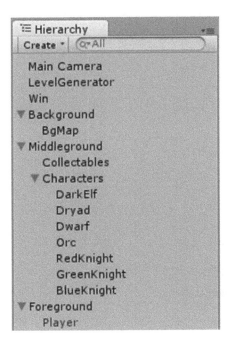

Figure 12.1 Several objects with MapSpawn scripts have been added to the Middleground to populate the Win scene.

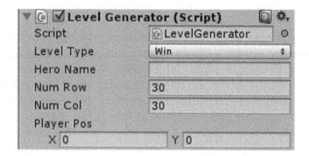

Figure 12.2 A LevelGenerator script facilitates the creation of the Win scene.

objects all around our map. Further, a LevelGenerator script is included to handle the generation of the Win scene (Figure 12.2). The existing LevelGenerator script has been modified to accommodate our Win scene, like so:

```
//LevelGenerator
//modifications to include Win scene

//add Win scene to LevelType enum
public enum LevelType {

        //map
        Map = 0,

        //dungeons
        Red = 1,
        Green = 2,
        Blue = 3,

        //win
        Win = 4,
}

//excerpt from Start() function
//check for Win scene
void Start() {

        /*
        Code omitted.
        */

        //check level type
        //win
        if (levelType == LevelType.Win) {

                //generate win
                GenerateWin();
        }

        /*
        Code omitted.
        */
}
```

```
//GenerateWin() function
//generate the win scene
private void GenerateWin() {

        //spawn
        //heroes
        SpawnObjectsWithTag("Hero");

        //knights
        SpawnObjectsWithTag("Knight");

        //collectables
        SpawnObjectsWithTag("Collectable");

        //retrieve all hero and knight characters
        List<GameObject> allChars = new List<GameObject>();
        allChars.AddRange(GameObject.FindGameObjectsWithTag
          ("Hero"));
        allChars.AddRange(GameObject.FindGameObjectsWithTag
        ("Knight"));

        //iterate through characters
        foreach (GameObject aChar in allChars) {

                //retrieve collider
                Collider2D collider = aChar.GetComponent<Collider2D>();

                //if valid
                if (collider) {

                        //disable collisions
                        aChar.GetComponent<Collider2D>().enabled =
                          false;
                }
        }

        //animation
        AnimateObjectsWithTag("Hero");
        AnimateObjectsWithTag("Knight");
}
```

This conveniently places all of our characters into the Win scene and animates them. Basically, this creates a situation where very many characters are spawned on the screen. They raise their arms to cheer on our returned heroes after they have defeated all of the dragons. It's a nice celebratory scene to congratulate the player for finishing our game. Beyond that, a Win object is created in the scene and has the aptly named Win script attached to it (Figure 12.3). The Win script contains this code:

```
//Win script
public class Win : MonoBehaviour {

    //whether input is enabled
    private bool _isInputEnabled;

    //init
    void Start() {
```

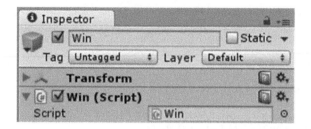

Figure 12.3 A `GameObject` is placed in the scene and has the Win script attached to it.

```
            //play music
            AudioManager.Instance.PlayClipFromSource(
                AudioManager.Instance.bgmWin,
                AudioManager.Instance.bgmSource
                );

            //fade music
            AudioManager.Instance.ToggleFade();

            //create dialogue
            InteractionSystem.Instance.dialogue.
              CreateDialogueWithText(new string[] {
                "Congratulations on your successful quest!",
                "Press ESC to return to the menu.",
                "Your coding journey continues..."
            });

            //show dialogue
            InteractionSystem.Instance.dialogue.Show();

            //hide dialogue
            StartCoroutine(InteractionSystem.Instance.dialogue.
              HideOnInput());

            //set flag
            _isInputEnabled = true;
        }

        //update
        void Update() {

            //check user input
            if (_isInputEnabled == true && Input.GetKeyUp(KeyCode.
              Escape)) {

                //toggle flag
                _isInputEnabled = false;

                //reset game
                StateManager.Instance.ResetGame();
            }
        }

} //end class
```

As you can see, the Win script plays a wonderful tune to the player and prints a message on the screen. It waits until a key press is made to exit. This lets the player enjoy the scene at will.

To load the Win scene, we must update the code inside our StateManager script's `SwitchSceneTo()` function. This function already checks whether the win conditions have been met. Thus, we simply load the Win scene once the player has met these conditions:

```
//StateManager script
//excerpt from SwitchSceneTo() function
/*
Code omitted.
*/

//check if all dungeons completed
if (dungeonData["Red"] == true &&
        dungeonData["Green"] == true &&
        dungeonData["Blue"] == true) {

        //load win scene
        SceneManager.LoadScene("Win");
}

/*
Code omitted.
*/
```

Once the player decides it is time to exit the Win scene, a call is made to the StateManager script's `ResetGame()` function:

```
//StateManager script
//ResetGame() function
public void ResetGame() {

        //reset data
        DataManager.Instance.ResetData();

        //switch scene
        StartCoroutine(SwitchSceneTo("Menu"));
}
```

Quite simply, this function calls to our DataManager to reset our game's save data and then proceeds to the main menu scene. In the DataManager, this is how our data are reset:

```
//DataManager script
//ResetData() function
public void ResetData() {

        //init save
        _Instance.currentSave = new DataSave();

        //save
        SaveData();
}
```

Conveniently, since we designed our DataManager script well, all we have to do to reset everything is create a new DataSave and resave our data. That sets everything back to the defaults. From there, if we proceed back to the main menu, it's as if the player is starting the whole game anew.

That's it. You have a beautiful Win scene to celebrate the player's victory. It's a great feeling for the player to complete your game and have a nice celebration afterward. Our game is complete, so let's proceed to export it for players to enjoy.

▌ Challenge: Play the Game

You've put a lot of effort into your game, and it's time to seal the deal. Let's look at the export options that Unity provides. Once we get the game into the proper format, it can finally be shared with a wide variety of players. The requirements for this challenge are:

1. Export your game.

2. Play your game.

Hint: Export for Windows

To export your game, start by going to the File > Build Settings ... menu in the Unity editor (Figure 12.4). The Build Settings window appears (Figure 12.5). You should see all of the scenes in your game in the Scenes In Build box.

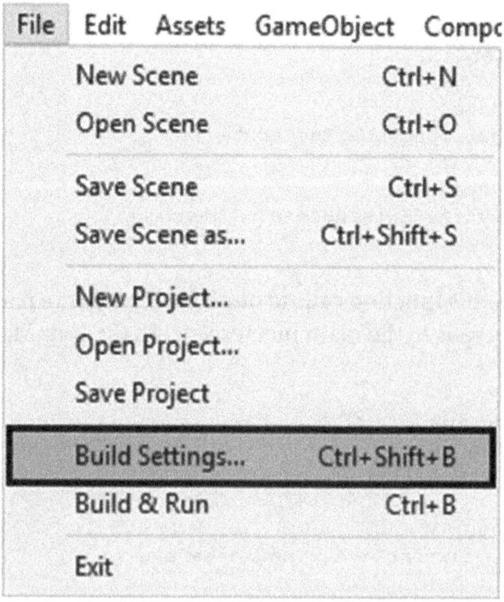

Figure 12.4 To export your game from Unity, go to the File > Build Settings ... menu.

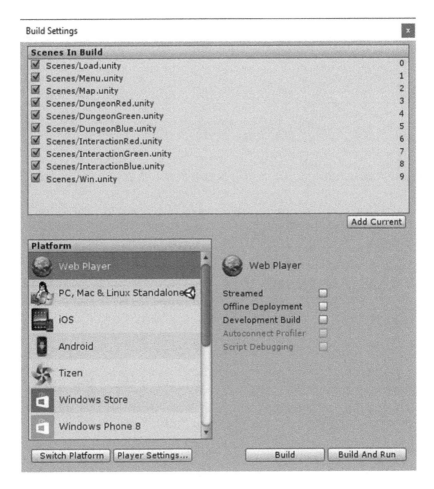

Figure 12.5 The Build Settings window offers several options for exporting your game.

If any are missing, open them and add them to the list. However, make sure that the Load and Menu scenes are listed at the top, since we always want the player to encounter these first. Meanwhile, in the Platform box, you will find several different options for exporting your game to different systems. Choose PC, Mac & Linux Standalone from the list. To export your game for Microsoft Windows, choose Windows in the Target Platform dropdown box (Figure 12.6). Then, click on the Build button (Figure 12.7). A standard file window will open. Choose a location and filename for your saved game. After saving, your game will take some time to compile. Subsequently, you will have an .exe file and a _Data folder. Note that you must keep the .exe and the _Data folder in the same location to play your game. If the _Data folder is missing, the game will not run. To play the game, double click on the .exe file. The game will open in its own window, just like any other application on your computer. Enjoy.

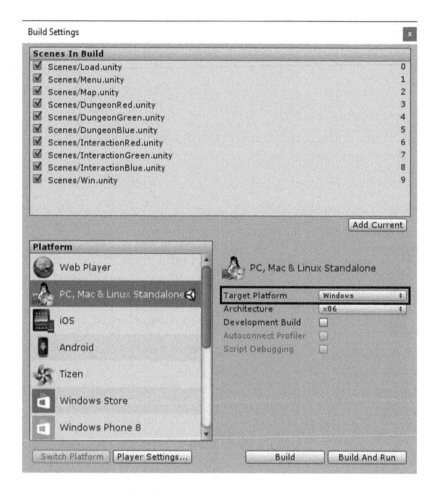

Figure 12.6 Choose Windows from the Target Platform dropdown box.

Hint: Export for Mac

The export steps for Mac are almost identical to the previous Windows description. Start by going to the File > Build Settings ... menu (Figure 12.4) and opening the Build Settings window (Figure 12.5). In the Platform box, choose PC, Mac & Linux Standalone. This time, in the Target Platform dropdown menu, choose Mac OS X (Figure 12.8). Click on the Build button (Figure 12.7) and choose a name and location to save your exported game. After your game finishes compiling, you will be left with a Mac package with the .app extension. Double click on the .app file to play your game. The game will open in its own window, just like any other application on your computer. Enjoy.

Hint: Other Export Options

Unity provides excellent cross-platform support, which makes it easy to put your completed game in the hands of players on a variety of systems. Besides

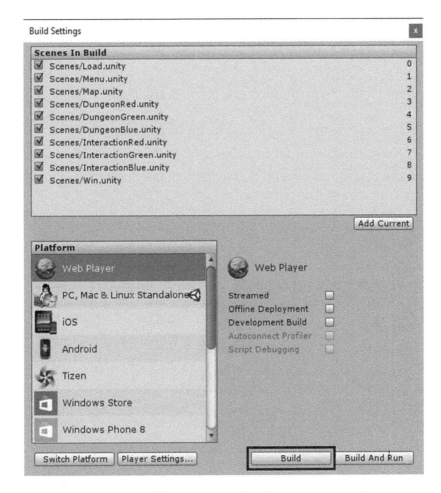

Figure 12.7 Click on the Build button to compile and save your exported game.

Mac OS and Windows, you can also export to the web, iOS, Android, Xbox, and PlayStation, among others. As appropriate, you may want to explore the other export options available to you.

On a side note, our game was specifically set up to export at a size of 1024 × 768 pixels (px). However, if you would like to further customize the game's final output, go to the *Edit > Project Settings > Player* menu (Figure 12.9). There, you can resize the game window, add a custom icon, and make several other modifications.

Example Solution: Play the Game

Follow the hints in the preceding text to get your game exported into the desired format. Before you share it around, take a final pass at playing every aspect of your game. If you find any bugs, fix them. If you find any minor touch-ups

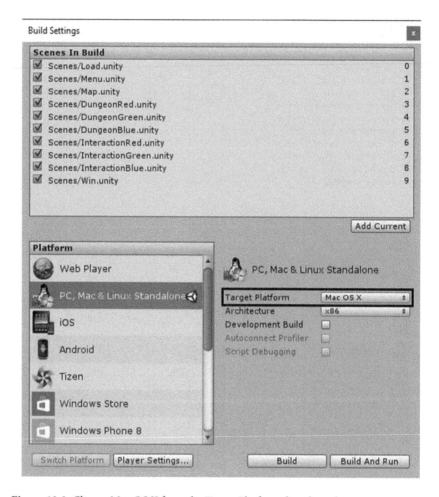

Figure 12.8 Choose Mac OS X from the Target Platform dropdown box.

that would make the game more pleasant and professional, make the necessary adjustments. However, most importantly, take the time to enjoy the fruits of your labor.

Summary

In this chapter, you created a celebratory scene that honors players when they complete your game. You also made preparations for resetting the game after it is won, which allows it to be played over and over again. Last, you exported your game in its final form for players to enjoy. Your updated development resume should include these game implementation techniques:

- Create a celebration scene for players who have won the game

- Reset the game, so it can be played again

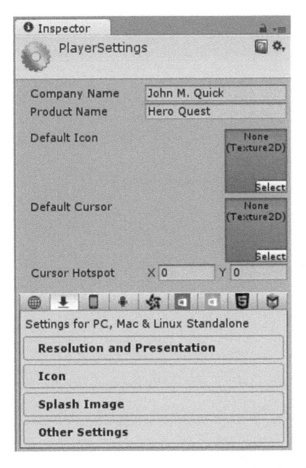

Figure 12.9 Several export customization options are provided in the *Edit > Project Settings > Player* menu.

- Add additional polish to the game to improve the player experience

- Export the final version of the game for players to enjoy

Congratulations on developing a complete, release-ready game! You have journeyed through the arduous game development process and built a magical world for Luna to explore. You've experienced countless coding and implementation techniques that will serve you well in future projects. By now, you should be prepared to implement a game of your own design. Why wait? Take your inspiration and bring it to life through code.

Index

Update() function
    alpha transparency, 232
    control functions, 13
    creating a main menu, 228
    dismissable dialogue box, 46
    fade in, fade out, 237
    frame animation, 273
    input functions, 39
    managing sound/music effects, 310
    Monobehaviour, 175
    moving the camera with Luna, 16
    stopping camera at boundaries, 21
    swapping the leader, 155
UpdatePos() function
    applying the animations, 293
    distance threshold, 25
    follow the leader, 160, 162, 166, 169
    movement logic design, 158–159
    smooth movement of camera, 26–27
    stopping camera at boundaries, 21–22
updates
    dismissable dialogue box, 37–38
    game data, 181
    scrolling text effect, 51–52
UpdateSprite() function, 269–270
UpdateText() function, 53, 55–56
UserCollision file, 42
UserCollision script
    applying the animations, 295
    asynchronous callback, 75–77
    collision detection, 152
    design implementation, 200, 206
    dismissable dialogue box, 46
    execute the choice, 79
    follow the leader, 158, 170
    functionality, 8
    making a choice, 71, 79–88
    managing information flow, 72
    music/sound effects application, 319
    presenting a choice, 70
    saving and loading game data, 172
    scrolling text effect, 58
    selection process implementation,
        77–79
    swapping the leader, 156
    timed dialogue box, 48
    timing coordination, 253, 255
    trigger collisions, 42
    updating lines of text, 52
user input, 225–226

UserMove script
    applying the animations, 289, 291
    follow the leader, 157, 169
    functionality, 8
    presenting a choice, 70
using statement, 37

V

variables; *see also specific variable*
    camera's target object, 14
    delegates, 72–73
Vector2 format, 263
Vector3 variable
    follow the leader, 167
    moving the camera with Luna, 15
    multiple animations, 283
    smooth movement of camera, 26
Vertical Layout Group
        component, 34
victory, *see* win conditions and scene
viewport space, 64
visibility
    changing dialogue box, 38
    selection box, 68
    variables, 24

W

WaitForChoice() coroutine,
        79–81, 131
WaitForSeconds() function
    applying the animations, 297
    loading screen design, 224
    testing the game, 146
    timed dialogue box, 47–48
    timing coordination, 252–254
while loop
    making a choice, 81–82
    selection process implementation,
        78–79
    turns implementation, 116
while statement, 41
win conditions and scene
    basic concepts, 327
    celebration, 137
    challenges, 328–334
    creating a win scene, 328–334
    design implementation, 198
    example solutions, 329–334, 337–338
    export formats, 334–337
    goals, 327